A BRIEF HISTORY OF
INDONESIA

SULTANS, SPICES, AND TSUNAMIS:
THE INCREDIBLE STORY OF SOUTHEAST ASIA'S LARGEST NATION

TIM HANNIGAN

TUTTLE Publishing

Tokyo | Rutland, Vermont | Singapore

ABOUT TUTTLE
"Books to Span the East and West"

Our core mission at Tuttle Publishing is to create books which bring people together one page at a time. Tuttle was founded in 1832 in the small New England town of Rutland, Vermont (USA). Our fundamental values remain as strong today as they were then—to publish best-in-class books informing the English-speaking world about the countries and peoples of Asia. The world has become a smaller place today and Asia's economic, cultural and political influence has expanded, yet the need for meaningful dialogue and information about this diverse region has never been greater. Since 1948, Tuttle has been a leader in publishing books on the cultures, arts, cuisines, languages and literatures of Asia. Our authors and photographers have won numerous awards and Tuttle has published thousands of books on subjects ranging from martial arts to paper crafts. We welcome you to explore the wealth of information available on Asia at www.tuttlepublishing.com.

Published by Tuttle Publishing, an imprint of Periplus Editions (HK) Ltd.

www.tuttlepublishing.com

Copyright © 2015 by Tim Hannigan

Library of Congress Cataloging-in-Publication Data

Hannigan, Tim, author.
A brief history of Indonesia : sultans, spices, and tsunamis : the incredible story of Southeast Asia's largest nation / by Tim Hannigan.
-- First edition.
    pages cm
Includes bibliographical references and index.
  ISBN 978-0-8048-4476-5 (pbk.) -- ISBN 978-1-4629-1716-7 (ebook) 1. Indonesia--History. I. Title.
  DS634.H35 2015
  959.8--dc23

2015011166

ISBN 978-0-8048-4476-5

Distributed by:

North America, Latin America & Europe
Tuttle Publishing
364 Innovation Drive
North Clarendon, VT 05759 9436, USA
Tel: 1(802) 773 8930; Fax: 1(802) 773 6993
info@tuttlepublishing.com
www.tuttlepublishing.com

Asia Pacific
Berkeley Books Pte Ltd
61 Tai Seng Avenue #02-12; Singapore 534167
Tel: (65) 6280 1330; Fax: (65) 6280 6290
inquiries@periplus.com.sg; www.periplus.com

Indonesia
PT Java Books Indonesia
Kawasan Industri Pulogadung
Jl. Rawa Gelam IV No.9, Jakarta 13930
Tel: (021) 4682 1088; Fax: (021) 461 0206
crm@periplus.co.id; www.periplus.com

Japan
Tuttle Publishing
Yaekari Building, 3rd Floor,
5-4-12 Osaki, Shinagawa-ku;
Tokyo 141 0032, Japan
Tel: 81 (3) 5437 0171; Fax: 81 (3) 5437 0755
sales@tuttle.co.jp; www.tuttle.co.jp

First edition
18 17 16 15   4 5 3 2   1510CM
Printed in China

CONTENTS

MYANMAR

NAYPYIDAW

Yangon

LAOS

HANOI

VIENTIANE

VIETNAM

THAILAND

BANGKOK

CAMBODIA

PHNOM PENH

Ho Chi Minh City

Gulf of Thailand

Hainan

Andaman Sea

Pulau Rondo

Sigli   Lhokseumawe

anda Aceh

Meulaboh   Takengon   Langsa

Labuhan Haji   Biniai   Medan

Pematang   Tebing Tinggi

Simeuleu   Siantar

Tuangku   Singkil   Bagan

Sibolga   Siapiapi   Melaka

Nias   Rantau   Dumai

Pini   Prapat

Batu Is.   Bukit   Pekan Baru

Tanahmasa   Tinggi

Padang Panjang   Sawah Lunto

Siberut   Padang

Sipura   Indra   Batu Ampar

Pura

Mukomuko   Saro Langun   Jambi

Pagai Selatan   Lubuk Linggau

Bengkulu   Batu   Palembang

Raja

Bintuhan   Terbanggi

Enggano   Besar   Bandar Lampung

Balimbing   Bakauheni

Strait of Malacca

Penang

MALAYSIA

KUALA LUMPUR

Melaka

SINGAPORE

Bintan

Tanjung Pinang

Riau Islands

Tembilahan

Singkep

Bangka

Pangkal   Tanjung

Pinang   Pandan

Belitung

Sumatra

SUNDA STRAIT

Serang   JAKARTA

Bogor   Bekasi

Sukabumi   Bandung

Anambas Is.

Siantan

Jemaja   Midai

Natuna Is.

Natuna Besar

Panarik

Subi

Serasan

Natuna Sea

Sambas

Singkawang

Ngabang

Mempawah

Pontianak

Sanggau

Sukadana

Ketapang

Kendawangan   Kotawaringin

Pangkalanbun

Sampit

BRUNEI
DARUSSALAM

BANDAR SERI
BEGAWAN

MALAYSIA

Kuching

Sintang

Borneo

Kalimantan

Mt. Raya

Palangkaraya

Nangapinoh

Longnawan

Tanjung Selo

Longiram

Samarinda

Muarateweh

Amuntai

Banjarmasin

Martapura

Tanah

Kandangan

Kota

Laut

Laut Kecil Is.

Masalembu Is.

Bawean

Java Sea

Kegean Is.

INDON

Kudus   Rembang

Cirebon   Gresik   Madura   Sumenep

Pekalongan   Semarang   Surabaya

Tegal   Surakarta

Purwokerto   Magelang   Madiun   Kediri   Jember

Yogyakarta   Malang   Banyu

Wangi

Bali Sea

Bali   Mataram   S

Denpasar   Lombok   Sum

J   a   v   a

INDIAN OCEAN

Cocos (Keeling) Islands
(Australia)

Christmas Islands
(Australia)

100 km
200 miles

Java

500 km
200 miles

Indonesia

Java (inset)

Bakauheni   Cilegon   Seribu Is.   JAKAR

Serang   Tangerang   Be

Pandeglang   Depok   Kara

BANTEN   Bogor   Purwa

Panaitan I.   Mt. Salak   2180m   Cia

Malingping   Sukabumi   WEST JA

Deli I.   Tinjil I.   Pelabuhan   Pangal

Ratu

Jampangkulon   Sindangbar

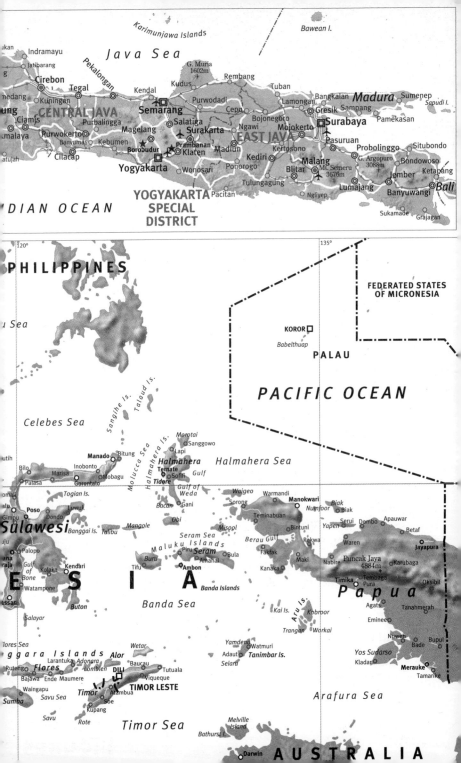

Preface

T he first time I arrived in Indonesia I went straight to the bookshop. I was an earnest young backpacker with a passion for history; I had three months of island–hopping ahead of me, and I wanted something to read on the journey.

I had spent much of the previous year travelling in India, and I had gorged myself on books about that country. There had been travelogues and reporters' memoirs that made light work of India's past; there were pop history accounts of the Indian independence struggle that read like airport thrillers, and any number of bright and breezy books tackling everything from the Mauryans to Mahatma Gandhi in a manner that any traveller could understand. Now I wanted to find the same sort of stuff about Indonesia.

I had touched down in Bali, at the height of the rainy season. The bookshop was on the top floor of a department store in the heart of Kuta, a bustling beach town on the west coast. I made my way between the racks of batik shirts, past wood carvings and painted scenes of rice fields, and entered the bright, book–filled space. At first glance things seemed promising: there were shelves full of books about Indonesia. But once I had skimmed the guidebooks and the language primers I found something strange: here, in a shop targeting tourists in the middle of Bali's brashest resort, many of the books on sale were academic tomes. There was certainly plenty of history, but most of it came weighted with heavy footnotes, and much of it tackled obscure topics. There were even serious works of sociology and anthropology on offer to the sunburnt shoppers. But when it came to pithy pop history page-turners and lightweight travelogues, there was a distinct deficit.

The few non-scholarly books available were mostly either memoirs of life in Bali, or reprints of things penned well over a century ago. Indonesia, it seemed, was something of a desert when it came to history books for general readers.

In the end I headed off on the ferry to Lombok with a wad of academic histories in my backpack. It did me good, for by the time I returned not only had I learnt a great deal—I had also developed a tolerance for heavy texts. Later I went back to that same bookshop, and to others in other Indonesian cities, and to libraries in London and Singapore. Light, entertaining books on Indonesia's past might have been in short supply, but there was a vast scholarly literature, and it was all fascinating stuff. Some of the best-known professional historians and anthropologists working on Indonesia also turned out to be brilliant writers, once you got past the academic conventions. But still, I would have preferred something a little easier to start with.

$$\odot-\odot-\odot-\odot-\odot$$

This book is not a work of professional scholarship or formal academic research. It is intended to be the kind of thing I was looking for in that Bali bookshop all those years ago: an entertaining first landfall in the archipelago of Indonesian history. It takes Indonesia's past and makes a story of it.

Dates, battles and kings have long since gone out of fashion with professional historians. They look instead to contexts and impacts, and find a deeper understanding therein. But you need a framework of facts before you can ever hope to consider the contexts, and so this book does have dates and battles and kings aplenty, as well as traders, missionaries, soldiers and revolutionaries, a few volcanoes, the odd stormy sea-crossing, and the occasional tiger. It also finds space for the views of the foreign travellers who have passed through Indonesia over the centuries—from Chinese pilgrims and Moroccan adventurers to English explorers and American tourists. Their impressions are often colourful and sometimes funny, but they also provide telling snapshots of the place at a particular point in time.

Narrative histories of this sort—not least those about a place as big as Indonesia—always simplify a good deal, and leave out a great deal more. So the Further Reading and Bibliography sections at the end of the book not only list the most important sources I have used; they also give suggestions for further reading on events passed over too quickly or bypassed altogether, as well as recommendations for books I have found entertaining and enlightening. There are endless opportunities for island-hopping in Indonesia, from shore to shore and from book to book.

◉ — ◉ — ◉ — ◉ — ◉

Before I started this journey through Indonesia's past, I had to tackle the thorny questions of spelling and nomenclature. The first was dealt with fairly simply. Modern Indonesian—the language known as *Bahasa Indonesia*—uses a refreshingly consistent and logical system of spelling. Once you know that an Indonesian C equates to 'ch' in English, all words are pronounced more or less exactly as they are written. And so I have used modern Indonesian spellings throughout, rather than the older Dutch-style spellings that were used until 1972. The only exception to this rule comes with the names of a few people from the early twentieth century. Some famous Indonesians born before the spelling reforms have had their names modernised in popular usage. Sukarno, for example, need not be called 'Soekarno' in the twenty-first century. The names of some others, however, are still usually written the old-fashioned way. In these cases I have stuck with the most common usage, but have added the modernised spelling in brackets the first time the name appears.

The question of place names was a little trickier. In some cases a place has had a formal change of name. Until World War II

Jakarta was called Batavia, and so until we reach World War II in this book, that is how it will be known. The island of Sulawesi was formerly known as Celebes, but the latter is probably just a Portuguese corruption of the former, so to avoid confusion it will be known as Sulawesi throughout.

One of Indonesia's trio of land borders cuts through Borneo. Today this huge, forest-clad island is divided between Indonesia, Malaysia and Brunei, and the provinces of·the Indonesian section are known collectively as Kalimantan. But the division is a modern one, a legacy of European colonialism, so I will use Borneo throughout this book to refer to the whole island, and Kalimantan only once we reach the second half of the twentieth century and start discussing the specifically Indonesian provinces.

At the eastern end of Indonesia lies another enormous territory, New Guinea, the second largest island in the world. Today it is split down the middle between Indonesia and Papua New Guinea. The western portion has been variously known as Dutch New Guinea, Irian and Papua. Each of those names has political connotations of its own, so will I use them only in the appropriate historical contexts. When discussing the place in general I will use the term 'West New Guinea'.

The biggest conundrum of all came with the name of the wider setting of this entire book—the galaxy of islands that now makes up the Republic of Indonesia. Many history books do speak of 'Indonesia' when discussing events in the distant past. But the word itself, a Greek contraction meaning 'the Indian Islands', was only invented in the mid-nineteenth century, and only came into common political usage in the early twentieth century.

The borders of modern Indonesia are simply those of the colonial territory that preceded it, the Dutch East Indies. But these islands existed long before either Europeans or Indonesian nationalists arrived on the scene, and there are many ancient connections that span the modern frontiers. The part of Borneo that now belongs to Malaysia and Brunei has had much in common with what is now called Kalimantan throughout its history, and for Dayak tribes of the interior the idea of a formal boundary cutting through the forest would have meant nothing. The Malaysian city of Melaka, meanwhile, was for many years the most important port in the region, a placed linked by trade and by blood to Java, Sulawesi and points east. The people of the Malay Peninsula have long spoken the same language—and have sometimes shared the same rulers—as their kinsmen across the water in Sumatra. To speak of an 'Indonesia' in the fourth, or eighth, or fifteenth centuries is not just anachronistic; it is to suggest that these other places and their people have no part to play in the story.

But if not 'Indonesia', then what?

In the nineteenth century the English explorer Alfred Russel Wallace called the region 'The Malay Archipelago', and the Scottish scholar John Crawfurd wrote of 'The Indian Archipelago'. These terms certainly had their appeal, and both Crawfurd and Wallace placed no political limits on their definitions of the region. However, their terms both contain inadvertent references to modern nations outside of Indonesia, and a faint whiff of imperialism to boot. But as I was pondering all this, it struck me: the problematic parts of the terms of Wallace and Crawfurd were the adjectives, not the noun. And so there it was: the Archipelago.

Throughout this book I use the term 'the Archipelago'. It encompasses all of what is now Indonesia, but it has no exact boundary until the nineteenth century, shading off north, east and west in a blur of mixed languages, cultures and ethnicities. In the early part of the story it can include northern Borneo, Melaka and the Malay Peninsula, when those places have a role to play. The terms 'Dutch East Indies' and 'Indonesia' appear only at the appropriate points, later in the narrative.

Look at a map of the world. Look at the great mass of islands that trails from the underbelly of mainland Southeast Asia. Squint, and you won't be able to see the red lines marking the political boundaries. This is the Archipelago, and this is its story.

Point of Departure:
The Archipelago

S omewhere in the middle of New Guinea, between the Muyu and the Ok Tedi rivers, there is a line in the forest. This is wild country, thick with greenery. To the north, where the rivers rise, are the Star Mountains. To the south the land slopes imperceptibly away towards the swamps and deltas on the edge of the Arafura Sea. This is the ancestral territory of the Yonggom people, hunter-gatherers who travel through the forest harvesting sago palms for their starchy flour and trapping the giant, flightless cassowary birds for their meat.

You cannot see the line on the ground amongst the leaf mould or in the high canopy of the trees, and if you were tracing one of the old Yonggom trails through the forest you would have no way of knowing that you had crossed it. But it is there on the map of the world, a scarlet strip running north to south and as straight as an arrow. The line is the 141st meridian east. It is also the eastern border of the Republic of Indonesia.

The distance from this point in the forests of New Guinea to Pulau Rondo, a speck of coral-fringed land off the northernmost tip of Sumatra, is a little over 3,274 miles (5,270 kilometres). This is about the same as the distance between London and Tehran, or between New York and Lima. Indonesia spans the gap between those far-flung points. It is the world's largest archipelagic nation and it is made up of more islands than anyone could possibly count: the official toll of individual landfalls within Indonesia's borders has ranged over the years from 13,667 to 18,307. The country is home to a quarter of a billion people, making it the fourth most populous nation on earth. It is also the world's biggest Muslim-majority state—though more than half of the entire population, and most of the Muslims, are crammed on to Java, an island no bigger than England.

Indonesia became an independent nation at the end of World War II. Since then, it has been ruled for two decades by a wild and passionate demagogue, for three decades by a cool autocrat, and since the turn of the twenty-first century by a bevy of democratic leaders. Its population has tripled in size and its economy has come close to basket case status, boomed spectacularly, imploded catastrophically, and then forged forward once more. The country has expanded its territories twice, and contracted once. It has seen riots, ethnic violence, and one unimaginable episode of mass killing, but it has never collapsed entirely.

Before Indonesia came into being the same territory was known as the Dutch East Indies, and men from the Netherlands held sway over much of it for several centuries. Before that, there was no single political entity stretching from Pulau Rondo to the 141st meridian east, but the region was not simply a mass of unconnected islands. There were great trading states in Java and Sumatra, with influence stretching to other shores. Before Islam became the dominant religion, many people in the region worshipped Shiva, and Vishnu, and Buddha, and before that still more of them worshipped their own ancestors. Over the centuries, the various islands have been visited and settled by people from India, China, Portugal and Arabia. All told, it is a very complicated place.

⊙—⊙—⊙—⊙—⊙

From its eastern anchor in New Guinea, the Archipelago, the mass of islands of which Indonesia is today the greatest part, runs westwards in two arcs. The northern arc is a chaos of twisted fragments. Beyond the northwest extremity of New Guinea itself, the small islands of Maluku are flung at all angles across a stretch of shallow sea. Further west is the tormented form of Sulawesi, and beyond that lies Borneo, a huge blot of an island. By contrast the southern arc is a vision of perfection, an arabesque of islands stretching from Tanimbar in the east, through Nusa Tenggara to Bali, Java and finally mighty Sumatra, rearing across the equator. These twin arcs of the Archipelago were born of fantastic geological violence in the deep past.

Some 200 million years ago the bulk of the world's landmasses formed two enormous continents. Laurasia lay to the north; to the south was what we know today as Gondwana, a jumbled jigsaw made up of Africa, Australia, South America, Antarctica and India. Between these two supercontinents was a stretch of turbid water known as the Tethys Ocean. At around the time that the dinosaurs were stalking the earth Gondwana started to break apart, and its fragments, carried on the deep convection currents of the earth's mantle, began to sail slowly away towards their current locations. One of the largest of these fragments was the Indo-Australian Plate, an enormous raft of rock with Australia at the stern and the Indian subcontinent for a bowsprit. It travelled north at a formidable rate, covering eight inches (twenty centimetres) a year at times, and squeezing the Tethys Ocean into an ever narrower space. Eventually, the Indian section of the plate ground into the Eurasian Plate, the greatest fragment of old Laurasia. The impact formed the Himalayas, lifting limestone sediments from the bed of the Tethys Ocean to the very summit of Mount Everest.

As the Indo-Australian Plate was driving northwards it was also pivoting towards the northeast, and another impact was threatening. It came some 70 million years ago as the Indo-Australian Plate ploughed into the Sunda Plate, an extension jutting from the underbelly of Eurasia, where Thailand, Cambodia—and, indeed, Indonesia—lie today. This was a thick, spongy plate, deeper but less dense than its counterpart, and the Indo-Australian Plate was forced beneath it, its leading edge driving down into the very mantle of the earth. Fragments from the outer skin of

the Indo-Australian Plate—chunks of sedimentary rock originally laid down below sea level—were scraped off at the subduction
zone and thrown up along the southern edge of the Sunda Plate
like flotsam. These fragments would eventually form the islands of
Timor, Sabu and Sumba, the high limestone peninsula that hangs
at the southern tip of Bali, and the banks of karst that stretch
through southern Java. The Sunda Plate itself, meanwhile, had
been cracked and torn by the impact, and through these fissures
the materials of the Indo-Australian Plate, rendered in the heat
below, were reborn, surging up to leave a rash of volcanoes just
north of the plate boundary.

The shifting of the plates was an incredibly slow process, of
course, unfolding over many millions of years. But the volcanoes
born of the impact could sometimes rise with incredible speed,
a new cone of black rubble emerging suddenly from the sea to
create a substantial new island over the course of just a few decades. And equally, these volcanoes could obliterate themselves
and all that surrounded them in a single, cataclysmic moment.
Where they didn't blow themselves apart, however, they formed
new lands, and in time they created the entire chain of the Archipelago's southern arc. Beyond this arc, meanwhile, a chaos of plate
fragments, fault lines and boundaries had formed the less orderly
islands of the northern arc.

If you look at a map of the Archipelago today there is a definite sense of movement, a clear contrast to the solid hulks of
Australia, Africa or mainland Asia. Individual islands seem to
dance before your eyes. It is a far from fanciful impression, for
there is still much movement here. The Indo-Australian Plate is
still driving beneath the Sunda Plate, and the volcanoes are still
fuming along the entire length of the chain. The plate boundary
produces endless earthquakes, as do the myriad shorter fractures
amongst the islands of the northern arc. There are few more dynamic landscapes anywhere on earth.

◉—◉—◉—◉—◉

Once the new lands had formed from the impact of the Indo-Australian and Sunda plates, it took no time at all for the first greenery to sprout amongst the black volcanic debris. Stretching across the equator, the Archipelago was a warm place, well watered by monsoon rains during the northern winter, and an apocalyptic volcanic wasteland could turn to jungle within a few seasons. There were chunks of old land mixed in amongst the new landfalls here, too, pieces torn from the original plates, and these already had their own forests and their own fauna. In fact, the dividing line between the Asian and Australian ecological spheres ran right through the middle of the Archipelago. In Sumatra and Java there were rhinos and apes and other big beasts of the Asian mainland. In New Guinea and the fragments of Maluku that had once been part Gondwana, meanwhile, there were marsupials, cockatoos and parakeets. The rise and fall of the sea levels over the millennia meant that there was a certain blurring of the boundary between these spheres, particularly in Sulawesi, where some fragments of the island had started life in Gondwana and some in Laurasia. But there were some absolutes: there have never been tigers east of Bali.

The Archipelago was a lush place. The long chains of smoking volcanoes and the subterranean fault-lines gave it a definite volatility, but it brimmed with bird and animal life. Its dark volcanic soils were formidably fertile, and its warm seas teemed with fish. All that it needed was the first people to turn up.

CHAPTER 1

FROM HOBBITS TO HINDUISM: PREHISTORY TO INDIANISATION

The little group moved quietly uphill through the trees. They were wiry men with long limbs and dark skin, carrying spears tipped with chipped stone and woven baskets loaded with edible things from the forest. They had been following the line of a thin river snaking through the hills, and they had spotted the cave from below. It formed a hollow in the western ranges of an island that the first Portuguese sailors, many millennia later, would call *Flores*—'flowers' in their own language. There were few dangerous animals in these forests, but three thousand feet above sea level it would be cold after dark, and the cave would make a fine shelter for the night. The men paused for a moment on the threshold. It was a vast space, with a vaulted ceiling of dangling stalactites. They made their camp—perhaps not too far back into the darkness—and sparked a fire from the dry things in their baskets.

The men were Melanesian hunter-gatherers, part of a wider population that was slowly picking its way through the forests of the Archipelago. The Melanesians were, as far as we know, the first modern humans to reach what is now Indonesia, some forty thousand years ago. They carried stone axes and they buried their dead. Sometimes they laid their hands on the walls of caves, then blew a thick spray of chewed ochre pigment against the rock to leave a ghostly outline of their presence. For the most part they moved through the open forests or along streams and shorelines, hunting out fruits and roots, fish and shellfish, and wild animals for meat. Eventually, in the more fertile landscapes, they settled into hut clusters and cleared the ground for a simple kind of agriculture.

Their movement through the Archipelago was generally slow: they had time and geography on their side, for during much of their period of expansion the sea levels were far lower than they are today. At the poles the icecaps had swollen, locking up huge quantities of the world's water, and you could walk from Thailand to Bali without getting your feet wet. Every so often, however, some unknown impetus prompted a more decisive journey, and the Melanesians took to the water on rough craft. The near ancestors of the little band, settling down for the evening in the Flores cave, had made the crossing over the current-charged Lombok Strait between Bali and what is now the island chain of Nusa Tenggara, a body of water so deep that it had never dried out. More of these crossings followed, and eventually the Melanesians would carry their journeys to New Guinea, and out into the long vapour trail of islands in the southwest Pacific.

But this group of travellers—crouched around the campfire in the limestone hollow which their distant descendants would call *Liang Bua*, 'The Cool Cave'—had no reason to believe that anyone had been here before them. The men could not have known that they had paused at one of the great S-bends of palaeontology, one of those rare traps—almost always a cave—where all the muck of prehistory accumulates in deep layers.

Perhaps one of their number went out at dusk to forage. Perhaps he heard something moving in the bushes and assumed it was a giant monitor lizard or one of the elusive dwarf elephants that lived in the deeper parts of the forest. But what he actually saw when he looked up must have sent a powerful pulse of shock deep into his core: it was a creature on the cusp between a *something* and a *someone*, staring back at him from the undergrowth.

It was dark and heavyset, with short legs and long, flat feet. Its brow sloped down into a broad face and its arms hung low at its sides. It was almost—*almost*—like a crude reflection of the Melanesian traveller himself, but for the fact that its head would barely have reached his waist. If they made eye contact it must have been a profoundly unsettling moment. Then the creature turned and hurried away into the trees with a strange, high-stepping gait, and the man shrieked over his shoulder to his friends in the cave that there was something out there in the forest…

◉—◉—◉—◉—◉

Though the inhabitants of Flores would tell tall tales of a short people called the *Ebu Gogo* long into the twentieth century, no one knew that the stories might have some connection with fact until 2003, when a team of Indonesian and Australian palaeontologists, digging in the damp levels of the Liang Bua cave, came upon a tiny 18,000-year-old skeleton, 'as fragile as wet blotting paper'. Elsewhere in the cave they found other bone fragments from the same creature, some dating back as far as 95,000 years, along with shards of worked stone suggesting that, whatever it was, it had been able to use simple tools. The individual specimens were simply numbered, and the putative new species was named *Homo floresiensis*. But the media, noting its three-foot-high stature and big feet, quickly dubbed it 'the Hobbit'.

In the subsequent years the scientific community fell to bitter wrangling over the precise nature of this forgotten population of tiny hominids. Some claimed that it was a late-surviving relic of the pre-human *Homo erectus*. Others insisted that the Ebu Gogo were simply modern humans suffering from a genetic disorder or a malfunctioning thyroid. Based on the long timescale of the creatures' existence and several crucial features of its skeleton, current consensus is edging towards the notion of a new species, more closely connected to the earlier *Homo erectus* than the later *Homo sapiens*, but all these arguments miss the most startling point.

We have long known that there were early humanoids in Java more than a million years ago. Their bones have been found along the banks of the Solo River. Thickset, heavy-jawed and beetle-browed, they are popularly known as 'Java Man'. But Java was connected to mainland Asia at various points, and no one credited these lumbering ape-men with much more than a meandering journey on foot, and technological skills extending no further than a few crude stone choppers. But the discovery of the Flores Hobbit proved that long, long before the Melanesians arrived—at least 95,000 years ago, and possibly as far back as 840,000 years—something almost human had made the first serious maritime journey in Indonesian history: across the Lombok Strait, the great Rubicon between the Asian and Australian ecological spheres. More remarkably still, that creature was still there, deep into the period of Melanesian travel in the Archipelago.

The Ebu Gogo myth notwithstanding, it is generally assumed that the Hobbits vanished some 12,000 years ago, around the same time that the dwarf Flores elephant died out, possibly due to a major volcanic eruption. But its unsettling presence in the forest offers a glimpse of the deep layers that lie beneath the shallow topsoil of tangible human history.

$$\odot - \odot - \odot - \odot - \odot$$

History has to start somewhere, however, and the arrival of the Melanesians in the Archipelago is the perfect point of departure. Not only were they the first modern humans in the region; their descendants still live in large swathes of eastern Indonesia today. Dark-skinned and curly-headed, Melanesian people predominate in the regions of East Nusa Tenggara, southern Maluku and New Guinea.

This Melanesian realm represents the outland of modern Indonesia, however, and most of the major set-pieces of the region's history were staged far to the west in the busy spaces of Sumatra and Java. The inhabitants of these places represent a far more recent series of landfalls in Southeast Asia, and they belong to the greatest tribe of maritime travellers the world has ever known—the Austronesians.

No one knows why they left; no one knows how many of them there were; but sometime around seven thousand years ago, a number of people set out towards the southeast from the damp interior of southern China. They headed not directly to Southeast Asia, but to Taiwan. This small teardrop of mountainous land was to prove the unlikely springboard for an epic expansion.

From around six thousand years ago, propelled most probably by local overpopulation, early Taiwanese Austronesians took to their boats—small, open outriggers for the most part—and headed south to the northern Philippines. They brought with them dogs and pigs, pottery made of red clay, and well-worked stone axes. They also knew how to tame buffalo and grow rice. Once they had reached the Philippines, the galaxy of islands beyond sucked them ceaselessly southwards. Some five thousand years ago they made it to Sulawesi, and half a millennium later—at about the same time that the Egyptians were working on the Great Pyramid at Giza—they made further journeys to reach Java, Sumatra, Timor and Borneo. From the latter landfall some of their number hopped back northwards across the South China Sea to settle in the southern corner of Indochina. Others turned sharply eastwards to find footholds on the northern foreshore of New Guinea, and then embarked on the most improbable of all their journeys, launching themselves into the apparent abyss of the Pacific Ocean to become the Polynesians. By the time the Anglo-Saxons were established in England and the Abbasid Caliphate approaching its apogee in far-off Baghdad, they had made it to Hawaii and Easter Island. Meanwhile, back to the west, other Austronesian seafarers had set out from the Archipelago on a voyage that would place the horizontal poles of their realm a full 8,700 miles (14,000 kilometres) apart: around 1,500 years ago they crossed the Indian Ocean and settled in Madagascar.

Historical distance has a telescoping effect, and this, coupled with crude maps and précising passages, can all too easily give an impression of the Austronesians coming in great waves—a waterborne Southern Mongoloid horde sweeping all aside as they rampage from island to island. The Austronesian expansion was indeed one of the swiftest and broadest in human history, but even so, more than four thousand years separated their first departures from Taiwan and the last of their major migrations to New Zealand. By then the Maoris, the Javanese and the Taiwanese aborigines were nothing more than distant linguistic cousins. Even within the Archipelago, where the journeys between islands were modest, they would have moved slowly over the course of many generations, and most Austronesians probably had no idea that they were participants in some globe-straddling migratory epic.

As the Austronesians settled into the Archipelago they formed villages—huddles of high-roofed huts in the green spaces between the volcanoes. They raised pigs and chickens and made pots, cleared patches of forest, and began to grow rice, and slowly developed into the Javanese, Balinese, Malays, and the other peoples of the western Archipelago. Theirs was a society of scattered settlements, a culture of clans, not kings. Wars—and there surely were wars—were small in scale and tribal in nature. There was no obvious political unity beyond that of individual communities, but there *was* a certain cultural continuity.

Given that most parts of the Archipelago have subsequently come under the influence of two or even three major world religions, it would be easy to suppose that no trace of what went before could possibly remain. But look at Indonesia in the right light and the original outlines still show through today. The most obvious places to start looking are in the remote eastern landfalls where neither Hindu-Buddhism nor Islam, still less Dutch colonialism, ever had much impact—places where a resolute handful still cling to the unsanctioned religious designation of 'other'. Sumba, in the nether regions of Nusa Tenggara, is one such place. Here, indigenous ancestor worship has only ceased to be the dominant religious tradition within the last two generations, and here, as in the old Austronesian world, there is a culture of clans and villages without dominant kings. The traditional belief system in Sumba is known simply as *Marapu*—'Ancestors'—and it is the forefathers who are given the active role in a spiritual world from which the Supreme Being has long-since disengaged. Village homes with a founding lineage are built with enormous towering roofs as both a symbol of long descent and as a temporal abode for the ancestral spirits, and the most important moment in life is death. The journey to join the ancestors is marked by epic funerals, the bloody sacrifice of a buffalo, and interment in monumental stone sarcophagi, eerily echoing the cromlechs and portal dolmens of prehistoric Europe.

None of this stuff is restricted to Sumba, however. Four hundred miles to the northwest, in Sulawesi's Tana Toraja, there are similarly bloody and grandiose funerals, and a nine-hundred-mile journey westward from there finds a clear echo of the sweeping, ship-like rooftops of the Toraja villages in the Minangkabau settlements of Sumatra. Even in Java and Bali, the places most thoroughly drenched with foreign culture, there are older traces. The old affection for tombs plays into a Balinese system in which formal Hindu cremation (with pomp and circumstance strikingly similar to that of Torajan or Sumban funeral rites) comes only *after* an initial burial in a village graveyard. In Java, meanwhile, the classic local architectural feature—the *joglo*, the towering pavilion roof—is in its original form simply the high-hatted home of those claiming descent from village founders, essentially identical to the clan houses of Sumba.

⊙—⊙—⊙—⊙—⊙

The Austronesians had arrived by water, and the sea lanes did not salt up in their wake. Small, fast-running outriggers criss-crossed the shallow seas from the earliest days, carrying modest cargoes—at first within the Archipelago, and then further afield. Here and there some radical new product was carried back to the islands from the Asian mainland. Around three thousand years ago a skilful society of metalworkers, the Dong Son, had developed in the north of what is now Vietnam. Amongst the fine bronze items that they forged through their cunning 'lost wax technique' were mighty kettle drums. By the middle of the first millennium BCE these drums were beginning to appear across the Archi-pelago, where the people of Java, Bali and Nusa Tenggara found a role for them in their own traditions as prestige objects, and even as coffins. Before long, ores were being shipped from the Archi-pelago to the Asian mainland, and metalworking techniques were being quietly transmitted back into the ports of Java and Sumatra. An international trade network was slowly coming together, and the Austronesians of the western Archipelago would soon find themselves at one of the most important maritime staging posts on earth, the point of contact between the Indian Ocean and the South China Sea, and the halfway house for seaborne traffic between the twin behemoths of mainland Asia: China and India.

By the dawn of the Current Era, goods gathered in or traded through the Archipelago were reaching Europe. Virtually no one traversed the entire length of this maritime trade route, however. It was a string of way-stations, and individual journeys were usu-ally short: southeast China to Sumatra; Sumatra to Bengal, then a series of short hops around the Indian coast and north to the Per-sian Gulf; up the Euphrates, then overland across the Syrian desert to the eastern Mediterranean. By the time a packet of Javanese camphor or Malukan cloves was delivered to a Roman apothecary, it might have been transhipped a dozen times or more.

The crews of all the boats that plied the trade routes were at the mercy of the winds. During the dry period in the middle of the year, a long easterly breeze drives out of the red heart of Australia and along the length of the Archipelago, before bending north towards China. During the sodden months of the northern winter, meanwhile, the flow reverses. In December a sailor setting out from southeast China could expect to make landfall in Sumatra in as little as two weeks, and to be in India a month beyond that. But once he got there he might have to wait six months for the winds to switch before he could head back in the opposite direction. At all the little entrepôts along the line temporary communities of seamen gathered at anchor, waiting for the wind. Half a year is a long time to kick your heels, and inevitably some of these sailors made themselves comfortable and never went home.

Small communities of Indians and Chinese developed in Archipelago ports. The locals accepted the occasional new technological trinket and took the odd linguistic loan. Indeed, they almost certainly allowed the outsiders' wives and concubines in return—for salty dogs have always been overwhelmingly male. But for the most part, they left this human flotsam and jetsam to get on with their foreign cultural practices undisturbed.

But as trade developed still further in the early centuries of the Current Era, there was an increasing impetus to form proper polities. If you didn't establish your own authority over a river-mouth port and the goods that passed through it, then somebody else—quite possibly a wily foreigner—would do so instead, and would grow rich on the profits. But the indigenous people of the Archipelago simply didn't have a suitable state mechanism of their own. Their traditional notion of tribal chief might work well enough out in the villages, but it was simply too modest to provide the linchpin for a nascent trading nation. Even their original

Austronesian honorifics—*ratu, datuk* and suchlike—lacked sufficient grandeur. They were faced with the options of either going quietly back to their clan-houses and letting history pass them by, or of making a pragmatic adaptation. A few canny chieftains seem to have made the latter choice, for when the first indigenous Indonesian kings appeared in the early centuries of the Current Era, they did so under the portentous foreign title of *raja*—a glittering moniker of Indian Sanskrit origin which was connected, via the Indo-European root, to the words 'regent' and 'regulate'. It was a term that brought with it a whole new culture.

$$\odot-\odot-\odot-\odot-\odot$$

The boat—a long, low Persian dhow with its huge lateen sail reefed in—swung to its mooring in the murky channel. It was the wettest part of the year, and the river was flowing furiously. But with a following wind the boat had made good time—crossing the full breadth of the South China Sea, negotiating the sharp turn at the bottom of the Malay Peninsula, and finally traversing the tidal stretches of the Musi River in all of twenty days. Now it had come to anchor deep inside Sumatra. The green levels of the island stretched away on all sides, and further inland to the west, towards the unseen bulk of the Bukit Barisan mountain range, there were banks of monsoon cloud. It was December 671 CE.

Standing on the deck of the dhow, looking out at the strange new prospect before him, was a Chinese man in the robes of a Buddhist monk. His name was Yijing, and he was thirty-seven years old. Yijing had been born in the city of Yanjing on the dusty levels where Beijing stands today. When he was seven, his family had sent him to a Buddhist monastery on the slopes of Mount Tai, a hulk of toothy stone rearing five hundred feet over the plains of Shandong. The boy grew up with his head in the clouds.

Yijing was, by all accounts, a profoundly religious child, and by the age of fourteen he had been ordained as a monk. He also seems to have been afflicted by a powerful sense of wanderlust, however, and a quiet life of contemplation in the chilly mists of Mount Tai was never on the cards. He developed a quiet obsession with the two great traveller-monks of early Buddhist China—the mighty fifth-century wanderer Faxian, and his later counterpart Xuanzang, the man who would inspire the Ming-era novel *Journey to the West*—and decided to follow in their footsteps to India.

However, in the later seventh-century, political turmoil in Tibet and Eastern Turkestan meant that the old overland trails traversed by Faxian and Xuanzang were firmly off-limits, so Yijing came up with an alternative plan: he would travel to India by sea. In November 671, he boarded the ship of a Persian trader in Canton (modern Guangzhou), and twenty days later they came to anchor on the Musi River, deep in the forests of southern Sumatra, at a riverine settlement which Yijing, struggling with the Indic consonants, called 'San-Fo-Qi'.

This place was not some old-fashioned Austronesian village of ancestor-worshippers, however. The town was already a substantial settlement, ringed by a palisade wall. More importantly for Yijing, it was the hub of a civilised religious culture:

> In the fortified city of Fo-Qi Buddhist priests number more than one thousand, whose minds are bent on learning and good practices. They investigate and study all the subjects that exist just as in [India]; the rules and ceremonies are not at all different. If a Chinese priest wishes to go to the West in order to listen and read, he had better stay here one or two years and practise the proper rules and then proceed to central India.

Parts of the Archipelago, it seems, had successfully turned themselves into mini Indias.

⊙—⊙—⊙—⊙—⊙

In the early centuries of the Current Era, Java, Sumatra, the Malay Peninsula and other parts of the western Archipelago had undergone a process of 'Indianisation' as new states formed under kings bearing Indian titles and confessing Indian faiths. The question of how exactly this process came about has long puzzled historians. European orientalists in the nineteenth century, hardwired with a sense of cultural superiority and hidebound by their own Greco-Roman concepts of civilisation, simply could not believe that 'the degenerate Javan' or 'the indolent Malay' had, of their own accord, raised the mighty monuments that dotted the Archipelago. They postulated a period of active expansionism with proselytising Indian colonists descending on Southeast Asia in droves. This idea has since been roundly discredited, not least because of the uniquely local features that Indian traditions developed in the Archipelago. But there is still some debate over how exactly the conversion did take place.

Much credit has traditionally been given to those little communities of Indian traders gathered in Archipelago ports. It was they, intermarrying with locals and displaying a compelling cultural sophistication, who converted the indigenous Austronesians, the theory goes. But there had been regular contact between the Archipelago and India for several centuries before the first significant signs of conversion ever appeared, and the long-standing presence of foreign traders alone is not enough to explain the change.

Local conversion myths, meanwhile, regularly feature a wandering holy man in the form of the Vedic sage Agastya, who comes striding through the rice fields, with his trident in hand, to convert some indigenous chieftain at a single stroke. This motif—of the wandering mystic and the miraculous conversion—is one that would come to be repeated a thousand years later during another period of cultural shift. But while there doubtless were a good few itinerant storytellers traversing the Archipelago during the period of Indianisation, they could not have done the job by themselves.

Other theories place the onus for conversion on the locals. Here and there some pretender prince, with ideas too big for the traditional role of village chief, might have seized control of a federation of hamlets or a growing port. Once he had done so he would have found himself in need of a political concept to bolster his new position as head of a proto-state. The Indian idea of kingship was perfect for the task. Not only was the notion of a raja or maharaja far more sophisticated than that of a village *ratu*; an Indian king was actually divine, an incarnation of a god, and as such magnificently unassailable. It was an intensely attractive job title for any man with political ambitions. What was more, by signing up to Indian cultural traditions, the ruler instantly tapped into a nascent internationalism. He allowed himself a cultural connection with other chiefs imbibing from the same Indic cup, everywhere from the Mekong Delta to the Arabian Sea.

Shifts of religious allegiance in Southeast Asia usually come from the top down, and the communities clustered around the new kings would have followed their lead, with concentric circles of diminishing influence extending into the hinterland. As literacy arrived in the Archipelago, it came first in the form of Sanskrit and Pali, and when local languages were first written down the medium was a version of the South Indian Pallava script.

Indianisation did not amount to a wholesale rejection of older traditions, however. The new kings of the Archipelago were pragmatic in their adoption of new customs. Though the Austronesian communities of Java, Sumatra and the surrounding landmasses accepted the broad fourfold Indian division of society into priestly Brahmins, knightly Kshatriyas, farming and trading Vaishyas, and common Sudras, they gave little space to obsessive stratification into infinite sub-castes. They were also always ready to take advantage of any latent flexibility, and to insert their old indigenous deities and practices into the new systems.

⊙—⊙—⊙—⊙—⊙

The faiths which seeped into parts of the Archipelago during the centuries of Indianisation are often crudely lumped together under the term 'Hinduism'. Indeed, this is the term that Indonesia's few million modern inheritors of the pre-Islam mantle use for their own faith today. But 'Hinduism' is a recent designation, first popularised by eighteenth-century European travellers, who used it as a reductive catch-all for the myriad interconnected traditions of the Indian subcontinent.

Roughly speaking, the states that formed around Archipelago rajas subscribed to one of four Indian religious traditions. Some, at an early stage, focused their worship on the Brahmins, the inheritors of the original Vedic traditions of north India. Kings only recently converted to a new religious outlook had much need of the priestly caste to bestow legitimacy. A fifth-century stone pillar from Kutai in eastern Borneo, one of the earliest Indianised states, records a raja called Mulavarnam showering gifts of gold and cattle on a local community of Brahmins. Later, worship of the god Vishnu developed a powerful hold, and later still it was Shaivism—devotion to the god Shiva—which held general sway. And by the time Yijing arrived in Sumatra in the seventh century and noted that 'Many kings and chieftains in the islands of the Southern Ocean admire and believe, and their hearts are set on accumulating good actions', the faith to which he was referring was his own Buddhist creed.

Buddhism, which emerged from the broader Indian tradition in the fifth century BCE, had the advantage of a more missionary bent than the other subcontinental schools, and it had found fertile fields in Southeast Asia. As for that muddy township on the banks of the Musi where Yijing scrambled ashore from a Persian ship at the end of 671, he may have known it as San-Fo-Qi, but its own inhabitants called it Srivijaya, the Buddhist trading state that would soon become the preeminent power of the Archipelago.

⊙—⊙—⊙—⊙—⊙

Yijing, sweltering in the heat of the tropics, found the Srivijayan capital a busy township. At its heart was the walled-off compound of the raja, an ambitious man by the name of Jayanasa. His palace was a series of wooden pavilions and platforms. Outside this inner sanctum were the wooden hutments of traders, artisans and minor courtiers, and scattered through these quarters and into the countryside beyond were the sanctuaries and temples of the Buddhist monks. Along the banks of the Musi, meanwhile, were rafts of moored boats, the scent of cooking and the chatter of children emerging from the rattan domes sheltering their middle sections. These were the floating homes of the *Orang Laut*, the 'Sea People' who plied Archipelago waters practicing a mix of trade and piracy.

At some point Yijing had an audience with the king, and he was well received. He settled down for six months and began to get to grips with the unfamiliar squiggles of Sanskrit and the more arcane details of Buddhist theology. Once the wet weather had passed, the king arranged a passage for him to the neighbouring city-state of Malayu, where he stayed for another two months. Then he crossed the narrow straits to yet another of these Indianised entrepôts—Kedah at the narrowest, northernmost section of the Malay Peninsula. Finally, in December 672, Yijing set sail once more and headed for India. He would spend almost fifteen years in the subcontinent, and during his stay he would achieve his ambition of visiting the holy places of Buddhism, of perfecting his own grasp of the holy languages and the holy law, and of meeting with many holy men. Eventually, in 687, he headed back to Srivijaya, bringing a bundle of accumulated Buddhist texts amounting to some half a million stanzas. In his absence the state had grown exponentially. Malayu was now a Srivijayan vassal, and Raja Jayanasa was clearly a man on the make.

⊙—⊙—⊙—⊙—⊙

Srivijaya, which first appears in historical records under Jayanasa's rule, had not been the first political entity to emerge in Sumatra. The island is a huge lozenge, angled across the equator and stretching some 1,050 miles (1,700 kilometres) top to toe. From its wild and wave-lashed western shore the land rises rapidly into the ridges and ravines of the Bukit Barisan, a spine of volcanic uplands running the entire length of the island. On the far side of this range the land levels out into slabs of low-lying forest and swamp, threaded by many meandering rivers and giving way eventually into the sheltered Straits of Melaka. By the dawn of the Current Era, this narrow band of water between Sumatra and the Malay Peninsula was already a crucial shipping route for traffic between the Indian Ocean and the South China Sea. It would remain so forever more, and over the coming centuries various ports would rise to prominence along its shores, growing fat on the transhipment business.

In the fifth century a minor regional power called Kantoli had appeared in the convoluted mesh of islands and deltas that flank the western shores of the Straits of Melaka. Kantoli, however, had merely dabbled in trade; it was its successor, Srivijaya, which first truly claimed the title of ultimate Straits entrepôt.

Srivijaya was not a nation in the modern sense, with defined geographical frontiers—and, indeed, neither were any of the other trading polities that came after it. Instead, it was the hub of a web of interconnected vassal ports that stretched up and down the Straits of Melaka, and out into the Archipelago. Those close to the centre might be kept firmly under the thumb, but the more distant vassals probably paid little more than lip service to their notional overlord, and were usually at the hub of their own smaller spiral of sub-states. Today Srivijaya is sometimes called an 'empire', but in truth the classic model of Archipelago power featured a grand, but geographically limited, central territory, and a scattering of regional franchises and sub-franchises. Srivijaya was more a brand than a bone fide nation state.

But still, in the immediate vicinity of southern Sumatra, Raja Jayanasa was an imposing figure. By the time Yijing returned to Srivijaya his host had not only conquered neighbouring Malayu; he had brought all the small islets of the Straits under his sway, and was tightening his grip on the sea lanes. He underscored these victories with some decidedly ominous threats, carved into celebratory stone columns and set in place in the newly annexed territories:

> All of you, many as you are, sons of kings, chiefs, army commanders, confidents of the kings, judges, foremen, surveyors of low castes, clerks, sculptors, sea captains, merchants and you washer men of the king and slaves of the king, all of you will be killed by the curse of this imprecation. If you are not faithful to me, you will be killed by the curse.

This might seem like the deranged bluster of an unhinged dictator today, but in the seventh-century Archipelago it showed how thoroughly Jayanasa had taken advantage of the Indian notion of divine kingship. He had invested in himself the power to strike down his foes with supernatural force. Above the chiselled threat was the carven hood of a seven-headed serpent beneath which holy water emerged from a narrow spout. Those submitting to the raja had to drink from the aperture, and it was in this liquid that the curse was carried. Transgressors, it was declared, would find themselves rotting away from the inside out.

⊙ — ⊙ — ⊙ — ⊙ — ⊙

The wandering monk Yijing, exhausted by a quarter-century of travel and translation, went home to China, where he died in 695. At the turn of the eighth century, Raja Jayanasa, too, passed on to whatever reincarnation his expansionist actions had earned him.

Srivijaya did not crumble on his death, however, and its subsequent kings found themselves at the crucial anchorage on a mighty web of trade that spanned the Archipelago. From the headwaters of the Musi, small canoes descended carrying gold and camphor; across the water from the river mouth, the miners of Pulau Bangka were digging pitch-black tin ore from the granitic bedrock; precious stones were spewing from the estuaries of Borneo; and from Java came pepper, slaves and rice (the latter a vital necessity, for Srivijaya only ever had a limited agricultural hinterland of its own). From even further afield there was fragrant Timorese sandalwood. Cloves and nutmeg came from Maluku, and at the very furthest limits of the network, Melanesian hunter-gatherers in the islands off western New Guinea, living lifestyles little changed since their distant predecessors had had that unnerving encounter with the Flores Hobbit, found that there was a foreign market for the fabulous feathers of the greater bird-of-paradise.

Srivijaya did not own or even loosely control all of this: it simply tapped into it. Arab travellers would later report that its kings had 'tamed the crocodiles' of the Straits of Melaka. This was probably not meant to be taken literally, for it was human rather than reptilian predators that the kings really had at their beck and call. They had harnessed the wiles of the piratical Orang Laut, the Sea People, and it was they, haunting the mouth of the Musi River, who were able politely to oblige any passing ship to detour upriver to the capital. But despite their paramountcy within Southeast Asia, the Srivijaya kings were happy to play the role of deferent vassal when it came to an even greater regional power. From Jayanasa's days onwards Srivijaya sent regular tribute to China, where local scribes recorded it as yet another barbarian fiefdom acknowledging the mastery of the Chinese emperor.

Given this tradition of tribute missions sent from Srivijaya, it might seem strange that it was India, rather than China, that set the cultural tone in the Archipelago. But in fact China's highly advanced political structure probably counted against it in this respect. In India there was no overarching control and no enduring institution of centralised power, and this may actually have fuelled the stream of cultural influence that seeped from its underbelly into Southeast Asia: the place was as leaky as a sieve. China, meanwhile, had storied thrones and imperial capitals, and over the centuries the whims of the centralised courts would render the country virtually schizophrenic in its relationship with the outside world. China would sometimes fling open its door to trade and travel, only to slam it furiously shut a generation later; it would unleash its own armada of monopolising seamen onto the Southeast Asian trade networks, only to haul them home and scupper their boats after a few voyages. The tribute system with which Srivijaya complied was in fact often the only way to continue trading during a bout of Chinese xenophobia. Shipments of Srivijayan ivory, birds' nests and spices would be accepted as 'gifts' by the port officials of Canton, and the favour would be returned in the form of metals, porcelain and silk.

⊙－⊙－⊙－⊙－⊙

All told, Srivijaya survived for some six centuries, but by the dawn of the second millennium CE it was already in decline—probably partly due to an inability to keep pace with the changing moods of China. As power at the centre began to wane, the outermost vassals of the Srivijayan network would have begun tentatively to test the waters with a few overlooked tribute missions and unacknowledged regal missives, and then, very swiftly, the threads would have snapped as outlying entrepôts reasserted their outright independence. The network contracted. Raids by bullying outsiders began to wrack the capital, and in 1025 the Cholas—a swaggering mob of pirates from South India whose economy was founded on plunder—sacked Srivijaya and many of its one-time vassals along the Straits.

At the end of the eleventh century the centre of the dwindling power shifted north from the Musi to the hub of Srivijaya's former vassal, Malayu, near the site of the modern city of Jambi.

There was a last flurry of temple building, with an array of red-brick monuments thrown up on the banks of the Batang Hari, but the flame was guttering. Before long it had gone out altogether.

By the time the Muslim sultans of Palembang established their own riverine kingdom on the Musi in the sixteenth century, neither they nor their subjects had the faintest idea that the ruins of a mighty state lay buried in the thick black soil beneath the foundations of their own city. But the Palembang sultans were, in their own small way, inheritors of a tradition of semi-divine kingship that had originated in Srivijaya—as were all the other kings of the Archipelago. Their common subjects, too, owed a considerable debt, for their own mother-tongue was a language that had first emerged from Jayanasa's realm. Southern Sumatra was the original wellspring of the Malay language, and it had been Srivijaya's dominance of the shipping routes that had first fuelled its spread as the lingua franca of the Archipelago, a role that it still claims today in its updated form as *Bahasa Indonesia*, the national Indonesian language, and the near-identical modern Malay spoken in Malaysia, Brunei and Singapore.

⊙—⊙—⊙—⊙—⊙

In the thirteenth century China suffered one of its periodic catastrophes: the Mongols swept southwards and usurped imperial power, overturning the old systems of tribute and diplomacy. By the 1360s, however, Mongol power itself had dissolved. As the courtiers of the new Ming Dynasty attempted to rebuild the Middle Kingdom, someone had the bright idea of calling in overdue tribute obligations from the islands of the distant south. In 1370, a full seven hundred years after Yijing's visit, an ill-informed Chinese diplomatic mission went looking for San-Fo-Qi.

Following the old monsoon trade winds, the officials eventually arrived in Jambi—to the astonished delight of the local rulers, who had long since gotten used to their own obscurity. They eagerly agreed to resume the tribute missions of old. Over the coming five years several embassies to China set sail from Jambi. The excitement rather went to the head of the local king, a man by the name of Wuni, and he began to believe that there might still be some flicker of life in the Srivijaya corpse. In 1376, he sent a request for Chinese acknowledgement as maharaja of a revived Srivijaya, and recognition as the greatest tributary chief in the Archipelago. In far-off Nanjing, the Ming officials had not yet grasped the real state of affairs in Southeast Asia, and the next year they sent a mission to acknowledge Wuni's improbable request. Unfortunately for the Chinese, they had reckoned without Java, the real centre of power in the fourteenth-century Archipelago. Before the Chinese reached Jambi, the Javanese got wind of the affair. They dispatched their own fleet, which tracked down the mission ship and slaughtered all the Chinese diplomats, before descending on Sumatra to teach the upstart Wuni a pertinent lesson and to obliterate whatever modest trace might remain of the magnificent Srivijayan heritage.

When word of the incident reached China, the Ming officials reacted with remarkable pragmatism. Instead of attempting to extract some sort of revenge for the death of their diplomats they decided to forget all about Sumatra, and to award the exclusive status of tributary to the Javanese king who had ordered the killing from his seat on the island that would be the lodestar of the Archipelago forever more.

CHAPTER 2

EMPIRES OF IMAGINATION: HINDU-BUDDHIST JAVA

T he plateau lies in the belly of an old volcano, 6,500 feet above sea level in the heart of Java. This is a broken landscape under a cladding of cold soil and pine trees, and there is still a smell of sulphur in the damp air. The name of this strange place is Dieng.

Sometime in the seventh century the first Shiva-worshipping temple builders came struggling up through the tiger-haunted forests to reach this spot, dragging their stonemasons' tools and their Indian-inspired blueprints. But they were not pioneers in an untrammelled world, for Dieng's name—*Di Hyang*, often translated today as 'Abode of the Gods'—is older than any Sanskrit-speaking arrival. *Hyang* is an ancient Austronesian concept of deity.

In far-flung corners of the Archipelago even today, away from the influences of India and Islam, mountains are the abode of ancestral spirits and fiery gods. From Gunung Dempo in Sumatra to the tricoloured crater lakes of Kelimutu in Flores, volcanic summits have always been sacred. As the seventh-century builder-priests paced out the plots for a new vision on Dieng's marshy, sulphur-scented levels, they were walking over an ancient place of power and pilgrimage.

◉ − ◉ − ◉ − ◉ − ◉

It would be easy to overlook Java. A slender slip of land, six hundred miles long and less than a quarter of that across, it rests beneath the equator at the point where the southern arc of the Archipelago bears away eastwards towards distant New Guinea. It is a fraction of the size of Sumatra or Borneo, and is some distance from the crucial shipping junction in the Straits of Melaka. At a glance, then, it is not the most likely candidate for the cradle of history. But peer more closely at Javanese geography, and something becomes apparent. The Archipelago-long string of volcanos that is moderately spaced down the length of Sumatra and scattered, island by island, through Nusa Tenggara bunches up dramatically here, with a legion of fiery peaks marching in tight formation along the entire length of Java. Dieng is just one of dozens of active or dormant Javanese volcanoes. They provide a spine for the island, and though their capacity for sporadic violence gives the place an uneasy edge, the eruptions have doused the soils with nutrients. The peaks snatch at passing weather systems and squeeze out their moisture, and the bowls of land between them are well-watered. Java is one of the most fertile places on earth. What's more, its mellow northern littoral is indented with safe river-mouth anchorages and brushed by easy trade winds.

There were already Indianised states here well before the rise of Srivijaya in Sumatra. They are glimpsed in the passing comments of Chinese scribes and travellers. In 412 CE, Faxian—the wandering monk whose story would inspire Yijing almost three centuries later—stopped by on his return from India in a West Java state that seems to have been called Holotan. As a good Buddhist, Faxian was none too approving of the state of religious affairs he encountered in Java: 'Heretic Brahmans flourish there, and the Buddha-dharma hardly deserves mentioning', he noted.

Later another state—this one called Tarumanagara—grew up in the same place, and there were others, hinted at in Chinese chronicles and traced in scattered stone pillars, marked with the wriggling worm-casts of the Pallava script. But the relics of these earliest Javanese states are remarkably thin on the ground, for the inhabitants built their homes and palaces of wood and thatch, and in the hot, wet climate these materials would last little more than a single monsoon once a kingdom had collapsed.

But by the seventh century, a new state had appeared on the northern coast of Central Java. When the Chinese heard of this polity they noted its name as 'Ho-Ling'. This may have been a corruption of 'Kalingga', or perhaps 'Areng', but whatever it was called it marked the beginning of a relay of royal realms in Java that has continued all the way to the present day. And under the Ho-Ling aegis an epic tradition began of religious architecture in a medium more permanent than mere wood.

⊙−⊙−⊙−⊙−⊙

Java's earliest stone temples sprang up on the Dieng Plateau in the second half of the seventh century. People from the surrounding hills had probably been making offerings to ancestral spirits at the steaming sulphur vents and cool caves here for many centuries, but these new places of worship were sophisticated miniatures of Indian influence and local innovation. The builders cleared spaces amongst the stunted trees, and raised carven blocks into squat but finely formed towers. Soon there were some two hundred temples scattered across the plateau and the surrounding hillsides. They were modest structures that were rarely more than twenty-five feet (eight metres) high. But their design set the pattern for a coming epoch: the leering *kala* ogres above the portals; the narrow access steps; the three levels of construction that symbolised the worlds of the mortals, the enlightened and the gods. And soon the royals of the rice lands below the Dieng eyrie would take these conventions and inflate them to a truly epic scale.

Down the steep slopes from Dieng along trails beetling back and forth through the forest, under the ribbed flanks of the Sindoro and Sumbing volcanoes and southeast across smoky foot-hills and deep green ravines, a returning pilgrim would come to the lush levels of Kedu. This bowl of low, well-watered land was hemmed with forested hills. To the east rose the hulk of Gunung Merbabu and its mighty twin, Merapi, angriest of all the volcanoes of Central Java. To the north an easy route led between the mountains towards the ports of the north coast, and snaking over the plain came the Progo River, a band of pale water which ran southwards, out of Kedu itself and across a triangle of rich, level land spreading south from Merapi. This was all fabulously fecund country. Palms stood in long ranks and the hillsides were thick with forest. The Progo was fed by myriad smaller streams, churning around bleached boulders and driving deep clefts into the limitless black soil, and the well-watered plots gave out a ceaseless cycle of crops across the seasons. It was a true land of milk and honey, and it would soon become the enduring cradle of Javanese civilisation.

By the early eighth century the main political action in Java seems to have shifted from the north coast to Kedu and the wider basin of the Progo. In 732, a local raja had his craftsmen raise an inscribed stone on a hilltop south of Merapi. It told of his rule over 'a wonderful island beyond compare called Yava'. This king was called Sanjaya, a title he would pass on to a storied dynasty, and the general term for the area of Java over which he claimed control was Mataram, a name that would come to have such a hold on the Javanese imagination that it would eventually be re-vived by a line of Muslim sultans nearly a thousand years later.

Unlike their Srivijayan contemporaries in far-off Sumatra, the royals of Mataram were not, initially, concerned with maritime trade. There were no safe anchorages on the southern shores of

Java, and the ports of the north coast were some distance away. What was more, they had no particular impetus for internationalism at this early stage: the region produced all they could possibly need. Rice and pulses grew in the irrigated fields, and the forests turned out fruits and seeds and dyestuffs. There were mines for salt, fish in the rivers, and a solid tradition of craftwork. Much of the excess produce did, eventually, find its way out to the ports, but it travelled by way of middlemen in the markets that rotated through rural settlements on a five-day cycle, and the rulers probably had little direct involvement in the trade.

The power of these Javanese rulers was rooted in water of the fresh, rather than salt, variety. Any given tranche of farmland had to be irrigated to keep its soils turning out crops through the fiery dry months in the middle of the year. Complex networks of dykes and ditches criss-crossed the countryside, and keeping them all free from leaks demanded cooperation across any number of banyan-shaded villages. The councils and collectives that managed these water networks were the earliest forms of organised government, and from time to time the chief of a particular network would decide to extend his influence beyond the head of his longest irrigation trench.

Villages became small kingdoms, and something not unlike the Srivijayan hub-and-spoke model of power developed in Central Java. A king would have his own timber-built palace, known as a *kraton*, with a clutch of directly ruled fields and hamlets close by. Ranged at a distance around this fulcrum were the seats of other feudal lords, vassals of the central chief but each with its own spiral of subject villages. Still further afield would be other fiefdoms owing only the most notional allegiance to the centre. Across the network the rudiments of a tax system were already in place. Each village owed a certain time-honoured portion of their crops to the overlord, and each community owed a tranche of their time too, a fixed amount of man-hours to be given over to labouring on the landlord's behalf. These obligations in time and kind might be owed only to the local village chief, or they might be passed all the way up the chain of command to the king himself.

The whole set-up allowed separate dynasties to travel side-by-side in the same region, vying for ascendency without annihilating each other. Over the generations the hub of the power-wheel might shift to some new village as a different dynasty won supremacy; the spokes leading to outlying vassals would realign, but the power structures and systems of tax and tribute would remain essentially unchanged. In Mataram there were two of these jostling lineages, twin clans which would leave the most monumental of marks on the Javanese landscape.

⊙ — ⊙ — ⊙ — ⊙ — ⊙

In 779 the son of the first Sanjaya king, Panangkaran, erected his own inscription amidst the green fields of Mataram. It was a rectangular slab, densely fenced with strips of Sanskrit, and it described his own realm as 'the ornament of the Sailendra dynasty'. Forty-seven years earlier, Panangkaran's father might have considered himself the biggest fish in the Mataram pond, but now the Sanjayas found themselves the underlings of the shadowy Sailendras, the 'Kings of the Mountain'.

Everything about the Sailendras is enigmatic: we know nothing about their background and precious little about their culture. The source of their power is uncertain, and even their ethnicity is a bone of contention. But perhaps the most incongruous thing about the Sailendras is their religion. Four centuries earlier, the scholar-monk Faxian had dismissed Java as a realm of 'Heretic Brahmans', and though there was a garbled origin myth in Ho-Ling involving a wandering Buddhist prince—from Kashmir, of all places—for the most part Java seemed well established on the Hindu side of the coin. But then in the middle of the eighth century, a fully formed clan of orthodox Mahayana Buddhists materialised in Kedu and established supremacy over all Mataram.

Their foreign faith clearly gave them a spiritual connection with Srivijaya, and it may be that the Sailendras had at least some direct familial link with Sumatra. That they used Malay instead of Javanese in some of their inscriptions certainly bolsters this idea. Some have even suggested that the Sailendras and the Srivijayans were one and the same, and that for some reason they had upped sticks in Palembang and headed south for an interlude in Java.

Whatever the case, within a few years of setting themselves up in Kedu the Sailendras had embarked on the most ambitious building project that Java had ever seen, an overwhelming undertaking that would leave the Shaivite sanctuaries of Dieng looking like the merest molehills. The structure—standing at the junction of the Progo and Elo rivers—amounted to 1.5 million blocks of chiselled grey andesite, and when it was finished it was the biggest Buddhist monument on earth. Its name was Borobudur.

Work on this epic edifice probably began around 760, and continued for some seventy years. The stone was quarried from the banks of the Progo, then hauled uphill to be set in the model of a monumental mandala. Nine concentric terraces were raised, the lower six square in form, the upper trio a set of shrinking circles culminating in a single stupa. The walls and balustrades of the lower terraces were covered with friezes in narrative order—more than 2,500 individual panels amounting in total to a strip of stories some three miles (five kilometres) long. They told tales from the massed library of Buddhist lore, along with snatches of local colour: a house built on stilts on the old Austronesian model with wooden plates on the supports to keep out clambering rodents; a ship running through a driven sea with straining outriggers and full-bellied lateen sails; weighing scales and earthenware water jars; pigeons on the rooftops and monkeys in the treetops.

The men who built Borobudur worked without a single blueprint, and each generation of Sailendra kings made their own modifications and innovations. Just how many people worked on the vast monument over the years is unknown—there are no contemporary inscriptions giving clear and practical details of its construction. Looking at the thing as it now stands it might be easy to conjure up images of Pharoanic megalomania, with legions of cringing slaves labouring under the lash to build the insane follies of a despotism. That there was no entrenched Buddhist culture out in the countryside of Central Java surely supports this notion—the labourers lugging two hundred-pound (one-hundred-kilo) blocks up from the Progo lived in a land where the elite had practiced Shaivism for centuries and where the rural peasantry concerned themselves with their own local spirits and deified forebears. All this business of Bodhisats was, quite literally, a foreign language.

But this may not be the full story: given the seven-decade timeframe of Borobudur's construction, a couple of hundred men, working when harvest cycles allowed, could have achieved a very great deal. The Sailendras in all likelihood simply called upon that traditional obligation to offer part-time labour to the overlord. Men who were used to giving a portion of their working life to building roads or roofs for the ruler, or helping in the planting of royal rice fields, found themselves deflected in the direction of the andesite quarries on the Progo River. And given the remarkably catholic approach to alien belief systems that Java has displayed over the centuries, they probably simply shrugged when presented with yet another outlandish pantheon, and got on with the business in hand.

Nowhere else in the Archipelago could have supported a project on this scale. Away to the north in Sumatra the Srivijayans might have had maritime mastery, but seated amongst the swamps they had to import much of their own rice, and they had direct rule over only a small population of traders and fishermen. They could hardly have conceived a project on the scale of Borobudur, let alone brought it into being.

The Sailendras vanished almost as abruptly as they had appeared. By the early decades of the ninth century their dynasty was in decline, and that other regal lineage, the Sanjaya, was making a comeback. The Sanjaya scion of the day, a man by the name of Rakai Pikatan, embarked on a Sailendra-slashing rampage through the rice fields, and the last Sailendra king, Balaputra, turned tail and fled to Sumatra to seek refuge with his co-religionists in Srivijaya. All that remained was the recently completed Borobudur, coated now with white plaster and glowing like a single molar in the green jaw of Java. This spectacular architectural legacy of the departed Buddhist overlords seems to have rather rankled with Rakai Pikatan. If the Sailendras could build something as remarkable as Borobudur, then so could he: to mark the Sanjaya resurgence, in 856 he ordered the building of Prambanan.

If the Buddhist interlude under the Sailendras had been an aberration in the Javanese narrative, then Borobudur itself was an anomaly in the local architectural tradition: squat and square and quite unlike anything that went before or after. The resurgent Sanjayas, however, went back to the architectural form pioneered in Dieng two centuries earlier. The Prambanan temple complex, built on the banks of the Opak River close to the spot where Rakai Pikatan had his palace, featured a trio of towering temples in the classic three-tiered Javanese style, but expanded on a monstrous scale. The central temple was 154 feet (47 metres) tall.

Over the coming half-century Central Java developed an unfettered addiction to temple building. In almost every potentially auspicious spot, every pleasing plateau or conspicuous confluence, a column of carven black stone was thrown up by the masons. The plains and hills around Prambanan are thick with these temples. Some are dedicated exclusively to Shiva; a few are given over to the Buddha. But something significant was underway at the time: Java, it seems, was chewing up and digesting these once divergent Indian traditions and turning them into something of its own—a syncretic faith in which worship of Shiva dominated, but into which a Vaishnavite thread was also woven along with all sorts of local strands, and where the Buddha was a paid-up member of the pantheon. This tradition, which first took shape in Sanjaya-ruled Mataram, is best described as 'Hindu-Buddhism'.

They heyday of Sanjaya-ruled Mataram lasted a mere fifty years. What brought it to an end is unclear, but the unconstrained royal passion for temple building may have eventually put an unbearable strain on the old systems of labour obligation. Here and there a family might have quietly decided to strip the rattan walls of their hut, load their buffalo, and head east to a new country where there were no temple-mad kings. Such a process would only have accelerated in the third decade of the tenth century, when a massive eruption of the Merapi volcano devastated Mataram and caked the countryside with cloying grey ash. It was certainly at around that point that the elite itself decided to pack up and move out, leaving the temples to the birds and shifting the centre of royal power in Java some four hundred miles to the northeast. The move would bring an unexpected boon: the two distinct power sources that had fuelled the previous polities in the Archipelago—the maritime advantages of Srivijaya and the agricultural wealth of Mataram—were about to intersect with spectacular consequences.

◉−◉−◉−◉−◉

The mountain rises sheer from the sweltering coastal plains of northeast Java. It is modest compared to the monsters of the interior—a mere 5,240 feet (1,600 metres). And it is long-dead: no sulphurous smoke issues from its crown and the water from its springs is icy cold. But it is perfectly formed. Its crown bursts through the blanket of forest, marked with deep grooves and catching at the running cloud, and lower down, each of its cardinal points is marked by a smaller outlying summit. Sailors passing along the channel offshore can see it even on days when the bigger peaks behind are cloaked in cloud. It is a mountain that has been catching the eye and the imagination for millennia, and there were surely sacred sites on its forested flanks long before Indian, Arabian or European traditions washed ashore here. Its name is Gunung Penanggungan.

Penanggungan is the northernmost sentinel of the Arjuno-Welirang massif, a hulk of high ground with a river basin opening on either side. To the east lies the Malang plateau, drained by the Kali Welang River and with the huge Bromo-Tengger massif rising beyond. To the west, meanwhile, a much broader river basin opens—the floodplain of the Brantas, East Java's longest river.

It was in these basins on either side of Penanggungan that royal power reconfigured in the tenth century, and the mountain became the sacred mascot of the new realms, claimed to be the tip of the mythical Mount Mahameru, home of the Hindu pantheon, broken off when the gods transported it from India to Java. This new, volcano-guarded wellspring of history still offered all the rich returns of field and forest which had fuelled the ruling dynasties of Mataram. But the Brantas delta also emptied into a sheltered sea with safe anchorages and steady trade winds. If a single centre point of the Archipelago can be identified, then this is probably it. The region was equidistant between the Straits of Melaka and the Spice Islands of Maluku. Makassar, the major gateway to eastern waters, was an easy sail away across the Java Sea, as were the river mouths of southern Borneo.

The various kingdoms and dynasties that bubbled up on the Brantas and around the flanks of Penanggungan over the centuries were essentially reincarnations of the same polity. But with each rebirth the power grew—shipping lines crept further across the Archipelago and beyond, and new vassals were collected on far-flung shores. The capital of these East Java kingdoms was usually somewhere around the point where the Brantas splits into its delta, approachable by boat from the sea and in full view of Penanggungan. This political hub was twinned with a port at the mouth of the Kalimas distributary, the site of the modern city of Surabaya. Trade goods of all kinds passed through this harbour, but the greatest boon was spices—for nutmeg and cloves from Maluku had already become a major global commodity. Soon, East Java kings were collecting tribute from distant islands, and even beginning to challenge the Straits of Melaka as the focus of Archipelago trading power.

The first truly great king to rise out of this bubbling cauldron—and, indeed, one of the first historical figures in the Archipelago to have a character and a narrative still clearly discernible today—was a man by the name of Airlangga.

⊙−⊙−⊙−⊙−⊙

Airlangga was the son of Javanese princess called Mahendradatta and a Balinese king called Udayana. Bali was a remote and rugged place that had kept its old Austronesian traditions strong. Its own chieftains had probably had little contact with royal Java in the days when the Mataram region was the centre of the local universe. But once Javanese power had reconfigured closer at hand on the Brantas delta, the trajectories of Java and Bali had become increasingly intertwined—as Airlangga's ancestry so clearly shows. There was, however, already the potential for neighbourly ill-feeling, and Airlangga's Javanese mother Mahendradatta would eventually be reincarnated as the most grotesque of all Balinese horrors—the mythical witch-widow Rangda.

Airlangga was born around 991, quite possibly in Bali itself, and his name meant 'Jumping Water', presumably as a nod to his strait-spanning ancestry. He would not be the only great Indonesian leader of mixed Javanese-Balinese ancestry—though it would be a full nine hundred years before his successor appeared.

He came to power in the early eleventh century after his father's kingdom had been destroyed in a conflict with Srivijaya. According to legend, the teenage Airlangga was the sole survivor of the old court, and after its destruction he sought refuge with a community of ascetics in the karst hills near the south coast. This motif of a youthful king-in-waiting serving out a period of exile amongst the jungle mystics would repeat over and over down the course of Javanese history, and would even find echoes in the political exiles of the twentieth-century independence struggle. In Airlangga's prototype tale the prince was tracked down to his remote retreat by a gaggle of dissolute Brahmans, who beseeched him to take up the royal mantle and resurrect the East Java polity. By the second decade of the eleventh century he had done their bidding and was back on the Brantas delta, ruling from a capital called Kahuripan and labouring under the spectacularly grandiose title of 'Sri Maharaja Rakai Halu Sri Lokeswara Dharmawangsa Airlangga Anantawikramottunggadewa'.

⊙—⊙—⊙—⊙—⊙

After Airlangga's death in 1049 his kingdom was divided be-tween his sons. In the received version of events the old king himself had ordered the partition in an effort to stave off a civil war upon his demise. In truth, however, the split may have been the result of just such a war, rather than a preventative meas-ure. It wasn't until the middle of the twelfth century that a king called Joyoboyo managed to put the divided realm back together. He ruled from a capital at Kediri on the middle reaches of the Brantas and had a sideline in popular prophecy. Joyoboyo codified the concept of the *Ratu Adil*, the messianic 'Righteous Prince' who would periodically emerge from the ether to save Java from catastrophe. Apocryphal versions of his predictions are still doing the rounds today.

In 1222, yet another new king forged yet another new royal capital at Singhasari, in the basin of the Kali Welang River, close to where the city of Malang stands today. If Airlangga and Joy-oboyo had provided the model for righteous princes and mystic kings-in-waiting, then this man, Ken Arok, offered an altogether less admirable prototype. He has gone down in legend as an orphan thief who wheedled his way into a vassal court of Kediri, killed the local lord, and then set about overthrowing Kediri itself. He was, in short, a *jago*—a term that literally means 'fighting cock' but which encompasses rebels, gangsters, upstarts—and the epitome of exactly what happens when a righteous prince goes wrong.

While power was ping-ponging back and forth between the jagos and the just, ever larger volumes of spice were being transshipped through the Brantas ports. Java's renown as a bustling hub of tropical trade soon spread throughout Asia, and even wandering Italians would pick up snatches of conversation about its riches. Marco Polo, travelling to China in the second half of the thirteenth century, reported that Java 'is of surpassing wealth… frequented by a vast amount of shipping, and by merchants who buy and sell costly goods from which they reap great profit'.

The pot of power in East Java was already coming up from a slow simmer to a rolling boil, but the fuel that would see it bubble right over came from an unexpected angle—a diplomatic mission despatched by a warrior king from the Mongolian steppe.

⊙ — ⊙ — ⊙ — ⊙ — ⊙

They could see the cone of Gunung Penanggungan from their ships, with the line of the Javanese coastline dark beyond a steel-grey sea. It was early 1293 and the Mongol commanders must have wondered what exactly they were doing in this strange place.

Three decades earlier, the Mongols had descended on China and set themselves up as celestial emperors in the form of the Yuan Dynasty. As Yuan Emperor, Kublai Khan—in between decreeing stately pleasure domes and trying to rein in the rampaging Golden Horde—set about sending missions to demand acknowledgment from the Southeast Asian vassals of the previous Chinese dynasty. He was particularly concerned about the Singhasari kingdom which, by the late thirteenth century, had its own vassals in Bali and Borneo, and which was even developing diplomatic ties with the Champa kingdom of Vietnam. Worried about what looked like a sort of proto-hegemony in the Archipelago, Kublai Khan despatched three missions to seek tribute from Singhasari. He sent the first in 1280, with another the following year. Neither met with much success, so in 1289 yet another diplomatic fleet departed on the monsoon trade winds, anchored off the Brantas delta, and sent a party ashore to negotiate with the then Singhasari king, a decidedly headstrong man by the name of Kertanagara. The visitors soon discovered that Kertanagara was not in the business of taking orders from anyone, not even the ruler with the best claim to the title of most powerful man on earth. What exactly he did to Kublai Khan's principal diplomat, Meng Qi, depends on who is telling the tale, but the unfortunate envoy certainly lost face, so to speak—Kertanagara either cut off his nose, branded his visage with a red-hot iron, or sliced his ears off. Naturally, the Great Khan did not react mildly when his humiliated ambassador came home: in 1293 he sent another fleet to seek revenge.

The avenging armada was enormous. Around a thousand vessels had come lumbering across the South China Sea from Canton under the command of a trio of multi-ethnic admirals—a Mongol, a Uighur and a Han Chinese. They extracted submission and tribute from petty polities along the way, and when they swung to anchor off the mouth of the Brantas delta and looked out on the distant outline of Penanggungan, they must have felt that they were undefeatable. However, the first local messengers who paddled out to meet them let them know that things in the region had changed since the departure of the red-faced envoy four years earlier. The troublesome king Kertanagara was dead and Singhasari itself had been toppled by a rebel prince called Jayakatwang, who had installed himself at the earlier capital of Kediri.

The Mongol commanders would later realise that at this point they ought to have swung their ships around and crept off as quietly as they could. Instead, they allowed themselves to be convinced by a son-in-law of the deposed Kertanagara to take part in a counter-revolution against Jayakatwang at Kediri. This son-in-law—whose name was Raden Wijaya—had a small fiefdom on the Brantas downstream from Kediri, and since the fall of Singhasari he had been quietly playing the role of malleable vassal. Now, however, he led the Mongol army up the river, overwhelming outlying Kediri garrisons. In April, with the last of the monsoon rains, the invaders surrounded the Kediri capital and forced an easy capitulation out of Jayakatwang.

Raden Wijaya very clearly carried the same jago genes as his Singhasari forebear, Ken Arok, for he now embarked on the most spectacular piece of treachery. Instead of politely thanking the baffled Mongols who had just done his improbable bidding, he turned against them and conjured up a country-wide uprising. The Mongols did their best to resist, but this land of rice fields and palm groves was no place for men of the open steppe, and they had no real idea what they were doing in Java in the first place. After two hard, sweaty months of guerrilla warfare up and down the lower Brantas, they scuttled back to their ships and fled.

The Mongols, who had sacked Baghdad and stormed all the way to the borders of Christian Europe, had been chased out of Java by a junior prince of a toppled dynasty. Raden Wijaya had good reason to feel proud of himself. He went back to his little capital—a village about twelve miles west of Gunung Penanggungan—and turned it into an empire called Majapahit.

⊙ — ⊙ — ⊙ — ⊙ — ⊙

The word 'Majapahit' rings like a bell through the halls of Indonesian history. The name of no other realm before or since resounds as this one does. This is, in part, down to the way in which it has been used and abused in the long centuries since its fall. Later Javanese kings, nineteenth-century European orientalists, and strident Indonesian nationalists have all retooled its reputation to fit their own prejudices and purposes. But despite the static of later fantasy that crackles around it, the historical Majapahit really was very impressive indeed.

Raden Wijaya (who ruled as 'Kertarajasa') died in 1309. He was succeeded by his son Jayanagara—by all accounts a rather sleazy character who had an unsavoury sexual obsession with his own stepsisters and who died in 1328 at the hands of a court physician he had cuckolded. Surprisingly, given his reputation, Jayanagara left no son of his own, and after his death there was a period of regency rule with queens at the head of the court. In 1350, however, a young prince named Hayam Wuruk ascended the throne.

By this time the Majapahit capital had grown from a village to a grand city. Some thirty miles up the Brantas from the sea, the kraton—the royal palace—was ringed by a wall of red brick. To the north, on the banks of the river, was the residential and trading city of Bubat, with a pulsing marketplace centred on a great square. There were all manner of foreign communities here, Chinese and Indian amongst them. The high-point of the Majapahit year was the celebration that marked Chaitra, the first month in the Hindu Saka Calendar. Festivities went on for weeks, with parades of princes dressed in cloth-of-gold. There were challenges of combat in the square at Bubat, and elaborate ceremonies in which the king received tribute then dished out lavish largesse in return. According to court chroniclers, towards the end of the festival things usually descended into a glorious tropical bacchanalia, with massed feasting on 'meats innumerable', and quaffing of heroic quantities of palm wine and arak until the point at which the entire population was 'panting, vomiting, or bewildered...'

Hangovers notwithstanding, the realm was remarkably well-run. On the Brantas delta the old and corrupt layers of taxation through local lords were simplified so that payment—in cash or kind—went straight to the kraton. Majapahit also had a thriving spiritual life. Both Buddhist monks and Shaivite priests were given their own quarters in the capital, and the surrounding countryside was studded with temples. Airlangga's old bathing temples on the slopes of Penanggungan got a new lease of life, and away to the south, in the beautiful countryside where the Brantas valley rumples up towards Gunung Kelud, an old Singhasari Shiva complex was updated and expanded to become the mighty temple of Panataran, a major focus of royal pilgrimages. There were already distinct local versions of the Indian epics the *Mahabharata* and the *Ramayana,* rewritten so that the escapades of the Pandava brothers and the adventures of Rama and Sita were now played out against a recognisably Javanese backdrop. Batik was already being crafted in village workshops, and complex traditions of music and dance were coming to fruition, as a visitor from the north of Sumatra described:

> Everywhere one went there were gongs and drums being beaten, people dancing to the strains of all kinds of loud music, entertainments of all kinds like the living theatre, the shadow play, masked plays, step dancing, and musical dramas. These were the commonest sights and went on day and night in the land of Majapahit.

These refined entertainments—the *wayang kulit* shadow puppetry, the masked *topeng* dances and more—would remain the cultural mainstays of Java and the lands that came under its influence forever more.

Feasting and frolicking cost money, of course, and the cash came mainly from trade. Majapahit had its own fleet—part merchant navy, part pirate armada—which traded out across the Java Sea and beyond, carrying, according to one account, everything from 'pig and deer dried and salted' to 'camphor and aloes'. The kingdom also consolidated and extended the network of offshore tributaries and vassals that had been stitched to East Java during

Singhasari days, and managed a good number of military conquests closer to home for good measure. All this did a great deal for Hayam Wuruk's reputation as a god-king, and soon his court chroniclers were tripping over themselves to heap superlative epithets upon his head:

> He is present in invisible form at the focus of meditation,
> he is Siwa and Buddha, embodied in both the material and
> the immaterial;
>   As King of the Mountain, Protector of the Protectorless,
> he is lord of the lords of the world …

In fact the real genius behind all this commercial and military glory was not Hayam Wuruk himself, but his *mahapatih*, his prime minister, a thundering Machiavelli of a man by the name of Gajah Mada, the 'Elephant General'.

⊙−⊙−⊙−⊙−⊙

Gajah Mada had first found favour under the debauched Jayanagara. It seems that he was a significant schemer from the start, for rumour has it that it was he who had incited the cuckolded court physician to kill his king. He was given the role of prime minister in 1331 in the regency period before Hayam Wuruk's coronation. During the lavish ceremony that marked his appointment, Gajah Mada made a vow. He would not, he declared, 'taste spice' until *Nusantara* had been brought under Majapahit sway.

'Nusantara' literally means 'the islands in between'. Gajah Mada probably meant by it something along the lines of 'the outer islands', but in time the word would form the key to the concept of the Archipelago as a single entity—if not a single nation. Today it is a synonym for 'Indonesia' itself.

By the time Hayam Wuruk was king, Gajah Mada had already made sure that Majapahit had more or less direct control over most of East Java, Madura and Bali, with a solid footing in Lombok and Sumbawa too. The Majapahit fleet had also become the main force in the Straits of Melaka. Over the course of Hayam Wuruk's reign, more links were forged across Nusantara.

Not everyone was prepared to acknowledge Majapahit suzerainty, however. A particular thorn in the Majapahit side was its West Java counterpart, the Sundanese kingdom of Pajajaran, a realm which had never submitted entirely to East Javanese rule. In 1357, in an effort to forge a bond, Hayam Wuruk contracted a marriage with a princess by the name of Pitaloka, daughter of the Pajajaran king. When the Sundanese wedding party arrived in the capital Gajah Mada informed them that the girl would be less of a queen than a concubine, and that the moment had come for Sunda to submit to its East Javanese overlords. The Sundanese were a proud lot, and despite the fact that they were camped out in Bubat, smack in the middle of Majapahit and surrounded by hostile forces, they refused. It was a brave but suicidal gesture. In response, Gajah Mada had the entire bridal party—including the bride-to-be—massacred. Naturally relations between Majapahit and Pajajaran would never be particularly cordial after that, and even today the ethnic Sundanese country of West Java, centred on Bandung, is the one part of Indonesia where 'Majapahit' is something of a dirty word.

$$\odot - \odot - \odot - \odot - \odot$$

In the *Negarakertagama*, the epic poem written out on strips of lontar leaf to mark the apogee of Hayam Wuruk's reign, a huge swathe of the Archipelago is claimed for Majapahit. Everywhere from the northern tip of Sumatra to the westernmost promontory of New Guinea gets a mention. It is a rundown that comes remarkably close to encompassing the entire Archipelago, and with the very notable exception of interior New Guinea and southern Maluku, it takes in all modern Indonesian territories and a little more besides. Any places in this vast maritime realm that failed to acknowledge Majapahit supremacy were, according to the *Negarakertagama*, 'attacked and wiped out completely'.

Inevitably, later nationalists would latch very firmly onto this aspect of Majapahit and claim it as a pre-colonial precedent for the existence of the Indonesian nation state. Some of the islands and outposts mentioned in the *Negarakertagama* do seem to have been directly conquered by Majapahit at some point, but for the most part the list of scattered vassals probably amounts to little more than a run-down of all the places with which Majapahit had ever traded.

Rather than a true empire in the European sense, Majapahit, like Srivijaya before it, was a cultural and economic brand. The extent of its direct rule and centralised authority probably stretched little further than East Java, Bali and Madura, but its pervasive presence on the sea routes and its remarkable cultural sophistication gave it incredible kudos throughout the Archipelago. If the Majapahit king could have his chroniclers claim ownership of some isolated dot of land in a lost eastern sea that no one from Java had ever even visited, then the petty chieftain of that same dot might well award himself hand-me-down Javanese airs and graces when he wanted to impress his subjects. Origin myths in remote places like Adonara at the eastern extremity of Nusa Tenggara, or the misty Pasemah Highlands of Sumatra, make a claim of royal Javanese descent, and art-forms, palace architecture, dress and even language across the Archipelago would display a conscious Majapahit influence for centuries to come.

Gajah Mada died in around 1364. Hayam Wuruk continued without him for another twenty-five years, commanding that final annihilation of vestigial Srivijayan power in 1377 and earning Chinese respect, rather than retribution, for the extermination of their mission to Sumatra. But by this stage Majapahit had probably already passed its prime. All royal houses and great businesses eventually decay—and Majapahit was both. The problem for the

East Java royals was probably that they had been *too* successful. The Archipelago economy had grown so vibrant under their aegis that the wealthy tributary chiefs of ports in Sumatra, Borneo, Sulawesi and beyond had every reason to strike out on their own the moment they suspected a weakness at the centre. Majapahit's energy had created the opportunity for the myriad entrepôt-states across the Archipelago that would ultimately usurp it. And the Majapahit-inspired atmosphere of internationalism would also provide the essential fertiliser for a cultural shift that would end the thousand-year process of Indianisation in the Archipelago.

⊙—⊙—⊙—⊙—⊙

In 1407, another Chinese fleet anchored off the coast of East Java. Unlike the Mongol armada 114 years earlier, it was not there to invade: its business was trade, treasure and tribute. It was quite unlike anything anyone had ever seen. A forest of brick-red sails stretched to the horizon over a flotilla of some three hundred ships. And if the size of the fleet was impressive enough, then the scale of the vessels themselves was truly staggering. The biggest amongst them were some 390 feet (120 metres) long with decks the size of football pitches. They were five times bigger than the Portuguese carracks that would begin to edge their way across the Indian Ocean in the following century. The fleet was a floating city of 30,000 men headed by seven imperial eunuchs and tended by 180 doctors and half a dozen astrologers.

Majapahit was still alive and kicking, and though its power had begun to atrophy in the western reaches of the Archipelago, it was still a place deserving of a visit from this, the first of a series of spectacular treasure fleets that the Ming Emperor, now ruling in place of the evicted Mongol Yuan Dynasty, would despatch to the furthest reaches of the Indian Ocean—and which would eventually carry the first giraffe back to China. The man placed at the head of these epic voyages was not the most likely candidate for the role of greatest seafarer in Chinese history. Zheng He (sometimes spelt as Cheng Ho) was the descendent of central Asian migrants, born in 1371 far from the sea in Yunnan and raised as a Muslim. As a small child he had been kidnapped by resurgent Ming troops, castrated, and dragged off to the north to serve as a eunuch at the imperial court. Despite his early emasculation, he grew to a formidable height and spoke with 'a voice as loud as a huge bell', becoming a key strategist in the Chinese court. When the first of the mighty treasure fleets sailed, Zheng He was placed in charge.

When Zheng He's men came ashore in Java they discovered a rather violent place. In a small skirmish 170 sailors were killed, and one of the fleet's chroniclers recorded that all the locals—'little boys of three years to old men of a hundred years'—were armed with deadly *kris* daggers, and that 'If a man touches [another man's] head with his hand, or if there is a misunderstanding about money at a sale, or a battle of words when they are crazy with drunkenness, they at once pull out these knives and stab…'

The unravelling authority of Majapahit was probably responsible for the edgy atmosphere, but the capital on the banks of the Brantas was still a bustling place. And it was still remarkably cosmopolitan. The sailors would doubtless have found other Chinese living around the market square of Bubat, as well as Indians, Sri Lankans, and people from the Southeast Asian mainland. There is no record of whether Zheng He himself ever came ashore, but had he done so he would almost certainly have encountered a few co-religionists in Majapahit, for by the beginning of the fifteenth century there were Muslims quietly settling in all over the Archipelago. Majapahit might still be rumbling on—and indeed it would be another hundred years before it finally breathed its last—but the Hindu-Buddhist centuries were coming rapidly to an end and the scene was set for the next great sea change in Southeast Asia.

CHAPTER 3

SAINTS AND WINNERS: THE ARRIVAL OF ISLAM

They had sighted the land when they were still far out at sea: a long, grey-green stain stretching out across the horizon of the Andaman Sea. It took shape as they edged steadily towards it over the course of the morning: a range of mountains rearing inland under banks of creamy cloud, and a strip of pale foreshore under an infinite rank of palms. Eventually the ship—a Bengali merchantman that had been lumbering southwards for twenty-five days since its last landfall—came to anchor in the shallows. There was a large village of thatch-roofed houses onshore, and as the ship swung to her anchor rope, small boats swarmed around it with villagers clamouring for a sale and holding up bunches of ripe bananas, fat mangoes, bulbous green coconuts and bundles of dried fish.

As the merchants and crewmen reached down from the deck and embarked on their first bout of commerce after a month at sea, one of the passengers looked out on the scene, noting its detail in his formidable memory and wondering what he would find here, in yet another strange land. He was forty-one years old and seven thousand miles from home. His name was Ibn Battuta, and now, after twenty years of travel, he had reached the Sumatran state of Samudra Pasai. It was 1345.

Ibn Battuta was a Moroccan Muslim, born in 1304 in Tangier—a town at the mouth of the Mediterranean and in view of the sierras of southern Europe. He was clearly a man afflicted with a truly spectacular case of wanderlust, for at the age of twenty-one, 'swayed by an overmastering impulse within me' and 'finding no companion to cheer the way', he had left his sobbing parents and headed eastwards. He was planning merely to complete the Haj, the mandatory Muslim pilgrimage to Mecca. But once Ibn Battuta was on the road, there was no stopping him. He wandered right, left and centre through the swelling realms of fourteenth-century Islam, eventually winding up as a *qadi*—an administrator of Islamic jurisprudence—at the court of Sultan Muhammad bin Tughluq in Delhi.

Many years later, back at home in Morocco after three decades on the road, Ibn Battuta would dictate the tale of his travels. It was a story full of colour, rich in the detail of life in far-off lands—and rich also with insights into the author's own character. He was a man thoroughly interested and engaged in the world around him, taking careful note not only of the dynastic and theological arrangements in far-flung sultanates, but also of what was sold in the markets, of how the people dressed and ate, and of what they said. He was, in short, a travel writer par excellence.

In 1345 Ibn Battuta had left India for Sumatra, where, once the babble of bargaining with the local hawkers had died down, an official came aboard the ship with the news that the local ruler would be delighted to make Ibn Battuta's acquaintance—for he, too, was a Muslim. Ibn Battuta was led inland between banks of lush greenery and wooden houses built on stilts. Several miles from the shore he came to the capital—'a large and beautiful city encompassed by a wooden wall with wooden towers'—where he was told to swap his Arab robes for a local-style sarong. Once the costume change was complete he was installed in a house in the middle of a garden and provided with a pair of slave girls. The custom of the country, he was told, was that he must bide his time for three days before meeting the sultan. The wait was hardly on-erous. Food, he noted, was 'sent to us thrice a day and fruits and rare sweetmeats every evening and morning'; the locals seemed to be good Muslims of the Shafi'i school of Law, and the slave girls were excellent company.

The following Friday he finally met the sultan, Mahmud Ma-lik az-Zahir, in the royal enclosure of the grand mosque. Once prayers were over there was a lavish entertainment laid on for the ruler and his guest:

> Male musicians came in and sang ... after which they led
> in horses with silk caparisons, golden anklets, and halters of
> embroidered silk. These horses danced before [the sultan],
> a thing which astonished me...

Ibn Battuta stayed with the sultan for two weeks before travel-ling onwards to China. He was very impressed with what he had seen. Samudra Pasai—a pocket of territory on the far northeast littoral of Sumatra in what is now the province of Aceh—was a hive of tropical commerce. Locals traded using tin cash and pieces of unrefined gold, and the hinterlands were rich with areca, aloes, camphor and all manner of fruits. Above all, as a sometime theolo-gian and a part-time zealot, Ibn Battuta was particularly pleased to find a small Muslim territory here at the ends of the earth. Sultan Mahmud, he declared, was 'a most illustrious and open-handed ruler, and a lover of theologians':

> He is constantly engaged in warring for the Faith and in
> raiding expeditions, but is withal a humble-hearted man,
> who walks on foot to the Friday prayers. His subjects also
> take pleasure in warring for the Faith and voluntarily ac-
> company him on his expeditions. They have the upper
> hand over all the infidels in their vicinity.

Away to the south in Java, Hayam Wuruk had not yet ascended to the throne of Majapahit and Hindu-Buddhist priests were still traipsing along the pilgrimage trails of Gunung Penanggungan. But here in Sumatra a new chapter in Archipelago history was already unfolding.

⊙—⊙—⊙—⊙—⊙

Islam had emerged from central Arabia in the early seventh century. Forged of a mixed Judaeo-Christian heritage and a desert Arab culture, it had swiftly spilled out from its Meccan wellspring, filling the Arabian Peninsula and the eastern Mediterranean, seeping up into central Asia, and leaching across North Africa. By the time Ibn Battuta was born, his native Morocco had been Muslim for some six centuries.

Even beyond the fringes of the territory under direct Muslim rule, the faith continued its journey. Sailors from the baking shores of Arabia had long ruled the waves of the Indian Ocean, and they carried the new confession out across clear blue waters. By the early eighth century, there were already communities of Muslims on the coasts of India. On land, too, trade and travel carried Islam eastwards, between the caravanserais of Oxiana and across the Hindu Kush and Tien Shan into China. Muslims of mixed Turkic and Chinese descent were soon settled in pockets across the Middle Kingdom—and also in its coastal cities, where the tribute ships from Southeast Asia came to anchor.

Obviously, then, there must have been Muslims visiting the ports of the Archipelago from an early stage. Way back in 671 the Chinese traveller Yijing had reached the capital of Srivijaya aboard what he called a 'Persian' ship—and by that time Persia was already under the sway of the Muslim Umayyad Caliphate. In subsequent centuries, a number of envoys from Buddhist Srivijaya were recorded in the Chinese annals under suspiciously Muslim-sounding names. These men were almost certainly not locals:

Srivijaya was a cosmopolitan place, and if there were Buddhist monks from the east camping out there to learn Sanskrit on their way to India, then there would likely have been a good few Muslim foreigners from the west too, offering their seafaring services to the king.

In Java, meanwhile, the oldest palpable trace of a Muslim presence comes in the form of a grave where an unnamed woman, daughter of a man called Maimun, was laid to rest some twenty miles inland from the north coast of the Hindu–Buddhist kingdom of Kediri in 1082. Who she was and what she was doing there is anyone's guess, but in the decades and centuries that followed, more of these incongruous tombs appear—a headstone and a footstone marking a narrow strip of earth and angled east–west in a best-guess approximation of the direction of Mecca. They stud the Archipelago in a cryptic pattern like the pins on some vast incident map.

By the early thirteenth century, there would certainly have been Muslim communities living in ports around the Straits of Melaka, out along the northern littoral of Java, and perhaps elsewhere, too. These maritime Muslims would have been of foreign origin. Some were probably Arabs, but others—probably the majority—hailed from elsewhere: Persia, Gujarat, Bengal and China. Like other traders and travellers before them they would probably have taken local wives, and these long-forgotten women would have been the very earliest converts to Islam in the Archipelago. They did not, however, start a trend, and the pockets of coastal Islam stayed quiet and inconspicuous as Hindu–Buddhist temples sprouted across Java, as Srivijaya rose and fell, and as Majapahit blossomed on the Brantas delta.

This all sounds rather familiar, and there are clear parallels between the arrival of Islam in the Archipelago and the arrival of the Indian faiths a thousand years earlier: the early presence of foreign traders professing a new religion; the old-established commercial communities in the ports; a centuries-long imperviousness on the part of the locals to their religious offerings; and then a sudden shift and a rush of state conversions.

The hows and the whys of the Archipelago's move into Islam ought to be much clearer than those of the earlier Indic change. There had been many centuries of literacy in the island courts, and if we know what they ate on feast days in Hindu-Buddhist Java, then surely we should have clear accounts of just why and when it was that they stopped eating pork. But a state conversion usually came with the rise of some new dynasty, and the rise of a new dynasty required the fall of an old one. The move from Hindu-Buddhism to Islam, then, almost always came at the point when conditions were at their most unsettled and when no one was bothering to take notes. In future centuries, local people would have to gather the small fragments of folk memory and make of them fabulous stories to explain just why they were Muslims.

$$\odot - \odot - \odot - \odot - \odot$$

It was the far north of Sumatra that offered Islam its first proper toehold in Southeast Asia. For a start, it was closer to the Muslim states on the other shores of the Indian Ocean than anywhere else in the Archipelago, and it would eventually come to be known as 'Mecca's Veranda' for its orthodoxy and its links with Arabia. The legend of how Islam came to Samudra Pasai, the north Sumatran sultanate that Ibn Battuta visited in 1345, is anything but orthodox, however.

According to the tale, the change came by way of a miracle as a heathen king named Merah Silau lay sleeping one night in his palm-thatched palace. The Prophet Muhammad appeared to him in a dream and—of all the strange things—spat in his mouth. When the baffled royal (who was presumably some sort of Hindu-Buddhist) woke, he found strange words spilling from his tongue. This was startling enough, but he had a still bigger shock when he examined himself and discovered that he had somehow been circumcised in his sleep! Merah Silau's subjects were understandably a little bemused by their king's bizarre new demeanour (he perhaps did not share with them the details of his alarming physical modification). However, all became clear shortly afterwards when a ship from Arabia arrived. Its captain informed the locals that the apparent gobbledegook Merah Silau had been babbling was in fact the *Shahada*, the Islamic Confession of Faith, and that their king was a ready-made Muslim.

Merah Silau—who ruled as Sultan Malik as-Salih—was a real king. His grave, not far from the modern city of Lhokseumawe, is dated to 1297. But tales of strange dreams aside, what exactly prompted these early conversions is unclear. There were certainly no conquests by alien armies under the banner of Islam. And though the presence of foreign Muslims in the ports obviously gave local kings and commoners their first sight of the new religion, the fact that they had been there for several centuries before the large-scale shift began suggests that they do not deserve sole credit for the change. As with the earlier introduction of Hindu-Buddhism, it was probably kingly pragmatism that provided the ultimate impetus.

By the end of the thirteenth century Islam had become increasingly ubiquitous across Asia, just as Hindu-Buddhism was beginning to go out of fashion. Ships sailing into the Archipelago from all corners of the Indian Ocean—and from ports to the northeast, too—were as likely as not to be captained by Muslims. In India, the original Hindu-Buddhist lodestar, more and more states were headed by Muslim kings. Even the emperors of China were despatching Muslim eunuchs on missions to the wider world. There was no other entity so obviously universal, and by signing up to Islam an Archipelago king would allow himself an obvious connection with many distant rulers—a natural bond of trade and sympathy, and a membership card to a new kind of internationalism. Soon, there were little pockets of Islam pop-ping up all over the Archipelago. On the west coast of the Malay Peninsula, Melaka was under Muslim rule by the late fourteenth century—after the local king underwent a similarly miraculous conversion to that of Merah Silau, if the stories are to be believed. Brunei, on the northern slant of Borneo, was officially Muslim from 1363. By the mid-fifteenth century, Islam had reached as far east as Maluku, where the ruling families of the tiny island seats of Ternate and Tidore converted in the 1460s. Before long, there were so many Muslim chiefs ruling so many tiny islands in this eastern region that Arab spice traders began to call the place *Jazirat al-Muluk*, 'The Islands of Kings'—from which Maluku takes its modern name.

By the dawn of the sixteenth century the Archipelago was undergoing a formidable change in complexion, and while we may not know exactly *why* or *how* it was happening, we do have a remarkable snapshot of the details on the ground—for it was at this point that an altogether new set of foreigners arrived in Southeast Asia—confessing, as it happened, yet another new religion.

⊙—⊙—⊙—⊙—⊙

On 20 May 1498, a fleet of four strange ships came to anchor off the coast of Kerala in the deep palm-clad south of India. The ships were broad-bellied, high-prowed carracks, square-rigged fore and lateen-rigged aft, with wind-shredded banners trailing from their topmasts. Their commander was a bull-chested man by the name of Vasco de Gama, and with this steamy landfall—six years after his compatriot Christopher Columbus accidentally stumbled upon the New World—he had completed the first successful European voyage to Asia.

The Portuguese were the first European nation out of the colonial starting blocks. They had advanced seafaring skills—borrowed in part from the Arabs of the Mediterranean—and a meticulous approach to navigation and record-keeping. As one

English missionary who hitched a ride on an early voyage to India noted, 'there is not a fowl that appeareth or sign in the air or in the sea which they have not written down'. They had crossed the Equator in ships before anyone else, and rounded the Cape of Good Hope in an era when much trade with Asia still travelled along the Silk Road. What prompted these improbable voyages was the heady scent of spice.

Spices from the Archipelago had been finding their way into Europe since at least the Roman era. But while Srivijaya and Majapahit had grown fat on shipping spice to all points of the Asian compass, the onward flow into Europe had always been controlled by ocean-going Arabs and their Venetian trading partners. The fortunes that these middlemen accrued were astronomical, thanks to market demand for spices. Nutmeg was particularly prized; it was touted not only as a flavouring but also as an aphrodisiac and a plague cure, and at times it was worth more than its weight in gold. Cloves and pepper, too, were rare and valuable commodities. In the mid-fifteenth century, under the energetic patronage of Prince Henry the Navigator, Portuguese sailors began their efforts to tap into the source of all these spices.

Within a decade of de Gama's first voyage, the Portuguese had set up a modest empire of mildewed white churches in Goa, and soon they were edging even further eastward. In 1511 they captured Melaka, the post-Srivijaya linchpin of trade in the narrow strait between Sumatra and the Malay Peninsula. It was, according to one of their number, the premier port on the planet: 'I believe that more ships arrive here than in any other place in the world, and especially come here all sorts of spices and an immense quantity of other merchandise'. Once they had established their base on the Straits, the Portuguese headed east to Maluku in search of the source of the spice.

On the side-lines of the trade, the Portuguese were making records of what they saw around them, and these accounts form the earliest European primary sources about the Archipelago. One

Portuguese document was particularly remarkable. It was written by a pharmacist with an exceptional talent for journalism, and it offered a detailed outside view of Islamisation in action.

⊙—⊙—⊙—⊙—⊙

In 1512, an apothecary from Lisbon arrived in the new Portuguese outpost of Melaka. He had been sent out to Goa the previous year to take charge of issuing ineffectual fever cures to the nascent Catholic community there, and had then shipped out further east. His name was Tomé Pires, and though he was a medicine man by trade, his real forte turned out to be reportage. During the three years he spent based in Melaka, he visited many corners of the Archipelago and noted down everything he saw. He also listened carefully to the reports of other Europeans and of the locals in the ports he visited. What really marked Pires out from virtually every other scribbling traveller of the age—from Ibn Battuta to Marco Polo—was his remarkable journalistic insistence on corroboration and fact-checking. This was not a writer to pass on as fact a third-hand tall tale of men with heads like dogs. If he heard a story, he needed it to be credible before he would credit it—and he needed to hear it from more than one mouth. His finished write-up was an astounding document called the *Suma Oriental que trata do Mar Roxo até aos Chins*, the 'Summation of the East from the Red Sea up to the Chinese'. Incredibly, the document was never published in his own lifetime. It was bundled away and forgotten after Pires left Melaka for China—where he seems to have died a mysterious death in a dungeon—and it would be four centuries before this mighty trove of humbly presented but scientifically gathered information was uncovered.

The first thing that Pires' account makes clear is just how spectacularly cosmopolitan the ports of the Archipelago had become by the sixteenth century. Melaka itself was a veritable human zoo:

Moors from Cairo, Mecca, Aden, Abyssinians, men of Kil-
wa, Malindi, Ormuz, Panees, Rumes, Turks, Turkomans,
Christian Armenians, Gujaratees, men of Chaul, Dabhol,
Goa, of the kingdom of Deccan, Malabars and Klings, mer-
chants from Orissa, Ceylon, Bengal, Arakan, Pegu, Siamese,
men of Kedah, Malays, men of Pahang, Patani, Cambodia,
Champa, Cochin China, Chinese, Lequeos, men of Brunei,
Lucoes, men of Tamjompura, Laue, Banka, Linga (they have
a thousand other islands), Moluccas, Banda, Bima, Timor,
Madura, Java, Sunda, Palembang, Jambi, Tongkal, Indragiri,
Kappatta, Menangkabau, Siak, Arqua, Aru, Bata, country of
the Tomjano, Pase, Pedir, Maldives.

Across the water, meanwhile, Sumatra was in the grip of a great
cultural change. A century and a half since Ibn Battuta's visit, the
east coast of the island between Aceh and Palembang was entirely
under Muslim rule. The far south was mostly still 'heathen', but
that, too, was rapidly changing. Samudra Pasai—which had, Pires
noted, given its name to the whole island: Samudra, or 'Sumatra'—had done well from the Portuguese seizure of Melaka. The
Catholic conquest had displaced many of the expat Muslim traders based there, sending them scurrying away to seek out new
footings in the Archipelago (and probably accelerating the speed
of Islamisation in the process). Many had gone to Samudra Pasai,
where there were now 'many merchants from different Moorish
and Kling [Indian] nations, who do a great deal of trade'. Inland,
the people of the Bukit Barisan mountain ranges had long resisted
conversion, but even that was now rapidly changing: 'In these
kingdoms there are in the island of Sumatra, those on the sea
coast are all Moors [Muslims] on the side of the Malacca Channel, and those who are not yet Moors are being made so every
day, and no heathen among them is held in any esteem unless he
is a merchant'.

Much is often made of the peaceful nature of Islam's entry into the Archipelago—the faith, it is said, spread here through trade and missionary zeal rather than through the sword. But both Ibn Battuta and Tomé Pires recorded Sumatran kings 'warring for the Faith'. The real significant point is not that holy war was unknown in the Archipelago, but that it was never carried out by foreigners. Initial conversion came at the foreshore; later on, local kings might push inland, conquering and converting as they went, and adding a new element in a manifold process made up of missionary work, settlement, intermarriage, trade and mysticism.

In the second decade of the sixteenth century, as Tomé Pires was scribbling away at his desk in Melaka, the process was at its height in Sumatra, and was rapidly gearing up in other parts of the Archipelago too. Within a decade Banjarmasin, on the underbelly of Borneo, would be Muslim. Buton, off the southeast promontory of Sulawesi, would convert in 1580. At the start of the following century the hub of eastern maritime power at Makassar, on the other southern leg of Sulawesi, would change its faith. According to subsequent legends, Makassar's seemingly rather slow conversion was down to a particularly passionate local penchant for pork. The Makassar chieftain insisted that he would never convert to a faith that banned the eating of succulent slabs of pig meat as long as the creatures were to be found roaming the forests of his realm. In the legend, an instantaneous extinction of porcine wildlife miraculously ensued, which was more than enough to convince the Makassarese to join the new religion. This was a particularly significant moment in the Islamisation of eastern Indonesia, for Makassar's influence was strong throughout this region, and within a few short years it would have shunted the westernmost islands of Nusa Tenggara—Lombok and Sumbawa—into Islam too.

These were all places that had come within the broader sphere of Majapahit in earlier centuries—and indeed the final stamp of Islam in the Archipelago would closely match the footprint of the earlier formal Hindu–Buddhist influence. The network of trade, the sophisticated courtly culture, and the swelling international- ism that had welled up out of the Brantas delta ultimately provid- ed the essential fertiliser for the new faith. In Java itself, however, the shift into Islam was unfolding rather differently.

$\odot - \odot - \odot - \odot - \odot$

Java on the eve of Islamisation was a land of beauty and sophisti- cation. It was a place where an advanced farming culture had ex- isted for thousands of years in a landscape of towering mountains and deep forests. Villages had taken on a timeless form—a refined rendering of the Austronesian prototype—and there was plenty of space for art and literature. A Majapahit poet in the fifteenth century described the scene in the *Siwaratrikalpa*, a tale of a sinful hunter wandering the forests of the island:

> His journey took him to the northeast, where the ravines were lovely to look down into;
> The gardens, ring-communities, sanctuaries, retreats and hermitages aroused his wonder.
> There lay large fields at the foot of the mountains, with crops of many kinds growing along the slopes;
> A large river descended from the hills, its stream irrigat- ing the crops.
> Now there was a village which he also viewed from above, lying below in a valley between the ridges.
> Its buildings were fine to behold, while the *lalan* roofs of the pavilions were veiled in the drizzling rain.
> Wisps of dark smoke stretched far, trailing away in the sky,
> And in the shelter of a banyan tree stood the hall, roofed with rushes, always the scene of many deliberations.
> To the west of this were mountain ridges covered with rice fields, their dykes running sharp and clear.

Tomé Pires recorded something not dissimilar—though in rather more prosaic terms—when he sailed from Melaka to Java for the first time. It was, he wrote, 'a land with beautiful air, it has very good water; it has high mountain ranges, great plains, valleys'. There were fish aplenty in the surrounding seas; the forests teemed with wild pigs and deer, and the people were 'very sleek and splendid'. It was, in short, 'a country like ours'. Javanese produce was magnificent too, and the rice was the best in the world—though there was 'no butter nor cheese; they do not know how to make it'. The women also impressed him: 'When they go out, they go in state looking like angels'. He was less sure about the men, however: 'The Javanese are diabolic, and daring in treacheries and they are proud of the boast of being Javanese'. They were also well-armed, with every man, rich or poor, obliged by Javanese custom to keep a traditional *kris* dagger in his house. And just as Zheng He's men had discovered a hundred years earlier, the Javanese were very sensitive about being touched: 'Do not make a gesture towards a Javanese from the navel upwards', Pires wrote, 'nor make as if to touch [his] head; they kill for this'. Tomé Pires also noted that in the second decade of the sixteenth century Java did not yet have anything like a Muslim majority.

The ports on the north coast of Java were true melting pots, however, full of Javanese becoming Muslim, and Muslims becoming Javanese. There were, Tomé Pires wrote, merchants of all nations settled in these ports: 'Parsees, Arabs, Gujeratis, Bengalese, Malays and other nationalities, there being many Moors among them'. But when it came to the interior, it was still the realm of a 'great heathen king' who went about his countryside with 'two or three thousand men with lances in sockets of gold and silver'. This, of course, was Majapahit, still lingering eight generations after the glory days of Hayam Wuruk and Gajah Mada.

The Hindu-Buddhist kingdom's power was much diminished; indeed, Pires noted that the Muslim rulers of the coast, even if they were of foreign origin, had 'made themselves more important in Javanese nobility and state than those of the hinterland'. But Majapahit could still lay a greater claim to represent the majority culture of Java. The island was still studded with active temples, and was still crawling with Hindu-Buddhist holy men: 'There are about fifty thousand of these in Java', Tomé Pires wrote; 'Some of them do not eat rice nor drink wine; they are all virgins, they do not know women'. Such was the hold of these wandering mystics, Pires declared, that even the coastal Muslims were inclined to pay them passing obeisance: 'These men are also worshipped by the Moors and they believe in them greatly; they give them alms; they rejoice when such men come to their houses'.

And yet within a century, Majapahit would have vanished altogether, and by far the greater part of Java would be Muslim. Just how this came to pass is unclear, but the local legends give all the credit to a clutch of shadowy figures who seem to have been following in the footsteps of Tomé Pires' army of ascetics. There were just nine of these new men, however, rather than fifty thousand; and they professed Islam rather than Hindu-Buddhism.

⊙—⊙—⊙—⊙—⊙

Javanese tradition today ascribes the Islamisation of the island to the exploits of the mythical *Wali Songo*, the 'Nine Saints'. Most do seem to have been real people: they have tombs that remain major pilgrimage centres in Java today. However, the presence of saintly bones in modern mosque courtyards is just about the only certainty in the tale of the Wali Songo; even pinning them down to a definitive list of nine is impossible. Some are clearly historical figures, even if they are thickly swaddled with later folklore. Amongst these is Malik Ibrahim, a foreign Muslim with purported origins oscillating from Persia to China, who settled at Gresik on the northeast coast of Java a full century before Tomé Pires' time and who found fame under the saintly name of Sunan Gresik. Others could be dismissed as a confection of ancient myths salted with a small pinch of Islamic lore—were it not for the fact that they have verified tombs of their own.

Perhaps the best way to look at the Wali Songo is as a metaphor for the early Islamisation of Java: a diverse array of men, some the temporal chiefs of little harbour kingdoms, some authentic ascetics wandering the byways touting Koranic quotations; some of Indian, Chinese or Arabic origin, some true sons of the Javanese soil; each doing his own little bit for the new faith.

The Wali Songo, and the wider movement they presumably represent, are often regarded as 'Sufi'. Sufism is the diverse mystic tradition within Islam, and the earliest Islamic manuscripts from Java are certainly of a mystical bent. But the popular modern perception of Sufism—all whirling dervishes and *qawwali* singers—mistakenly makes the term a synonym for earthy heterodoxy, a colourful counterpoint to the dour business of mosques and scriptures. Given the eclectic, heterodox and at times downright heretical complexion of later Javanese Islam, the idea of wild-eyed holy men spreading a left-field version of the faith between the palm groves and volcanoes is hard to resist. But just as in Christianity and Judaism, Islam's meditative and ascetic traditions are often rooted in the most strictly orthodox readings. It has always been perfectly possible to be both 'Sufi' *and* 'Fundamentalist', and though Java's earliest Islamic texts may well be mystical in approach they are generally orthodox in attitude. A colourful heterodoxy would typify traditional Javanese Muslim culture in the coming centuries—with old Indian epics still forming the literary lodestone; with modes of dress and carriage infinitely distant from those of Arabia; and with Muslim sultans reputedly consorting with mythical mermaid queens. But this probably represents the culmination of a long process of later synthesis rather than the original style of Islam espoused by lamplight in the velvety Javanese darkness by the wandering Wali Songo.

◉—◉—◉—◉—◉

The first major Muslim state to rise out of the Javanese cruci- ble was Demak. For most of its length the north coast of Java—a region known as the *Pasisir*, 'the Littoral'—is a slab of level land giving way gently to the muddy shallows of the Java Sea. But just over halfway along this strip of shoreline, Java bulges suddenly around the flanks of a single isolated volcano, Gunung Muria, ris- ing 5,250 feet (1,600 metres) to a ragged crater. Today, the towns that stand around the base of the peak—Kudus, Jepara, Demak and Pati—are moderately prosperous backwaters. Old rivers have silted up, shunting the foreshore outwards and leaving places that once were ports marooned several miles inland. In the sixteenth century, however, this quiet quarter was the anteroom of Muslim Java.

In his account Tomé Pires vividly describes how small Mus- lim-ruled maritime states had grown up along the Pasisir:

> [Foreign Muslims] began to trade in the country and to grow rich. They succeeded in way of making mosques, and mollahs [sic] came from outside, so that they came in such growing numbers that the sons of these said Moors were already Javanese and rich … In some places the heathen Javanese lords themselves turned Mohammedan, and these mollahs and the merchant Moors took possession of these places … These lord pates [*patis*] are not Javanese of long standing in the country, but they are descended from Chinese, from Parsees [in this instance simply 'Persians' rather than people of the Zoroastrian religion] and Kling [Indians]…

Something like this seems to have happened in the little port of Demak sometime late in the fifteenth century. A foreign Mus- lim, most probably Chinese, gained control of the port, and this man's son, remembered by the name of Raden Patah, was one of those who was 'already Javanese and rich'. But it was the sub- sequent king of Demak, Trenggana, who brought the state to its brief bout of glory. He came to the throne in the early 1520s and swiftly pushed the influence of his maritime kingdom east and west along the coast. He annexed other ports along the central stretch of the Pasisir, and then, sometime around 1527, he overran Majapahit, the decayed and increasingly irrelevant relic of Hindu-Buddhist Java. Sixteen years after that, Demak troops swarmed up sweeping mountainsides, chased the shaven-headed priests away from the bathing temples, and took possession of the sacred mountain, Gunung Penanggungan.

And that, to all intents and purposes, was the end of Hindu-Buddhist Java. It would be a few years before the Sundanese country in the west of the island made the change (Tomé Pires had noted that foreign Muslims were generally unwelcome in Sundaland 'because it is feared that with their cunning they may do there what has been done in [Central and East] Java'), and the strange ghost-state of Blambangan in the far east of Java would stay Hindu-Buddhist until the eighteenth century. But the baton had clearly been passed.

Trenggana of Demak died in 1546 while trying to extend his rule still further east along the Pasisir beyond the Brantas delta, and once he was gone his kingdom swiftly fragmented. For the rest of the sixteenth century, various Muslim-ruled micro-states flared up along the coast, and then in the interior too—each smoking and crackling for a generation, but ultimately failing to catch fire. It was not until the dawn of the seventeenth century that the true inheritor of the Majapahit mantle emerged—a state that successfully completed the synthesis of old tradition and new Islam, and that came to control more of Java than any realm that had gone before. Its name was a storied one that had first been used almost a millennium earlier—and its location, too, was steeped in old glory. The religion might have changed, but in Java the past would not be forgotten, least of all in the new incarnation of the ancient state of Mataram...

⊚—⊚—⊚—⊚—⊚

In the mid-sixteenth century, somewhere in the vicinity of the weather-worn temple complex at Prambanan, a minor Muslim-ruled state emerged. It was known as Mataram after the ancient realm that had existed in the same region; its ruler was called Ki Gede Pamanahan, and he had a son called Senopati.

According to later myth, sometime in the 1570s Senopati retreated to the wilder parts of Central Java, out amongst the sacred bathing places and bamboo groves, and started to practice mystic asceticism. There is a clear echo here of the older tale of Airlangga's mystical apprenticeship with the ascetics. This—and indeed another thread of the tale claiming a Majapahit ancestry for Senopati—shows that the shift to Islam had required no wiping clean of the slate of stories. Java was no palimpsest.

Senopati's meditative efforts were effective, it is said, and he ultimately attracted the attention of a figure from Javanese mythology who had successfully survived the Islamic conversion—*Kanjeng Ratu Kidul*, the so-called Queen of the Southern Ocean, an aquatic deity of particular potency. She took the young noble deep beneath the waves of the Indian Ocean, taught him how to make both love and war, and then returned him to dry land, where he promptly bumped into the meandering Muslim missionary, Sunan Kalijaga (presumably this one-time member of the Wali Songo—who would have been well over 100 years old by this stage—felt that he ought to provide a counterbalance to the Goddess and all her fishy heresy). He told Senopati that his coming conquests were nothing short of the Will of Allah. Success was assured. Senopati went home and swiftly turned his father's modest estate into the greatest kingdom that Java had ever known.

Senopati certainly seems to have existed—he has a tomb, dated to 1601 and sited in the graveyard of his capital at Kota Gede, on the edge of Yogyakarta, a city founded by his descendants. But the man who really brought Mataram to greatness was his grandson, who came to the throne in 1613. His name at that stage was Raden Mas Rangsang, but today he is remembered by the title he took towards the end of his reign: Sultan Agung.

Sultan Agung appeared on the stage at a time when true Javanese dominance of the Archipelago sea lanes was no longer a possibility. There were other powerful players by this time, and unlike the rulers of Majapahit or Srivijaya he would not attain uncontested maritime mastery. But he ruled from the stupendously fertile country between Gunung Merapi and the Southern Ocean, and the new Mataram quickly came to exercise a more extensive and organised degree of power over Java itself than any kingdom that had gone before.

In an inordinately short space of time, Sultan Agung forced his frontiers east and west from his new palace at Karta, up to the north coast, out into the rebel badlands of East Java, and westwards to the fringes of Sundanese country, crushing any number of smaller polities in the process, including the feisty city-state of Surabaya near the original site of Majapahit.

Sultan Agung must have considered himself to be enjoying all the divine beneficence of both Allah and the Queen of the Southern Ocean at this point, so when he embarked on a project to crush another trading city at the other end of Java, he surely felt that success was equally certain. But by the third decade of the seventeenth century a radical new element had entered the Archipelago, and the feverish outpost in question—a port on the Ciliwung River formerly known as Sunda Kelapa—was the kernel of a brand new sort of colonialism...

CHAPTER 4

SPICE INVADERS:
THE EUROPEANS
ARRIVE

T he four ships limped into Banten Bay looking more pitiable than threatening. Their sails were ragged, stained with welts of mould and mildew. If anyone amongst the crowd of buyers and sellers at the riverside market outside the walls of the port city at the head of the bay looked up and saw the pathetic little fleet advancing they might have wondered at its provenance before pressing on with their errands. Ships from foreign parts had been dropping anchor off Banten for millennia; a new arrival was nothing to get excited about. It was June 1596.

Banten lay on the most westerly indentation in Java's north coast. This had once been the heartland of Holotan and Tarumanagara, and three generations earlier the locals had been Hindu–Buddhists. But in the 1520s, a Muslim army from Demak had conquered Banten. Now it was an independent polity under a ruler by the name of Maulana Muhammad who was enjoying the considerable trade revenues of this crucial staging post—for Banten was above all else a pepper port.

Pepper was the most versatile and high-volume of Archipelago spices. It had been brought to Southeast Asia from southern India two millennia earlier, and along with the more elusive nutmeg and cloves it soon became the mainstay of the spice trade. The other spices grew only in the remote groves of Maluku, but pepper spilled in green strings from the plantations of Lampung in southern Sumatra, and from the hills of Banten itself. The harbour there was full of trading ships from Arabia, China and India—and a good few Portuguese carracks and caravels, too.

In the century since Tomé Pires had made his notes, the Portuguese had settled into the Archipelago scene. In some ways they were the founding fathers of European colonialism in Southeast Asia. They had cast a brittle arc of Catholicism through the easternmost islands, taken chilli, potatoes and papaya to local kitchens, and added their own dash of Latin spice to the semantic stew of the Malay lingua franca. The modern Indonesian words for butter and cheese (*mentega* and *keju*), flags, tables and windows (*bendera*, *meja* and *jendela*), shoes and shirts (*sepatu* and *kemeja*), churches (*gereja*), and even Sunday (*Minggu*), were all Portuguese borrowings. Indeed, Portuguese itself remained an important common language in the Archipelago until the nineteenth century.

But the Portuguese had been more thoroughly assimilated into the Archipelago trading communities than the other Europeans who would follow. Living at impossible distances from Lisbon, they had settled into Southeast Asia with little prospect of ever going home. They had taken local wives and concubines, and within a few generations to be 'Portuguese' in the Archipelago often meant little more than to be a Catholic and to speak a pidgin version of the language.

In 1596, however, the Portuguese were still the foremost Europeans east of Africa, and they were well established in the foreigners' quarter of Banten, a jumble of lodgings and warehouses outside the city walls. But the four ramshackle ships that had swung to their anchors in the milky waters off the mouth of the Cibanten River that bright June day were not Portuguese. A voyage from their bases in Melaka or Goa was a relatively short affair; these boats looked like they had been floating around the least salubrious of the seven seas for months. As a gaggle of emaciated men with bleeding gums and broken noses stumbled ashore from the ships' launches, the locals must have gawped. They had never seen such a pathetically decrepit party of sailors. Appearances, however, can be deceptive: these men were the forerunners of an empire. The Dutch had arrived in the Archipelago, and they were about to set the tone for the coming centuries.

$$\odot - \odot - \odot - \odot - \odot$$

This first Dutch expedition to Indonesia had sailed from Amsterdam the previous year. The canny businessmen of northern Europe had long cast a jealous eye on the spice incomes of the Portuguese. Stories of the Spice Islands of Maluku and of astronomical incomes accrued from small shipments of nutmeg were rife amongst Dutch seafarers, and as their own naval technology caught up they started to plot their own adventures. A group of Dutch investors trading as the *Compagnie van Verre*, or 'Long Distance Company', spared no expense in setting up their fleet. They were hoping for a spice fortune in return and they did not baulk at fitting out their ships with the latest maritime technology. They spent months discussing routes and compiling pre-emptive reports, even engaging in industrial espionage, sending men to sniff around the Lisbon docksides in search of navigational secrets. And then, having done all this, they decided to send their four ships to sea under the command of incompetent reprobates...

With a hothead by the name of Cornelis de Houtman at the helm of the flagship, the fleet and its accompaniment of 249 sailors headed out from the Netherlands towards the Atlantic in April 1595—and immediately got lost. They drifted in the wrong direction as far as Brazil before doubling back east and finally wallowing around the southern tip of Africa. By the time they entered the Indian Ocean the ships were already in a sorry state, and men were succumbing to scurvy and dysentery on a daily basis. And as if disease and decay weren't enough to contend with, all sense of order had collapsed as men and officers turned violently against one another. By the time they arrived at Banten the crews had been decimated by sickness and their own bad behaviour, and the ships were floating carcasses.

But as interesting newcomers in town, the Dutch received a certain amount of polite attention. The resident Portuguese gave them an introduction to the king, who received them in his palace and signed a treaty, as he was inclined to do with any ocean-going traders who came his way. But this was as far as friendly relations went. The Dutch were put out to discover that, apart from the locally-grown pepper, the only spices available in Banten were sold at artificially inflated prices by the resident merchants. They grumbled noisily about this, caused trouble in the markets, and when Cornelis de Houtman managed personally to insult the inner circle of the court, they were ordered to leave. The Dutch were quite happy to comply, but first, in the words of one of their number, 'it was decided to do all possible harm to the town...'

The hundred or so Hollanders who had survived the scurvy and the infighting now embarked on an outburst of wanton vandalism. They opened fire with all their cannon; they captured, tortured and killed dozens of locals; they sent missiles into the palace, and then, 'having revenged ourselves to the approval of our ship's officers', they ran up their rotten sails, departed from the shell-shocked and smouldering Banten, and went wandering aimlessly along the Javanese coast.

Somewhere near Surabaya a party of local pirates came on board and killed several of the crew, thus bringing down an orgy of destruction on their own beachside villages by way of retribution. Onwards the Dutchmen sailed, with vague designs of crossing the Java Sea towards Maluku. As they passed the low coast of Madura, a local prince sailed out from the shore to greet them with a flotilla of streamer-bedecked barges. The Dutch opened fire, killed the entire Madurese welcoming party, stripped the jewels from the prince's fingers, and threw his corpse to the sharks.

But even the distraction of massacring the locals was not enough to engender unity amongst de Houtman's men: their ships were no longer seaworthy and they were now bickering violently over the advisability of continuing to Maluku. It was eventually decided to burn the most worm-eaten of the ships, to consolidate the fractious crews, and to abandon the expedition. They made one final stopover in Bali, and somehow managed to rein in their destructive inclinations long enough to be impressed by the king of the Balinese Gelgel kingdom: 'a good-natured fat man who had two hundred wives, drove a chariot pulled by two white buffalos and owned fifty dwarves'.

Bali had given no space to the new Islamic vogue and had remained staunchly Hindu-Buddhist. In fact, it had probably received a kind of cultural boost as a consequence of the Islamisation of Java. Oft-told tales of a mass exodus of Hindu-Buddhist courtiers and artisans, fleeing the rampaging Muslim zealots of Demak and finding refuge in Bali, are apocryphal to say the least, and don't stand up particularly well under scrutiny. The obvious artistic continuity between Hindu-Buddhist Java and Sultan Agung's Mataram clearly demonstrates that there had been no iconoclastic purge of the island. More importantly, the fall of Majapahit had been a slow atrophying over generations, rather than a single catastrophic defeat. Demak's ultimate overrunning of the capital was little more than a symbolic formality. However, with no remaining point of cultural orientation in Java, Bali would certainly have gone from being a peripheral vassal to the centre of the Hindu-Buddhist universe, and there were some cultural refugees from amongst the aristocracy and priesthood of old Java who turned up in the Gelgel court. Bali was the only major chunk of Majapahit-claimed Nusantara that would never convert to Islam.

Whatever the nature of its cultural and religious make-up, the Dutch seamen seemed to like Bali, despite its total lack of spices.

De Houtman decided to call it 'Young Holland', and two sailors stayed behind when their compatriots departed.

And with that the first Dutch expedition to the Archipelago headed home. They had done little but trail offense and bloodshed in their wake, and by the time the three surviving ships limped back into Amsterdam in 1597, there were only 89 of the original 249 sailors still alive. If appearances were anything to go by, the Netherlands' imperial adventure ought to have ended there. But incredibly, despite the ruin of the fleet and the fact that they had never even reached the Spice Islands, de Houtman's expedition had managed to turn a small profit. So astronomically high were the prices paid for spices in Western Europe that the tiny quantity of mouldy cloves and second-rate nutmeg that the sailors had picked up in Banten, and during brief stops on the Sumatran coast during the homeward journey, were enough to cover all the costs of the expedition. They even provided the shareholders of the Compagnie van Verre with a small return on their investment.

There was every reason for a return voyage.

◉ — ◉ — ◉ — ◉ — ◉

News of the financial success of de Houtman's voyage sparked excitement in the Dutch merchant houses. If you could return a profit without even reaching the Spice Islands, then just imagine the riches if you actually made it as far as the nutmeg groves of Maluku! What followed was a period appropriately known as the *Wilde Vaart*, the 'Wild Voyages'. Ship after unregulated ship headed east. They belonged to a burgeoning crop of rival companies and most of them returned successfully. In 1599 the first Dutch fleet actually reached Maluku, and racked up a magnificent 400 percent profit in the process. Having made amends for de Houtman's earlier vandalism, four rival Dutch spice agencies set themselves up in Banten, while back in the Netherlands there was always ready cash to finance another expedition to the Archipelago.

The Wild Voyages had nothing to do with colonialism. The glory of king and country meant little to these sailors, nor did territorial gains. What mattered was profit, and if accruing it meant behaving like a pirate, then so be it. Though they managed polite relations with at least some of the local chieftains in Maluku, the arrival of a shipload of Dutchmen in an Archipelago port was often cause for the locals to pack up their wares, hide the alcohol and lock their womenfolk safely out of harm's way. Even many years later, when an organised and territorial kind of colonialism had begun to develop, the Dutchmen were, as far as many locals were concerned, boorish thugs. A treaty signed by a later generation of Hollanders with the Banten sultanate contained clauses demanding that measures be taken to stop Dutchmen stealing from the markets, behaving in an 'unseemly' fashion in mosques, molesting women, and leering lecherously at the royal ladies when they performed their open-air ablutions at the riverside.

The Dutch were by no means unique in their bad behaviour. The Portuguese had committed many an outrage—as, of course, had the armies of local kingdoms. The British, too, were as prone as anyone to debauchery and violence when they came ashore.

Ships sailing under an English flag had actually beaten Cornelis de Houtman to Southeast Asia by two decades—the royally sanctioned privateer Sir Francis Drake had filled his hold with Malukan spices on his return voyage from South America in the 1570s, and during the years of the Wild Voyages there were plenty of English ships racing the Dutch for the Spice Islands. It was a free-for-all that risked precipitating a collapse of the European spice market. Back in the Netherlands the investors were well aware of this, and so in the early spring of 1602 the rival trading houses came together to form a monopoly. They called it the *Vereenigde Oostindische Compagnie*, the 'United East India Company', better known as the VOC.

At its inception, the VOC was an entirely commercial affair. Like the English, who had started their own East India Company two years earlier, the Dutch in many ways stumbled into possession of an empire by accident, as trade and profit became hopelessly tangled with the political complexities on the ground. In fact, it was the eventual transition of the VOC into a conventional colonial project that turned it from a golden egg-laying goose into a dead economic duck.

In the beginning, however, the Company was an institution with enormous potential. Its shareholders were obliged to invest in the VOC itself, not in individual expeditions—an innovation designed to bring an end to the destructive get-rich-quick motivations of the Wild Voyages. It was run from Amsterdam by a board of seventeen directors, known as the *Heeren XVII*, the 'Seventeen Gentlemen'. Like the equivalent English East India Company, they had a government charter that gave them a semblance of sovereign power and the right to sign treaties in the name of the Netherlands, but they were essentially free to do as they pleased in the Archipelago.

Before the building of the Suez Canal and the invention of steam it could take two years to get a message to Southeast Asia and to receive the reply. The Seventeen Gentlemen were well aware of this, and so in 1610 they created the post of governor-general for their head man in the Archipelago. The governor-general was not supposed to be an imperial viceroy; he was supposed to be an area manager with executive powers, and for the first decade from the VOC headquarters in Ambon—the biggest port of Maluku which the Dutch had captured from the already declining Portuguese in 1605—that's exactly what he was. But then, in 1617, the Seventeen Gentlemen appointed as their representative in Asia the first man of real consequence. He was thirty-one years old and his name was Jan Pieterszoon Coen.

Coen was a stern man with angry eyes and flying moustaches. He was born in the windy fishing town of Hoorn on the Dutch coast and brought up in the strictest of Calvinist traditions. He went out to Asia early and rose quickly to the top of the VOC

ranks. He was on the scene in 1607 when dozens of Dutch traders were killed in an uprising by the inhabitants of the Bandas—
the tiny Malukan archipelago that was the world's sole source of
nutmeg. He had harboured a deep dislike of the locals ever since.
He was no friend to the Netherlands' English rivals either. Even
before he was appointed governor-general, he was in the habit of
sending outrageously belligerent letters to the Seventeen Gentlemen, sneering at their soft-touch policies and demanding more
aggression towards competitors.

Quite what manner of person Coen was depends entirely on
your perspective. From a financial point of view he was the hothead who—with his doctrine of 'no trade without war, no war
without trade'—overstepped the mark and kick-started the slow
but ceaseless descent of the VOC into bankruptcy. For later patriotic Hollanders he was the man who launched an empire—and
for their nationalist Indonesian counterparts he was the first of
the rapacious colonial exploiters. For seventeenth-century English traders, meanwhile, he was little short of demonic, a ruthless
rival who clattered over the decks on cloven hooves and presided
over the worst Dutch perfidy in the history of the spice trade.
One thing is certain however: if Cornelis de Houtman, staggering
scurvy-ridden up the Banten beach in 1596, marks the symbolic
arrival of Dutch colonialism in the Archipelago, then Jan Pieterszoon Coen, twenty-one years later, represents its real beginnings.

$$\odot - \odot - \odot - \odot - \odot$$

On 30 December 1618, the tall masts of fourteen English ships
hove into view off the mouth a muddy river called the Ciliwung
on the north coast of Java, fifty miles east of Banten. The estua-
rine settlement there had originally been called Sunda Kelapa—a
name which referred to the local abundance of coconuts—but
in 1527, according to legend, it had fallen to Sunan Gunungjati,
a wandering member of the Wali Songo from Cirebon. The port

had originally been an entrepôt of the Hindu–Buddhist state of Pajajaran, but by the 1520s Pajajaran was as faded as Majapahit and the conquest can hardly have been one of high drama. However, Sunan Gunungjati (or whoever it was that really oversaw the seizure) must have had a penchant for hyperbole: they renamed the new possession Jayakarta, meaning 'Victorious Deed'. By 1618 Jayakarta was the seat of a minor vassal prince of Banten who was in his way a small embodiment of the new synthesis that was increasingly defining Javanese culture—a Muslim with a Sanskrit name, Wijayakrama.

Since 1611, the VOC had maintained a small outpost on the banks of the Ciliwung opposite Jayakarta's modest fortification. The English, too, had their own fortified warehouse beside the township, and although it was hardly a place to excite the fantasies of urban planners, Jan Pieterszoon Coen, in his new role as Dutch governor-general, had taken a shine to Jayakarta as a spot suitable for a future Dutch capital in the Archipelago. The old headquarters at Ambon, despite being in the thick of the spiceries, was too far from other key staging posts. The long-established Banten, meanwhile, was still bristling with rival trading factions, and a base there was always dependent on the goodwill of its young king, Abu al-Mafakhir, and his wily uncle, the regent Pangeran Arya Ranamanggala. Coen had decided that Jayakarta—or Jaccatra, as both Dutch and Englishmen mistransliterated it at the time— with its sheltered location and accessible river channel, would make a nice alternative. But now, with the arrival of that English fleet under the command of an admiral called Thomas Dale, it was about to become the setting for an absurd four-way conflict.

Prince Wijayakrama of Jayakarta had been troubling the Banten court, behaving in a fashion not befitting a deferent vassal. What was more, the Bantenese were unsure about the advisability of allowing a major Dutch outpost to develop on the fringes of their realm. Turning to the time-honoured tradition of getting someone else to do your dirty work, they had encouraged an

English naval fleet then harboured in Banten to sail down the coast, unseat Wijayakrama and evict their Dutch rivals. Relations between the English and the Dutch were far from friendly at the time. Coen was making great efforts to obliterate England's own Spice Islands outpost on the minuscule Banda islet of Run, and he had every intention of banishing them from the Archipelago altogether. Admiral Dale found that his own motivations intersected very neatly with those of the sultan. He headed for Jayakarta.

In the event, the siege of Jayakarta was scarcely more fitting of its glorious epithet than the minor conquest nine decades earlier. The fleets of Coen and Dale danced delicately around each other for twenty-four hours before the outnumbered Dutch departed abruptly for Ambon in search of reinforcements. Dale then came ashore and managed to team up with Prince Wijayakrama to besiege the remaining Hollanders.

The VOC's Jayakarta outpost was tiny, and with Coen's fleet gone it was defended by a skeleton crew of soldiers and traders. After a muddy and malarial month during which little action took place, they were ready to surrender. However, at this point a new army appeared from the west. Back in Banten, the king and the regent had realised that the upshot of the shenanigans in Jayakarta was likely to be either an entrenched Wijayakrama, or a minor Dutch fort replaced with a major English one. They sent their men to settle the score. Both Dale and Wijayakrama reacted in an understandable fashion—the English took to their boats and bolted, while the Javanese gathered their grumbling courtesans and fled to the mountains. And the Dutch remained more or less besieged.

For the next three months very little happened. The Dutch eked out their days in the fort getting drunk and dying of malaria. On 12 March 1619, however, one of the unnamed defenders roused himself sufficiently from the torpor to come up with a fanciful new name for the place in honour of a Roman-era Germanic tribe by the name of the *Batavi*. When Coen returned in May with a fully armed fleet, all fired up for a victorious deed of his own, he found that the English had gone, the Bantenese had largely lost interest, and that Jayakarta was now called Batavia. He needed only to come ashore, burn the palace, the mosque and every other Javanese building in sight, and the Dutch would be in possession of both a location and a name for their grand East Indies capital.

$\odot - \odot - \odot - \odot - \odot$

Batavia was known as 'the Queen of the East'. At the head of the town stood a stocky, four-cornered fort with cannon-lined ramparts. Behind this there was a grid of smooth-flowing canals flanked by heavyset buildings with whitewashed walls. For a place with a feverish climate occupied largely by slaves and the kind of Dutchmen Coen himself described as 'the scum of the earth', it was rather pleasant.

From this little pocket of tropical Europa the Dutch consolidated their control of trade in the Archipelago. Within a year of the founding of the city, the last English redoubt in the Banda Islands had been wiped from the map; in 1641 the Dutch ousted the Portuguese from Melaka; and by 1682 the VOC was powerful enough to press an advantageous treaty on the once-feared Banten court ordering all English traders to be kicked out for good.

But if all this paints a picture of a colonial Dutch power approaching supremacy, it is worth taking note of how very little of the Archipelago they actually controlled in the late seventeenth century. At this stage they were, in some ways, simply a trading power on the old Srivijayan-style hub-and-spoke model. Though they held sway in much of northern and central Maluku, elsewhere they were usually a token presence at best. Sumatra, Borneo and Nusa Tenggara were essentially untrammelled, and even in Java, Dutch possessions only amounted to an arrow-shaped abscess of orange-daubed territory around Batavia. There were other Dutch outposts in all of the major ports on Java's north coast, but most of the island was firmly under the sway of indigenous kings—Banten in the west, and Sultan Agung's mighty Mataram reigning over the rest. The Dutch domain was the merest pimple on the flank of Java.

⊙–⊙–⊙–⊙–⊙

Sultan Agung tried hard to squeeze the tiny colonial pustule of Batavia, but he failed to squirt the Dutchmen out into the Java Sea. For all their territorial insignificance, the Dutch had one mighty advantage—the very factor that had carried them the seven thousand miles to the Archipelago in the first place: a maritime mastery.

Mataram first besieged Batavia in 1628. Sultan Agung had already overwhelmed Surabaya and all the other city-states strung along the Pasisir, and he had an army of some 160,000 men. Batavia should have proved no great challenge. But the Dutch base was 300 miles (480 kilometres) from the Mataram court and the roads were terrible. It took months to get the attacking army in place, and it proved near-impossible to keep them fed and watered once they were there. The Dutch, meanwhile, were free to come and go as they pleased by sea throughout. After a lengthy stalemate, the Mataram commanders were executed by their own troops for their incompetence, and the Javanese army trudged home over the hills.

They returned the following year and spent a further two months outside the walls of Batavia. But again, Dutch naval superiority made the siege hopelessly ineffectual, and the Mataram forces gave up once more. Dutch losses were negligible, but the second siege did at least defeat one sturdy constitution. On 20 September 1629, just twelve days before the Javanese pulled out for good, Jan Pieterszoon Coen succumbed to dysentery, doubtless spitting vitriol about the spinelessness of the Seventeen Gentlemen to the very last.

⊙–⊙–⊙–⊙–⊙

Even with Jan Pieterszoon Coen hastily interred in the sticky riverine soil of Batavia's rapidly filling Christian cemetery, the VOC was still set on its course of political and territorial advance—and concurrent financial decline. In the coming decades, the Dutch expanded their toeholds in the Javanese ports into pockets of territory, and eventually came to control the whole of the north coast. They established tenuous outposts on the fringes of Borneo, and they also managed to cow the dominant indigenous power of the eastern Archipelago, the Makassarese sultanate of Gowa. In West Java, meanwhile, the once powerful Banten was made into a virtual client state, its successions decided by the VOC.

The Dutch were not yet in a position to overwhelm Mataram, but after Sultan Agung died in 1646 the kingdom was never quite the same. In the subsequent decades the VOC proceeded to act as a self-interested mercenary to the courts of Central Java whenever there was an internal uprising or a disputed succession. By the eighteenth century it was unthinkable for any conflict to arise in the still-sovereign Mataram territories without Dutch troops being called upon to back one side or other, and when internal tensions became insurmountable in the 1750s and the realm ended up definitively divided between the feuding courts of Surakarta and Yogyakarta, the VOC were the powerbrokers. The story of this strange episode, however, belongs to the next chapter.

While all of this was happening, Batavia had continued to grow. In 1624 it had had a total population of just 8,000; by 1670, the city was home to around 130,000 people, with 27,000 of them living inside the walls. No more than 2,000 of these were Europeans; the rest were a mix of immigrants, chancers and slaves from across Asia. There were communities of Arabs and Indians, and there were also large numbers of Portuguese-speaking Catholics. These so-called Black Portuguese, along with other Asian Christians and emancipated slaves, were known by the Dutch as *mardijkers*—a term originally from the Sanskrit *maharddika*, meaning 'eminent man'. Batavia was also home to thousands of Chinese.

Jan Pieterszoon Coen had recognised the value of Chinese economic expertise from the very start. He encouraged the Chinese to come to his new capital, and allowed them to trade freely at a time when not even Dutchmen were permitted to set up private businesses. The Ming Empire had lifted its own ban on Chinese citizens travelling overseas for private trade just one year before the first Dutch fleet reached Java, and soon not only traders, but also settlers, labourers and entrepreneurs, were heading for the Archipelago. Before long, the Chinese accounted for almost a quarter of Batavia's entire population—and the most productive quarter at that.

As had always been the way when foreigners settled in the ports, a new climate, new foodstuffs—and above all, new women—had created a Chinese creole culture. In truth, they were often closer in lifestyle and language to the indigenous populations around them than to their cousins on the Chinese mainland, as one of their own number explained: 'When the Chinese remain abroad for several generations without returning to their native land, they frequently cut themselves off from the instructions of the sages; in language, food and dress they imitate the natives and, studying foreign books, they do not scruple to become Javanese'. Those who were Muslim may well have lost their sense of Chinese identity altogether and melted into the wider local populations. Others, however—creolised and Malay-speaking though they often were—still remained identifiably Chinese.

The Dutch had very quickly developed some deeply negative opinions of the indigenous people of Java, and had attached to their 'national character' a string of unflattering epithets, foremost of which was 'lazy' and its various synonyms. The locals had been banned from living within the city walls of Batavia from the moment they were built. But the Chinese elicited more complex reactions. There was much to praise in the apparent Chinese sense of industry, and they had quickly become essential to the running of the VOC's operations. But whenever a particular ethnic group can be identified with wealth, then opprobrium won't be far behind, and European commentators dished out lashings of contempt along with backhanded compliments. Given such attitudes, it was little wonder that jealousy of the Chinese could tip over into outright violence from time to time.

In 1740, the arrival of bands of wandering Chinese freebooters on the outskirts of Batavia sent panicked rumours through the Chinese and European communities of the city. The Dutch believed that the Chinese were plotting to rebel and annihilate them; the Chinese took whispers of deportation to mean they were all to be shipped over the horizon and tipped into the sea.

Tensions rose rapidly, and when word spread that there had been some kind of altercation with the freebooters and that Dutchmen may have been killed, the entire non-Chinese population of Batavia went on the rampage. A Dutch resident of the city named Ary Huysers recorded what happened:

> An instantaneous cry of murder and horror resounded through the town, and the most dismal scene of barbarity and rapine presented itself on all sides. All the Chinese, without distinction, men, women, and children, were put to the sword. Neither pregnant women nor suckling infants were spared by the relentless assassins. The prisoners in chains, about a hundred in number, were at the same time slaughtered like sheep. European citizens, to whom some of the wealthy Chinese had fled for safety, violating every principle of humanity and morality, delivered them up to their sanguinary pursuers, and embezzled the property confided to them. In short, all the Chinese, guilty and innocent, were exterminated.

That last sentence was not hyperbole: Huysers really did mean *all* of them. There had been around ten thousand Chinese residents inside Batavia's walls before the massacre.

One result of the slaughter was that the few surviving Chinese from outside the walls, together with their vagabonding countrymen whose arrival had precipitated the carnage, ricocheted off around Java, prompting rebellion and uproar wherever they went, and dragging the VOC forces into yet more military entanglement with the decaying Mataram court. The other result was that Batavia received an economic and social blow that it could ill afford—for by the middle of the eighteenth century the city, the Company, and the empire it ran, were unmistakably in the pits.

$$\odot-\odot-\odot-\odot-\odot$$

The rot had probably set in more than a hundred years earlier, the moment Jan Pieterszoon Coen committed troops and cash to territorial gains. The cost of maintaining an ever-expanding network of residencies and military outposts was enormous, and as the outgoings spiralled the returns dwindled. The Council of the Indies—the clutch of administrators who sat in session with the governor-general twice a week in Batavia—would justify military entanglements in the internal affairs of local courts by way of the advantageous treaties that were usually signed as a result. But treaties couldn't be traded for hard silver in the docks.

To make matters worse, the bottom had fallen out of the spice trade. Nutmeg and cloves were still regarded as pleasant flavourings in the kitchens of Europe, but they were no longer a condiment that people would risk lives and pay in gold to obtain. Smuggling of seedlings out of Maluku, meanwhile, meant that France and Britain were now producing their own crops in their own Indian Ocean territories. This should not have been a problem: the Archipelago was turning out plenty of other export commodities, and with its maritime dominance the VOC was the preeminent presence on the regional commerce networks. Rice was traded back and forth along Asian shipping routes; indigo was being grown in treaty territories; cane sugar plantations had sprouted along the Javanese Pasisir; and in 1696 coffee had been introduced to the green highlands behind Banten.

But on a wider scale, the economy of the entire region had slumped. Japan—a traditional market for tropical wares from the Archipelago—had closed its doors to foreign trade. The British, meanwhile, were proving increasingly adept at bypassing both Dutch and local traders in the carriage of goods from India and points west to Chinese entrepôts. Visitors in the eighteenth century reported that the Batavia roadstead was still 'always full of the flags of all nations, attracted by the profit they are sure to make by it', but individual fortunes accrued by canny captains could not make up for the VOC's crippling deficits. By the 1770s, in the entire Archipelago only the VOC stations in the north Java ports were making any money, and the Bandas—one-time honey-pot of the spice trade—were sucking up fifteen times their annual earnings in running costs.

The slump was not only down to circumstances and misman-agement; corruption was also a precipitating factor. Jan Pieterszo-on Coen's complaint that only 'the scum of the earth' would settle in Batavia was typical of his caustic character, but he had some justification. As far as Europeans were concerned, the Archipelago was at the insalubrious ends of the earth, and for the most part the only people who would actually want to go there were those with the worst possible motives. The VOC seemed to attract all the flotsam and jetsam of Europe, and plenty of German, French, Danish and even Scottish vagabonds joined its ranks. There were severe punishments for corruption in the VOC rule book, but they were rarely enforced, and across the Archipelago European residents gave themselves over to graft on a grand scale.

A party of British visitors, passing through Indonesian waters in 1770, glimpsed provincial corruption in action at one of the VOC's most isolated outposts. On 21 September the good ship *Endeavour*, under the command of the celebrated Captain James Cook, dropped anchor off the north coast of the miniscule island of Sabu, halfway between Timor and Sumba in the far southeast of the Archipelago. Cook and his crew were heading home after their successful first voyage. They were short of supplies and they had happened upon Sabu by chance.

Even today Sabu is one of Indonesia's most isolated spots, an unlikely flake of stony land drifting far to the south of the main Nusa Tenggara chain. It was still more remote in the eighteenth century, but it was already home to a lonely VOC resident. He was a German by the name of Johan Christopher Lange.

Lange had been installed on the island in the wake of a treaty-signing between Dutch forces and the Sabunese chieftains in 1756. He had been provided with a pair of mixed-race assistants—a Timor-born 'Black Portuguese', and the son of a Dutchman and a local woman by the name of Frederick Craig—but the Company seemed largely to have forgotten about him. He had, as far as Captain Cook could make out, gone three-quarters native: 'he sits upon the ground, chews his betel, and in every respect has adopted their character and manners; he has married an Indian woman of the island of Timor, who keeps his house after the fashion of her country'. As for Lange's job, 'It is hard to say upon what footing he is here', Cook noted:

> [H]e is so far a Governor that the Natives dar[e] do nothing openly without his consent, and yet he can transact no sort of business with Foreigner's [sic] either in his own or that of the Companys [sic] name nor can it be a place of either honour or profit...

Lange may have been officially forbidden to make any profits out of his posting, but that wasn't going to stop him trying. Trembling on the beach as the Englishmen rowed ashore, he must have viewed their arrival as the greatest windfall of the decade. Cook and his crew rapidly set up a bustling barter market on the beach. Sabunese villagers, dressed in lengths of their dark homespun *ikat* cloth, emerged from the groves of lontar palms and were soon cheerfully exchanging new muskets for chickens, buffaloes and cups of *tuak*—the palm wine that was their drink of choice ('a very sweet agreeable Cooling liquor' Cook called it). A cashless economy was not what Lange had had in mind, however. He stomped off home through the palms to come up with a plan.

When Dr Daniel Solander, one of the *Endeavour's* biologists, wandered up to the tiny Sabunese capital at Seba, he encountered a flustered Lange who told him 'that the People were almost in rebellion on account of the Radjas permitting us to trade with goods instead of money'. Solander was not remotely alarmed by this tall tale, and he had already noted how very pleased the locals were with their new muskets. He hung around to watch an ama-teurish display from the local soldiers that Lange hastily hustled into action with the intention of scaring the Englishman. The botanist found the sight of the *ikat*-clad army bumping into each other and stumbling over their spears so funny that he stated that he 'desired he might see the exercise of their Sabres also'.

'You had better not desire it', spluttered the exasperated Lange, according to Solander's account; 'the People are very much enrag'd'.

Lange had been marooned on Sabu for a decade; no wonder his methods were crude. Cook's party, meanwhile, had crossed the Pacific successfully and had shown a great aptitude for peaceful encounters with men of many lands. The scaremongering 'had no part of the design'd effect'. Solander, Cook and the other officers knew exactly what Lange was after, so in the interests of a smooth passage, 'tho sore against his will', Cook agreed to pay some very confused locals the grand sum of ten guineas for a pair of buffalos, before carrying on with the bartering. It was all it took, and 'In the Evening Mr Lange came down to the Beach softened by the money which no doubt he had received: he who was in the morn as sour as verjuice was now all sweetness and softness'.

By now the Englishmen were beginning to feel rather sorry for the pathetic resident. They gave him a small keg of beer, and the next morning they departed for Java, leaving the corrupt German behind, a forlorn figure waving from a lonely beach.

◎—◎—◎—◎—◎

Lange was one small man lining his own threadbare pockets on one small island, but his behaviour was replicated throughout VOC realms. Corruption was so endemic that it had become almost officially normalised: to obtain an administrative post, a junior Company merchant might be expected to make a payment to the appointments board totalling almost ninety times the value of his monthly salary. The death of one chief VOC cashier in Batavia revealed that a million guilders had vanished from the treasury on his watch, and by the late eighteenth century graft had become so normal that Company staff were actually being formally taxed on their illicit incomes. One VOC official, supposedly on a salary of sixty guilders a month, filed a self-assessed tax return for a staggering thirty thousand guilders.

Those who weren't engaged in energetic graft, meanwhile, were either dying or depressed. Even the Queen of the East had lost her glamour. Late eighteenth-century accounts of Batavia convey an appropriately *fin-de-siècle* atmosphere, but without any of the last-gasp hedonism. Although new waves of Chinese entrepreneurs had taken over the shop-houses left empty in the wake of the 1740 massacre, Batavia's total population had dwindled. Many corners of the city had been abandoned, and the once smooth-flowing canals were choked with sewage and general detritus. Indeed, Batavia had become 'one of the most unwholesome spots on the face of the globe'.

The mortality was horrific. A new European arrival in Batavia, it was said, had barely a 50 percent chance of surviving his first year, and a bleak sort of cynicism seems to have infected the survivors:

[L]ittle signs are shown of emotion or surprise, on hearing
that the companion of yesterday is to-day no more. When
an acquaintance is said to be dead, the common reply is,
'Well, he owed me nothing;' or, 'I must get my money off
his executors'.

European Batavia's once burgeoning social scene had withered
away, and even when it came to romance there were slim pickings.
As far as the stuffier colonial gentlemen were concerned there
had always been a chronic shortage of marriageable women in the
Indies. Way back in the 1620s, in one of his rancorous missives to
the Seventeen Gentlemen, Jan Pieterszoon Coen had complained
that 'Everyone knows that the male sex cannot exist without
women … if your Excellencies cannot get any honest married
people, do not neglect to send underage young girls'.

A ready supply of wholesome Dutch teenagers was never
forthcoming, however, and the tiny handful of white women that
the VOC did convince to head east turned out to be far from
respectable, prompting officials to admit that they were 'of no use
for the man on the street and expensive and prejudicial to the interests of the Company'. At one point in the seventeenth century,
the Seventeen Gentlemen managed to recruit a few purportedly
married couples from the Netherlands and sent them out to settle
at Ambon in Maluku. However, these couples turned out to be
no sort of civilising influence, as a furious Coen reported in yet
another of his vitriolic missives: 'you will have heard … how ill
your good intentions have turned out, that is, with the arrival here
of the married couples. Our reputation has suffered badly and the
[locals] are absolutely scandalised by them, because of their bestial
living, their constant drunkenness and lewdness'.

Between 1602 and 1795, the VOC sent some five thousand
ships from the Netherlands to the Archipelago, carrying a total of
around a million Europeans, the vast majority of who were male.
Inevitably these early generations of Dutchmen, just like other

foreign settlers before them, had availed themselves of local wives and concubines, from either the old-established mestizo Portuguese community, or from amongst the Javanese, Sundanese and others. As a result, Batavia and the other big VOC-held cities became home to large populations of mixed-race Indo-Europeans, and by the late eighteenth century this community was the standard source of colonial wives. These Java-born women were often illiterate. Most spoke pidgin Portuguese or Malay by preference. Many knew no Dutch at all, and European visitors were generally disapproving, with one declaring that 'the handsomest would scarcely be thought middling in Europe'.

All of this—the corruption and collapse, the disease and the dearth of marriageable women—had combined to cast a pall of constant gloom over Batavia. The VOC, and indeed the entire concept of 'company colonialism', seemed to be dying. And as it expired there were new signs of life in the indigenous courts—in Central Java the Mataram heirs of the Majapahit mantle were stirring.

Taking all this in isolation, observers of the late eighteenth-century Archipelago might have been forgiven for predicting that the Dutch were set to go the same way as the Portuguese who had come before them—swamped by their surroundings, their institutions overwhelmed, their very ethnicity diluted to the point of vanishing, and ultimately amounting to nothing more than another dash of spice in the Southeast Asian stew.

But as the nineteenth century reared up over the horizon of history, a new global connectivity was coming into play that would allow the zeitgeist of Amsterdam, London and Paris to rattle the walls of Batavia and Yogyakarta. And even as the East India companies of both Britain and the Netherlands lumbered wearily towards extinction, a fresh impetus was being forged in the crucible of a war-torn Europe. With Napoleon on the rampage and with Enlightenment sensibilities finding strange new form in an aggressive expansionist impulse, the true age of European empire in the Archipelago was only now about to begin.

CHAPTER 5

THE CLASH OF CIVILISATIONS: FROM COMPANY TO EMPIRE

T he low country of Central Java lay to the west under a fine lavender haze. This had been the cradle of the mighty Sanjaya and Sailendra dynasties a thousand years earlier, and the countryside was still studded with their blackened and crumbling temples. Now it was the seat of the Muslim incarnation of Mataram—a sweep of green ground, thick with forest, dappled with flooded rice fields and speckled with villages. From this vantage point on the slopes of Gunung Lawu the panorama seemed peaceful. In truth, however, the countryside of Central Java was scarred and seething, wracked by decades of rebellion and rancour. But on this day—15 February 1755—a drastic step was being taken to bring the troubles to an end.

The two Javanese royals, sitting a few feet apart at a heavyset table carried into place for this meeting at the little village of Jatisari, could hardly bring themselves to look at one another. Every effort had been made to make the setting agreeable—a gamelan orchestra was in full flow and ranks of courtiers were watching quietly from the sidelines. But still, the two Javanese royals were overcome with emotion. It was left to the host, a Dutchman, to ease things along. Nicolaas Hartingh, governor of the VOC's north coast territories and official point of contact with the Mataram court, spoke in flowing Javanese. This, he declared, was a special moment: after decades of turmoil there was finally peace in Java. He took the hands of the two men—Susuhunan Pakubuwono III, and his uncle Mangkubumi, officially recognised just a few days earlier at a spot higher up the mountain as the first sultan of what was to become Yogyakarta—and called for three glasses of beer. Nudged gently onwards by the Dutchman, the royals swore to fight each other no more. All three men raised their glasses and drank.

After almost two hundred years, Mataram, the first truly great Javanese kingdom since the fall of Hindu-Buddhist Majapahit, had been cleaved in two—with a Dutchman as the powerbroker.

$$\odot - \odot - \odot - \odot - \odot$$

At his death in 1645, Sultan Agung had bequeathed to his descendants the most extensive indigenous polity that Java had ever known. Despite his failure to crush Dutch Batavia in the 1620s, Agung had consolidated his power in the Javanese heartlands, and made Mataram a major exporter of rice to other, less fertile corners of the Archipelago. But as soon as he was interred in his hilltop tomb at Imogiri, a sacred site south of the capital on the road to the coast, his heirs set about making a mighty mess of the kingdom. For the next hundred years, the Mataram court lurched from crisis to crisis. According to the Javanese chroniclers, Sultan Agung's heir, Amangkurat I, was a 'king who had sunk to the level of the beasts', and he was by no means the only inept and unpleasant scion of the dynasty. The Islamic title of 'sultan' had been dropped at Agung's death for the Javanese honorific *susuhunan*, and over the decades a procession of struggling susuhunans took to shunting the Mataram capital, complete with its sacred banyan trees, to fresh locations in search of auspicious new starts. But though the court moved from Karta to Kartasura to Surakarta, the troubles continued. There were uprisings and intrigues, famines and natural disasters, and the court was sacked by rampaging Madurese warlords on several occasions. And all the while the VOC was becoming ever more entangled in the internal affairs of the state.

By the beginning of the eighteenth century the Dutch were a near-permanent presence as powerbrokers in Mataram. Many of the more traditionally-minded Javanese aristocrats were re-sentful and suspicious of the presence of these non-Javanese and non-Muslims; they were unconscionable infidels from whichev-er side of the well-established Javanese dualism you approached the question. But floundering kings couldn't resist calling upon Dutch firepower whenever there was a troubled succession or a threatened rebellion. The Dutch, meanwhile, had their own best interests at heart. They never attempted actually to annex Mata-ram; they simply used their powerbrokering position to ensure that whichever king occupied the throne was a man that they could work with, and to ensure that ever more favourable treaties were signed. It was a kind of imperialism by stealth, unfolding organically over the generations.

By the middle decades of the eighteenth century, however, the state of crisis in Mataram had reached an impasse that not even Dutch assistance could surmount. The reign of the king of the day, Pakubuwono II, had been an unmitigated disaster. He had faced endless upheavals; at one point he had ended up on the run with rebels rampaging through his Surakarta kraton, and by the 1740s he was embroiled in the biggest rebellion of all.

The revolt had been started by an ambitious princeling by the name of Mas Said. He was, it was said, a very small man, but he more than made up for it with a surfeit of compensatory energy. A VOC official reported that 'fire and vivacity radiate from his eyes'. Part jago, part Ratu Adil, he hated the Dutch, despised the decayed corruption of the court, and claimed that the Queen of the Southern Ocean was on his side. He joined forces with an even more impressive rebel prince, Pakubuwono II's half-brother Mangkubumi. Before long they were rampaging through Central Java at the head of an army of 13,000 malcontents. This time the Dutch could not help. The rebellion was simply too big, and what was more, the VOC itself was in a state of terminal decline.

It is unsurprising, therefore, that at this point Pakubuwono II seems to have given up the ghost. Dying was apparently the only way out, and he set about the terminal task with considerable enthusiasm. When the Dutch governor of the coastal regions came to visit him on his deathbed in late 1749, the king made a quite spectacular offer: he would cede his entire kingdom to the VOC if only it would earn him a final moment of peace.

The colonial officials were understandably flabbergasted by this unprecedented offer, but they battered out a treaty nonetheless, and hustled the crown prince onto the throne as Susuhunan Pakubuwono III, leaving the old king to die in peace five days later. This did not amount to the inception of a new, Dutch-ruled Mataram, however, for at exactly the same time, at a tented rebel court a day's ride to the southwest, a wildcat enthronement had taken place. Mangkubumi had also been declared Susuhunan Pakubuwono Senopati Ingalaga Ngabdurahman Sayidin Panatagama, King of all Mataram. The conflict, it seemed, was intractable.

By the 1750s everyone was exhausted. Pakubuwono III was as miserable as his father; the VOC had troubles enough of their own, and Mangkubumi had fallen out with Mas Said, turning the whole sorry business into a monumental stalemate. Some sort of solution, no matter how unpalatable, was essential. Nicolaas Hartingh, a smooth operator and a fluent Javanese speaker, was the VOC's man on the scene by this stage. During the fiery dry months of 1754 he set up a correspondence with Mangkubumi's rebel court at Karta, and by the time the year spluttered out in a succession of monsoon downpours they had come up with a radical solution: they would cleave the kingdom in two.

And so, on 13 February 1755 at Giyanti—a misty, murky spot perched high on the slopes of Gunung Lawu—Mangkubumi met with Hartingh to sign a contract. It gave the rebel a jumbled half of the Mataram realm, and half of the twenty-thousand-dollar rent which the VOC had agreed to pay for what was still notionally Mataram territory on the north coast. Two days later, the whole party rode down the lower slopes to that spot at Jatisari where a gamelan was playing and Pakubuwono III was waiting with tears in his eyes. From now on what had once been Mataram would have both a susuhunan and a sultan.

$\odot - \odot - \odot - \odot - \odot$

In the received version of history that is taught today in Indonesian high schools, the Treaty of Giyanti is the ultimate example of imperialist divide and rule tactics, depicting the horrible Hollanders at their very worst. Those in possession of a more fertile imagination and a firm grip on Indonesia's favourite literary clichés will tell you that Nicolaas Hartingh, with his slick language skills and glib turns of phrase, was the *dalang*, the puppet-master, in whose hands the Javanese royals had been rendered into *wayang kulit* shadow puppets, held up against the screen of history with a volcano for a back-light. It's a nice idea, but it's not really true. The idea of splitting the realm had been as much Javanese as Dutch—and they had the story of Airlangga's supposed partitioning of his own Kahuripan kingdom seven hundred years earlier as a precedent. They had almost certainly not expected the arrangement to be permanent. Instead, just as in Airlangga's day, it would allow breathing space before the complete kingdom eventually reconvened under some new 'Righteous Prince'. There is nothing to suggest that, as they rode away from Jatisari in the cool mists of February 1755, either the Javanese kings or the accompanying Dutchman ever supposed that this time things would prove to be different.

⊙–⊙–⊙–⊙–⊙

As sultan, Mangkubumi presided over a grand new capital close to the original Mataram seat at Karta. Officially founded in 1755, it was named Ngayogyakarta Hadiningrat. The first part of the name was taken from Ayodhya, the mythical birthplace of the god Rama (Mangkubumi is often regarded as the man who presided over the perfection of Java's synthesis of Islam and other, older cultural threads). From the outset it was better known as Yogyakarta, and it quickly became a burgeoning wellspring of Javanese culture and power. Up the road in Surakarta, too, peace had allowed a certain vigour to return to kraton life. Meanwhile, Mangkubumi's one-time rebel sidekick Mas Said had also come in from the cold, and for his belated loyalty he had been granted a kingdom within the kingdom—direct hereditary rule over a pocket of four thousand households within Surakarta territory.

The VOC, meanwhile, was on its very last legs. In the outer reaches of the Archipelago the Dutch had reduced many of their unprofitable outposts to mere token presences—sometimes little more than a single feverish resident. Closer to the centre, corruption and incompetence were endemic, and in the new bifurcated Mataram—which they had helped to create—the Dutch often ended up looking decidedly lacklustre alongside the resurgent Javanese. In Yogyakarta, bumbling incompetence meant that it took the VOC some twenty-five years even to build a small fortress, while the Javanese managed to throw up a three-mile curtain wall around the entire city in a matter of weeks. Mangkubumi's 'most notable physical trait', it was claimed, 'was the habit of answering importunate Dutch requests with an enigmatic smile'.

Had things continued in this fashion, then perhaps the sons and heirs of Mangkubumi might have been able to shake the Dutch off altogether, and even to have reasserted outright indigenous sovereignty over Java, with the outer islands of the Archipelago following suit. But in 1789 something dramatic happened

7,500 miles from Java: on a July day in Paris, a mob of revolutionaries attacked a fortification rather larger than the one the VOC was trying to build in Yogyakarta. The storming of the Bastille and the launch of the French Revolution would set in train events that would rattle the rafters in many corners of the globe. In the Archipelago they would alter the course of history.

◉ — ◉ — ◉ — ◉ — ◉

Strange new currents had been flowing through the salons of Europe for a century. Today we look back on this period as 'the Enlightenment', and enlightened it often appears as any lingering medievalism is swept aside in a deluge of scientific and political enquiry. Abolitionism, the French Revolution, the Declaration of the Rights of Man, the political and economic ideals of Thomas Paine, Adam Smith and others: all emerged from this heady ferment. On paper the key philosophical notions of the age appear impeccable; indeed, they seem more suited to inspiring an end to nascent imperialism than to presaging its true beginnings. But something is implicit in the idea that 'Men are born and remain free and equal in rights': if that thought was the exclusive luxury of the educated young thinkers of northern Europe, then the notion that those young thinkers were at the apex of civilisation was inevitable…

Out of the Enlightenment came the ideas of European intellectual and moral superiority and the spurious moral imperative that would underpin both the British Raj and the Dutch East Indies—the idea that 'we know what's best for them', which in turn generated the contemptuous notions of 'the ignorant native' and 'the Asiatic despot'. The ultimate upshot was all the hubris and racism of high nineteenth-century imperialism.

It would be a mistake to view the older style of company-based European involvement in Asia as benign by comparison, however. In its commercial motivations it was often little more than piracy, and as Cornelis de Houtman's 1596 shenanigans show, it could frequently descend into the most appalling barbarity. But it did allow space for pragmatism, acculturation and—crucially— the tolerance of authentic indigenous sovereignty. Now that was all about to change. The nineteenth-century zeitgeist would arrive in the Archipelago with an almighty bang in the persons of two men—one Dutch, and the other English.

◉—◉—◉—◉—◉

At the end of 1794, a French army came thundering across the Low Countries to invade the Netherlands. At the same time an internal revolution with republican sympathies unseated the fifth Prince William of Orange. He fled across the water to find succour with his royalist friends in England, and a Napoleonic government was set up in his stead.

One of the first things that the new administrators of the Netherlands did was to cast a critical eye over the accounts of the VOC. What they found there was horrific. The Company had been cooking its books for the best part of two hundred years. The expectations of the investors had been met with an endless relay of short-term loans, and the whole edifice amounted to a monumental 134 million-guilder debt. The *Heeren XVII*, the Seventeen Gentlemen who had presided over the chaos, were unceremoniously evicted from their chambers, and on the first day of the first month of the first year of a brand new century the VOC was formally disbanded, and both its pestilent assets and its staggering debts were turned over to the Dutch-Napoleonic state. Nobody, however, knew quite what to do with them.

There were certainly plenty of ideas floating around as enlightened thinkers attempted to bend revolutionary ideals to distant tropical circumstances. The most notable proposals came from a man named Dirk van Hogendorp, who had served in both British India and Dutch Java. He had decided that the traditional VOC approach of indirectly extracting labour and payments from the peasants in the Archipelago through local middlemen ought to be overturned. Instead, van Hogendorp believed, the villagers should be made individually responsible for the land they worked. This, if you slipped a rose-tinted lens before your eye, could be made to fit with fashionable ideals about the Rights of Man, but more importantly it would allow a colonial government to extract taxes directly from the commoners without having to work through the calcified layers of a co-opted indigenous elite.

The political situation in Europe meant that putting such ambitious ideas into practice was a little tricky: the Napoleonic Wars were in full swing, and the Netherlands had become a de facto enemy of Britain, meaning its overseas territories were fair game for English attack. Low-level naval warfare in the Indian Ocean was hampering communication between Batavia and Amsterdam, and colonial finances were decidedly precarious. In 1806, however, Napoleon installed his brother Louis on the throne of the Netherlands, and the new ruler decided to despatch to the Archipelago a new governor-general thoroughly steeped in the ideals of the day. His name was Herman Willem Daendels.

Daendels has gone down in history as 'the Thundering Marshal', the very epitome of the swaggering Dutch imperialist. He had lofty ideals and a short fuse: he once threatened to shoot the Dutch envoy to the United States, who he profoundly disliked, if he were ever to set foot in the Indies. But he was nothing if not radical. Born in 1762 in the medieval town of Hattem, out in the flat countryside of the eastern Netherlands, he had studied law at the University of Harderwijk. A fully paid-up adherent to Napoleonic ideals, he had been sent to the Archipelago with specific instructions to shake the colony out of its corrupt lethargy. For the previous two hundred years every single governor-general had already served time in the Archipelago before his appointment. Some had even started out as common soldiers in the VOC army or as cabin boys on Dutch trading ships. But this new sixty-sixth governor-general was a high-flying executive, parachuted in directly from Europe on a mission to overturn age-old practices. In doing so, Daendels would demonstrate all of the uncompromising energy—and all of the fiery temper—of his long-dead predecessor, Jan Pieterszoon Coen.

He arrived in Batavia in the wet January of 1808 when the city was at its diseased and mud-splattered worst, but he lost no time in kicking the enervated inhabitants from their slumbers. He ordered that the crumbling, mosquito-filled fort at the head of the city be demolished at once, set about building modern cantonments in the less feverish fields to the south, and filled the new barracks with a rapidly expanded army of local recruits bolstered with Napoleonic regiments from Europe. All this activity alone was enough to put plenty of noses out of joint in the old-established Dutch community, but worse: Daendels had been ordered to 'cure the abuses which had crept in under the company'. He started to take a moral stand against the slavery that had been a feature of Archipelago life for centuries (though only when it served his purposes—at one point he ordered the purchase of 750 slaves from Bali to serve as soldiers), and he began to enforce the long-ignored anti-graft measures. None of this made him particularly popular with the more entrenched of the European residents, but it was the high-ranking Javanese who really reacted rancorously to Daendels and his radical anti-feudalism.

Out of combined enervation and necessity, the VOC had always farmed out the administration of its territories to local regents, drawn from the mid-ranking Javanese aristocracy. These administrators had largely been allowed to behave as feudal lords, as though they were vassal princes under an indigenous kingdom rather than the salaried staff of a European merchant company. They made up the very layer of administration that van Hogendorp had suggested be removed. It was inevitable that Daendels would look unfavourably upon them. They were aristocrats, after all, and in the Napoleonic scheme of things aristocrats were generally for the chop. He was not able to actually send the regents to the guillotine, but he did begin to treat them as what they technically were—government-employed civil servants.

Daendels even went so far as to regard the post-Mataram courts of Surakarta and Yogyakarta in a similar light. The old and uneasy compromise in which the Javanese could think of the Dutch as deferent allies was to be overturned. Daendels wanted no mistakes about who was in charge. He radically rewrote the rules for his residents at the royal courts. No more were they to take the role of Dutch ambassadors to a sovereign power—and no more were they respectfully to remove their hats when approaching the sultan or the susuhunan! They were instead, he wrote, 'to give the rulers an impression of the power and splendour of the present Royal government in Holland and of the protection of the great Napoleon, and to inspire them with awe and respect'. Unsurprisingly, this all went down spectacularly badly in Central Java, and for a long spell Dutch and Javanese teetered on the brink of outright hostilities.

But before he'd had time to really stir things up with the courts, the new governor-general also had to embark on the most ambitious engineering project that Java had seen since the temple-building heyday of the Hindu-Buddhist era. He had arrived with instructions to construct a modern road along which troops could be moved at speed all the way from one end of Java to the other. It was certainly needed—the slow advance of the Mataram armies along atrocious mountain trails had been one of the reasons that early Batavia had withstood the sieges of the 1620s. In the subsequent two hundred years there had been little improvement, and almost all communication between Batavia, Semarang and Surabaya still went by sea. But with British frigates now prowling the Java Sea from their outposts on the Straits of Melaka, an alternative was essential, and Daendels presided over the building of a 870-mile (1,400-kilometre) highway, running from Merak in the west, through Batavia, up to the mountains around Bandung, back to the coast at Cirebon, and then all the way along the Pasisir to Panarukan in the east. It was called *De Grote Postweg*, the 'Great Post Road'.

The job was done in a year, and Daendels was obliged to abandon all his haughty ideals about the Rights of Man to see it through. His original job description had instructed him to 'improve the lot of the common man and protect him from arbitrary treatment', but now Daendels called on the very Javanese regents that he held in such disdain to organise forced labour for the Great Post Road project. Tollgates along the completed sections of the road were leased to the most profit-minded Chinese and European usurers on hand, and government lands were sold off to rapacious private investors to raise construction funds. The death toll—a toll paid almost entirely by the local communities along the route of the road—was enormous. Labourers died in their thousands as they hacked away at green hillsides or raised embankments over malarial flatlands, but there could be no doubt that the Great Post Road was an engineering triumph. Its real significance was not realised at first, however: it had been meant to facilitate defence against attack from the seas, but in fact it provided the vital thread that would eventually bind the disparate parts of Java into a single, bone fide colonial possession.

Daendels would not get to see that particular project through, however. He had made endless enemies amongst the old guard, and when word of his apparent megalomania reached Europe, his masters became rather nervous. In 1810 they ordered his removal on the grounds of 'rapacity, brutality and incompetence'. He was replaced the following year by another Napoleonic officer, Jan Willem Janssens. But Janssens would survive little more than three months in his post before the arrival of the man who would properly pick up the baton that Daendels had set down—and that man was no Hollander. He was a highly ambitious young English civilian by the name of Thomas Stamford Raffles.

⊙—⊙—⊙—⊙—⊙

On 4 August 1811, a fleet of eighty-one British warships dropped anchor in the murky waters of Batavia Bay, and a massed force of eleven thousand English redcoats and Indian sepoy soldiers came splashing ashore through the shallows. The idea of a British assault on Dutch possessions in Southeast Asia had been batted around in the debating chambers of London and Calcutta ever since Napoleon first sent his troops into the Netherlands in 1794. But with more pressing priorities elsewhere, the project had been delayed for a decade-and-a-half. The Archipelago had fallen off the British map since the steamy days of the spice race, and their own East India Company's properties in the region amounted to nothing more than the Straits backwater that was Penang, and Bengkulu—a knuckle of atrociously unhealthy and unprofitable land on the west coast of Sumatra, which the British had occupied since 1685. But in 1811 a fleet finally set sail from India, and bore down on Batavia.

Remarkably, the British Government did not actually want to take control of the proto-colony for itself. Colonialism, they recognised, was a costly business, and the instructions issued to Lord Minto, the British governor-general in Calcutta, were to overwhelm the Dutch forces, destroy their fortifications, dish out their guns and ammunition to the locals, and 'hand the island over to the Javanese'. At this crucial moment, on the very threshold of the colonial century, the Archipelago came within a whisker of being freed from European colonialism altogether. That things panned out so very differently was entirely down to a spectacular piece of disobedience: Lord Minto decided to ignore the orders. He felt that in far-off London 'the disruptive and calamitous consequence to so ancient and populous a European Colony, the property and lives of which must fall as sacrifice to the vindictive sway of the Malay [sic] Chiefs … have not been fully contemplated'. He would therefor unilaterally embark on 'the modification of all their orders'.

Lord Minto's concern for the Dutch civilians in the Archipelago was doubtless genuine, but more importantly he'd had his head turned by Raffles, an East India Company clerk who had been serving out his apprenticeship in the sleepy administration of Penang and who had developed the romantic idea that Java and the surrounding islands could be turned into some sort of economic and ideological Eden under an enlightened British administration.

The invasion was over within a few weeks. Despite Daendels' efforts to expand the colonial army and improve fortifications and communications, the rotten VOC structures and attitudes were still in place; local recruits deserted at a rate of seventy a day, and the entire Dutch defence rapidly collapsed. Jan Willem Janssens signed a formal capitulation in September 1811, and Java and the other Dutch territories in the Archipelago were handed over to Britain. Lord Minto then installed Raffles—aged just thirty and with virtually no practical experience of government—as his lieutenant-governor in Java and the other former Dutch possessions in the Archipelago, with free rein to do as he pleased.

If Daendels had represented the bruising, bully-boy facet of the new nineteenth-century imperialism, then Raffles was in some ways a personification of its intellectual aspect. 'Knowledge is power', he once wrote, 'and in the intercourse between enlightened and ignorant nations, the former must and will be the rulers'. Today he is popularly remembered in Indonesia for cataloguing the relics of Java's Hindu-Buddhist past and for producing one of the first major orientalist texts on Southeast Asia, the hulking two-volume opus that is *The History of Java*. But in fact Raffles did just as much chest-thumping as Daendels. He shared the same essential sympathies, declaring that 'a much more regular, active, pure and efficient administration was established by Marshal Daendels than ever existed before'. He was also every bit as inclined as his predecessor to furious disputes with his detractors.

Raffles was also as unprepared to tolerate true indigenous sovereignty as Daendels. With the strange sense of personal insecurity that often marked his character, he worried that the Yogyakarta sultan in particular looked 'upon us as a less powerful people than the [Dutch-Napoleonic] Government which proceeded us', and decided that it was 'absolutely necessary for the tranquillity of the Country that he should be taught to think otherwise'. He quickly decided that some sort of crushing military assault was essential to establish his authority. Less than a year into his tenure he got his way. The British had learnt of a tentative correspondence between the estranged Mataram courts of Surakarta and Yogyakarta, in which the then susuhunan of the former was attempting to provoke the then sultan of the latter (Mangkubumi's heir, Hamengkubuwono II) to rise up against the European presence in Java. In light of this it really ought to have been Surakarta which felt the wrath of Raffles. However, the Englishman had correctly identified Yogyakarta as the grander of the two courts, and he swung for the sultan with all his might.

Before dawn on 20 June 1812, an expeditionary force of 1,200 English and Indian troops came storming out of the VOC-built fortress north of the Yogyakarta kraton. They jogged steadily across the *alun-alun*, the banyan-studded ceremonial square in front of the royal gateway, flung up bamboo ladders, and surged over the curtain wall. The British were outnumbered by a factor of ten to one, but so taken aback were the Javanese by the turn of events that the defence collapsed almost immediately. By mid-morning the sultan and the crown prince had been arrested and a wild orgy of looting had erupted.

The dethroned sultan was exiled, and his son installed as puppet king in a hasty coronation in the old Dutch residency. During the ceremony the princes and courtiers were forced to kneel and kiss Raffles' knees in the ultimate act of submission. It was the first time in the two hundred years since Cornelis de Houtman's ramshackle fleet hove into view off Banten that Javanese aristocrats had paid such humiliating obeisance to a European. A treaty was hammered out, giving the British all manner of rights in what had once been sovereign Mataram territory and telling the new sultan that 'His Highness acknowledges the supremacy of the British Government over the whole Island of Java'. Two days later Raffles wrote a celebratory letter to let Lord Minto in India know what had happened:

> The blow which has been struck at Djocjo Carta, has afforded so decisive a proof to the Native Inhabitants of Java of the strength and determination of the British Government, that they now for the first time know their relative situation and importance. The European power is now for the first time paramount in Java.

In the coming years Raffles proceeded to crush other Archipelago courts. The minor Javanese sultanates of Cirebon and Banten were brought under the colonial yoke, as was the outlying island of Madura. Courts further afield—in Borneo, Bali and Bone—also came under fire. There had been wars between Dutch and local forces since the earliest days of the VOC, of course, but those battles had always been fought for a tangible end—control of a particular avenue of trade, in most cases. These new 'chastisements' were principally an assertion of dominance. The local kings were being taught a lesson.

Once Raffles had cowed the courts of Java, he turned to another issue which had also been on Daendels' reformist roster: land revenues. The new 'land rent' system that Raffles attempted to enforce in Java (the British did not have a sufficient territorial footing to put it into play elsewhere in the Archipelago) sidestepped the local regents just as van Hogendorp had demanded, and gave the peasantry direct responsibility for their individual plots. But the Englishman then went one step further: he wanted rent paid to his government in cash, not in kind.

In practice the new system was a catastrophe. The values on which the land rent was based were arbitrary and astronomical, and rents were never properly collected. What was more, most of rural Java had never known a proper cash economy; the farmers had no money with which to meet these radical new demands, and so the institution of the Chinese moneylender and an endemic debt culture came into play on a large scale in the countryside for the first time. But whether successful or not, the attempted reforms had at their heart a crucial new concept: a colonial economy based on much more than just trade, with revenues directly extracted from the Archipelago through an organised system of European government.

Like Daendels before him, Raffles' overreaching ambitions eventually got the better of him. He, too, was removed from his post in 1816 on grounds of incompetence, financial mismanagement and alleged—though never proven—corruption. Napoleon had by this time been defeated in Europe, Dutch sovereignty had been restored and friendly relations between Britain and the Netherlands re-established. Not long after Raffles was shipped out of the Archipelago the territories were handed back to the Hollanders.

Both Daendels and Raffles had been very much of the intellectual moment, but rather ahead of their time on the ground in the Archipelago. Between them they had pushed the colonial economy still further into the red, and antagonised virtually every member of the traditional elites, both Dutch and Asian. Even Raffles' claim of European paramountcy ultimately proved hollow. But they had brought vital new ideas into play, ideas that would, within a few short years, be made good. Nothing would ever be the same in the Archipelago again. The Nusantara of Majapahit and Mataram was giving way to the Dutch East Indies, and that entity in turn would provide the blueprint for Indonesia itself. The indigenous powers would not go down entirely without a fight, however.

⊙—⊙—⊙—⊙—⊙

The city of Palembang lies some forty miles from the sea, deep in the green levels of southeast Sumatra. Today it is a big and earthy town, a thumbprint of bright light on a dark patchwork of palm oil plantations. There is a pungent whiff of diesel and durian to the place. For all its 1.7 million inhabitants, it feels a long way from anywhere, and the roiling band of the Musi River still seems like the most obvious way out.

This, of course, was the old seat of Srivijaya, but that fact was quickly forgotten once the Buddhist trading state disappeared. Palembang fell off the map altogether until the sixteenth century, when a vagabonding Muslim—an exile from Demak in Java, according to local legends—came ashore and created a new sultanate on the north bank of the Musi.

The Palembang sultanate had a strange pedigree. It made much of its Javanese origins; some sort of Javanese remained the language of the court in this, the original wellspring of the Malay language, and even today Palembang Malay has some of its vowels rounded by a distant Javanese influence. But the place also drew in Arab traders, and the sultans took Arabic names and claimed Arab genes as well as Majapahit bloodlines. Although Sultan Agung of Mataram had claimed the town as his vassal in the early seventeenth century, it remained an isolated place. It had no agricultural wealth to speak of, and it would have offered little to would-be colonialists but for one thing: Palembang had tin.

Off the mouth of the Musi lay a pair of rugged islands—Bangka and Belitung—and streaking their hard granite bedrock were deep veins of tin ore. The tin was mostly shipped out to China, where it was used as a silvery backing for the spirit money to be burnt in temple offerings, and it raised a respectable revenue for the sultanate. The VOC had noticed this, of course, and in the 1720s an ambitious young Palembang prince had noticed their noticing. He took advantage of Dutch commercial interests to call in European backing for a coup against the then sultan. The coup was successful; he took to the Palembang throne himself, paid the

VOC a mercenary's fee of eighty slaves and 400,000 dollars, and signed a treaty that allowed them a trading post opposite his palace and an annual delivery of tin at a fixed price in silver. It was a perfect example of the way the old company style of colonialism could, from time to time, work for the mutual benefit of local kings and European traders. But in the nineteenth century there was no way that that sort of equitability could continue.

Palembang's troubles had started with Thomas Stamford Raffles in 1810. With a keen eye on the tin-rich islands, the British had energetically attempted to convince the then sultan, Mahmud Badaruddin II, to tear up his treaty with the Dutch and to evict the European trading community from his territory well before any British warships reached Batavia. The reason for this demand was never explained to the sultan, of course: Raffles and his boss, Lord Minto, knew well that should the Napoleonic Wars ever come to an end, then any Dutch territory they had seized would likely be handed back to its former owners. But if Palembang was to declare unilateral independence ahead of any British action in the Archipelago, then there would be a legal argument for any subsequent British annexation of the tin islands to stand in perpetuity. The sultan, however, was a canny man himself, and he prevaricated until he knew the outcome of the 1811 invasion. As soon as word of British successes reached him, he did exactly what he felt had been asked of him: he declared independence and evicted the two-dozen Dutch traders from his territory with extreme prejudice—they were all dead by the time they reached the mouth of the Musi.

The British, by this time ensconced in Batavia, cooked up a storm of manufactured outrage in response and despatched a fleet to Palembang. The city unravelled in a horrific outbreak of rioting even before they arrived. Sultan Badaruddin fled to the jungle; the British placed his younger brother, Najamuddin, on the throne; then annexed Bangka and Belitung—as had been planned all along—and sailed off into the sunrise. The new sultan, however, was rather unpopular, and a profound sense of injustice continued to simmer in what was left of the Palembang aristocracy—so much so that a subsequent British official there decided to return the exiled Badaruddin to the throne in 1813, apparently with Najamuddin's happy acquiescence. Unfortunately this resident, William Robison, had never had much favour with his chief in Batavia, and when Raffles found out what he had done he insisted that things be flipped around yet again: after a month back in the Palembang palace Badaruddin was evicted once more and his brother returned to the throne.

The end of the British interregnum in 1816 did not bring an end to the ridiculous game of musical chairs in Palembang. The incoming Dutch administration immediately began flexing its muscles and making hostile gestures at the court. Najamuddin found himself unseated and exiled to Batavia. Incredibly, the Dutch now put Badaruddin—the very man who had murdered their countrymen seven years earlier—back onto the cursed throne for the third time. And at this point Badaruddin decided he'd had altogether too much. He declared absolute, outright independence once again.

The sheer absurdity of the Dutch and British meddling in Palembang—where a mutually beneficial treaty between the VOC and a local court had held good for most of the previous century—shows just how much things had changed by the early decades of the nineteenth century. Europeans had long been entangled in the politics of Archipelago courts, but now they felt able—and, indeed, compelled—to arbitrarily change successions with little more than a snap of their fingers and with scant regard for local circumstances. The results in this instance were horrific, with years of fighting before the Dutch eventually toppled Badaruddin for the last time and shipped him off to exile in far-off Maluku, which would soon become a favoured dumping ground for unseated sultans.

This time, the Dutch thought the better of reinstating Najamuddin: they made his son king instead. For an uneasy couple of years they let him rule along the lines of the old treaties, before deciding that this would not do. In 1823 they evicted him from his palace and turned it into the official Dutch residency, giving him a pension and a ceremonial role by way of recompense. Najamuddin junior and his disgusted courtiers then attempted to poison the Dutch garrison, now encamped in a palace that had been strictly off-limits to all non-Muslims until a decade earlier. A final bout of fighting erupted, before this last sultan of Palembang, too, was shipped out to Maluku. In the thirteen years since Raffles' first demand for a break with the Netherlands there had been no fewer than five changes at the head of the sultanate, every one of them decided by Europeans. Untold thousands of locals and Dutchmen had been killed in the process.

Palembang was not the only source of trouble for the Dutch in Sumatra. In the cool green highlands of Minangkabau they had become entangled in a local conflict between the traditional rulers and staunch Muslim reformists. These reformists were dour, turbaned men known as the *Padris* after Pedir, the Acehnese port from which pilgrim ships to Mecca traditionally sailed. Inspired by the Wahhabi fundamentalists who had conquered the holy city of Islam in 1803, the Padris had attempted to follow suit in Minangkabau, trying to stamp out gambling, cockfighting, and the matrilineal inheritance customs of the hills. In 1821 the old anti-Padri rulers had decided to hand the country—over which they no longer had control—to the Dutch, who thereby inherited a fiery civil war. It would take almost two decades for colonial troops to quash the zealous Padri armies and to capture their spiritual leader, Imam Bonjol, the Archipelago prototype for an Islamist insurgent.

Elsewhere in the Archipelago, the resurgent Dutch faced all manner of small wars. In south Sulawesi the Bugis princes refused to go quietly into vassaldom, and even in Maluku, oldest of all European toeholds in the Archipelago, there was significant unrest in the years following the British interregnum. But it was in Java, the great lodestone of the Archipelago, that the old order would make its most formidable final stand.

⊙–⊙–⊙–⊙–⊙

On a hot May day in 1824, a feisty thirty-eight-year-old prince from Yogyakarta had a vision. He was a slim man with high, broad cheekbones, and he had recently stopped attending the affairs of state in the kraton. Yogyakarta had long recovered from the violence and looting of the British interregnum, but, the prince felt, the dynasty had been overtaken by debauchery and corruption.

The vision came to him as he was meditating in a cool cave in the limestone hills near his home at Tegalreja, out in the rice fields to the south of the city. He was a staunch Muslim—unusually staunch in fact, by the standards of his courtly contemporaries—but he was not averse to dabbling in the more esoteric aspects of Javanese mysticism, and he had often received supernatural visitations. This, however, was something entirely out of the ordinary: the vision was of none other than the Ratu Adil, the messianic 'Righteous Prince' who had been haunting the imagination of Java since the days of King Joyoboyo in the twelfth century. In the story of the vision that the prince later shared with his followers, the Ratu Adil issued him with an ominous instruction: 'The reason I have summoned you is for you to set my army fighting. Let Java be conquered immediately!'

The prince had been born Raden Mas Mustahar, but he would be remembered forevermore by his official princely title: Pangeran Aria Diponegoro.

⊙–⊙–⊙–⊙–⊙

Diponegoro was born at dawn on 11 November 1785, the first son of the man destined to rule as Hamengkubuwono III, the puppet sultan appointed by Raffles after the sacking of Yogya-karta in 1812. His mother was a concubine rather than a queen, so he was never a serious contender for the throne. That should not have stopped him rising to a very senior position within the court, but there had always been something a little odd about Diponegoro, and the difference only deepened when at the age of seven he was plucked from the women's quarters of the kraton and taken away to live with his great-grandmother, Ratu Ageng, in her rice-land retreat at Tegalreja. Ratu Ageng was a formidable woman who had headed the sultan's corps of fearsome amazon fighters in her youth. Since her widowhood she had been playing at being a gentlewoman farmer in a mansion with a garden full of caged songbirds and old Hindu-Buddhist statues. Little Dipo-negoro was raised on her tales of the glory days of Mataram, and steeped in the traditional ways of royal Java.

But as well as learning what it meant to be royal, the young Diponegoro fraternised with the people of the countryside, learnt about cock-fighting and popular magic, and came into contact with both traditional mystics and those roguish young village men who would quickly turn rebellious during times of unrest. By his teens he had also developed contacts in the *pesantren*, the seminaries out amongst the palm trees where scholars taught a more orthodox Islam to the sons of farmers. These pious men, known as *santri*, had their own power and influence.

When Diponegoro returned to the Yogyakarta court as a young man he did not like what he saw. He had experienced the humiliations during Raffles' rule at first hand, and things had not improved with the return of the Dutch in 1816. The incoming governor-general was a man with an admirable sense of decency. If Daendels and Raffles had been a few years ahead of their time with their proto-Victorian imperialism, then Godert Alexander Gerard Philip, the Baron van der Capellen—an upright man with blond hair and foxy sideburns—was the best part of a century early with his ethical concerns. He was frustrated from the very start by the cold capitalism of the reconstituted Dutch East Indies, and he once complained that 'whenever I see that in the Netherlands people understand liberalism to mean the protection of European landowners at the cost of the native population, and that the latter, who are so dear to me, are completely lost from view in order that a few speculators and adventurers can succeed in their plans, then I must declare myself an ultra anti-liberal'.

Those speculators and adventurers had been doing rather well in Central Java. Both Daendels and Raffles had allowed tranches of private land in what had originally been sovereign Mataram territory to be leased out to European and Chinese investors. Diponegoro had refused to lease out his own Tegalreja estates—which he had inherited from his great-grandmother Ratu Ageng at the age of eighteen—but plenty of other local aristocrats had been more than willing to receive large cash sums in return for control of their traditional holdings. A considerable degree of debauchery had crept into the local high society, and the rent payments often went on fast living and imported European luxuries. Meanwhile, the local farmers, who had previously worked the land on their own terms, usually suffered once a foreigner with an eye for a quick cash crop profit moved in. They found themselves suddenly transformed from de facto landholders to disenfranchised labourers on commercial plantations where coffee and indigo had replaced rice. The system, in the words of one critical Dutchman, 'deprived the Javanese peasant of his property rights and debased his status to that of a coolie'.

Worse still, the colonial authorities had given licenses to businessmen—almost invariably ethnic Chinese—to run tollgates along the highways of Java, where often exorbitant fees were extracted from every passing peasant. Unsurprisingly, then, the countryside was beginning to slide into a sort of low-level anarchy as desperate men gave themselves over to the marauding bands of jago, those petty gangsters who had been a part of the Javanese scene since before the days of Majapahit.

In 1821 the harvest failed and, as if that wasn't bad enough, a global cholera pandemic hit Java and the rest of the Archipelago towards the end of the same year. Then, twelve months later the Gunung Merapi volcano blew its top and devastated the surrounding countryside. By this stage apocalyptic prophecies and millenarian visions were doing the rounds in the villages and markets, and many people were beginning to suggest that it was time for the Ratu Adil to show his face in Java. The court of Yogyakarta, meanwhile, was in a state of perpetual crisis.

If there was a fair degree of debauchery going on in aristocratic circles, it was more than matched by the senior Dutch staff at the residency in Yogyakarta. Besides the usual drinking, they seemed to particularly enjoy all manner of sexual shenanigans, with one resident declaring of his deputy that 'in general his conduct with numerous Javanese women and girls was not only extremely improper but sometimes even attended by insults' (though the resident in question also conceded that his own sexual misconduct 'had excelled over his predecessors and contemporaries').

The disgusted Diponegoro would later declare of this period that 'Dutchmen had trotted into our kraton as though it was a stable and had shouted and called as though it had become a market'. By the time of his visitation from the Ratu Adil he had broken from the court and gone home to Tegalreja, where he was quietly nursing his sense of outrage, keeping up his contacts with the santri, the mystics and the jago, and planning an almighty rebellion.

The final spark came at the start of the dry season in 1825. Diponegoro's own retainers clashed with a column of workmen sent out on the orders of the Dutch resident to repair a road that skirted his Tegalreja lands. What started as a petty argument quickly turned into an armed stand-off, and when on 20 July Dutch officials sent a party of soldiers to arrest the recalcitrant prince, they instead precipitated a war. As the Dutch troopers set fire to Tegalreja, the prince escaped with his men. He was last glimpsed by the Europeans fleeing through the rice fields on a beautiful black horse: 'He was clad entirely in white in the Arab style. The end of his turban flapped in the wind as he made his horse prance… dancing in the midst of his lance-bearing bodyguard'.

Central Java descended into carnage.

⊙ ⁓ ⊙ ⁓ ⊙ ⁓ ⊙ ⁓ ⊙

Diponegoro's Java War would last for five bloody years. Fully half of the princes of Yogyakarta went over with him into rebellion, and forty-one of the eighty-eight senior courtiers followed suit. This was in no small part down to a recent ill-considered attempt by the well-meaning van der Capellen to tackle the deep-seated social problems in the region: he had outlawed the leasing of land to foreigners in the court territories, thus depriving many of the dissipated aristocratic landlords of their cash and priming them for rebellion in the process.

The Dutch and their notional ally, the Yogyakarta sultan, lost control of the countryside almost at once, and the city was besieged. Diponegoro had taken not just princes and courtiers with him into insurgency; he had also taken the white-turbaned minions of the pesantrens and the gangster bands of the rural jago. His rebel forces were an unholy alliance of zealots, traditionalists and criminals, and they rallied remarkably to the task of guerrilla warfare. Tollgates were burnt to the ground; Dutch and kraton outposts were ambushed; and a semblance of alternative authority through taxation and market management was even set up. Dutch tactics, meanwhile, were singularly ineffective. A third of their forces were dead by 1827.

It has never been entirely clear what Diponegoro himself expected to gain from his rebellion. He had become the embodiment of all manner of divergent traditions and aspirations—Islamic, Javanese, anti-foreigner, millenarian and more—but at times he struggled to maintain a balance between these contrasting forces. At the outset, his rebellion was principally an uprising against the decayed and debauched Yogyakarta court; later Diponegoro would talk of evicting all the Europeans from Java. At other times he cleaved closely to Islam as a standard and talked of establishing some kind of kingdom of the faith. In his more pragmatic moments, however, he seemed mainly to want simply to reassert the old circumstances of the eighteenth century, with the VOC camped out on the north coast, free to trade there as they pleased, while the Javanese continued undisturbed in the heartlands according to time-honoured tradition. But Diponegoro did not realise that the eighteenth century had passed; Daendels and Raffles had been no aberration, and the world no longer ended on the marches of Java.

At the end of the 1820s the Dutch changed tactics. They set up small, fortified outposts all over the rebellion-wracked countryside, sturdy cubes of stone that could act as springboards for columns as fast-moving and sure-footed as those of the rebels—and better armed to boot. There were more than two hundred of these outposts by the end of the decade, and around each a small pocket of security grew, to the relief of a peasantry exhausted by the years of war. Diponegoro's rebel army, meanwhile, had slowly gone to pieces, the santris falling out with the traditionalists, and an increasing number of princes and aristocrats sneaking away as they sniffed the way the wind was blowing. Diponegoro ended up almost alone, a ragged, righteous prince traversing the mountain trails and shivering through bouts of malaria in village huts. At the end of Ramadan in early 1830, he came in to the small upland town of Magelang to negotiate with the Dutch.

Diponegoro himself—not to mention later patriotic Indonesians—would subsequently claim that the actions of the Dutch commander, General De Kock, were a betrayal, and that the prince had met in good faith for discussions on equal terms. But he must surely have known that his demand to be made the chief of all Islam in Java would never be accepted. On 28 March 1830, he was arrested in the Dutch residency at Magelang, bundled into a coach, and shipped off into exile, muttering, it was reported, 'How did I come to this?' He lived out the rest of his days across the water in Sulawesi, dying at the age of sixty-nine in the Dutch fortress at Makassar.

⊙–⊙–⊙–⊙–⊙

Diponegoro's war was the biggest and bloodiest of the myriad small reactions to the resurgent Dutch in the decades following the British interregnum. Some eight thousand Europeans had died, along with as many as quarter of a million Javanese, and the countryside of what had once been Mataram had been ravaged. But all of these rebellions—from Palembang to Ambon and from Java to Minangkabau—ultimately failed. They were hopelessly one-sided—and not just in terms of military technology. On the local side there were men who were still fighting based on ancient ideas of identity—as Javanese, Minangkabaus, Bugis or Palembang Malays. If they had any notion of an Archipelago-spanning Nusantara, it would have been abstract in the extreme, and even Islam had proved to be the shakiest of unifying standards. The Dutch, meanwhile, were fighting for something bigger. By the time the Java War was over, the Dutch East Indies was much more than an idea: it was a veritable entity. And what was more, with enormous war debts to recoup, it was time for it to start paying its way...

CHAPTER 6

RUST EN ORDE: THE DUTCH EAST INDIES

T he road unspooled ahead across soft, green countryside. It was the wettest part of the year—the late months of 1834—and the air was clean and cool. Skeins of cloud hung over the landscape, and the interlocking ridges floated on a cushion of haze. This was the heart of the Priangan highlands, the hulk of up-thrown country that forms the hinterland of West Java. In earlier centuries, this had been the stomping ground of the old Sundanese kingdoms, and the name of the place—a contraction of *para-hyang-an*—contained that same ageless Austronesian idea as the Dieng Plateau, further west along the same mountain chain: *hyang*, expressing the concept of deity. This was an abode of ancient gods. But for all its misty mysticism, and for all its apparent fertility, the man making his way along the road could see that something was amiss.

The man's name was Louis Vitalis. He had been born in France into a merchant family of Greek descent, and had come out to Java in the service of the Dutch. He was an inspector employed to tour the countryside and to take notes of the conditions. He had been sent here to investigate concerns raised by Otto Carel

Holmberg de Beckfelt, the Dutch resident in overall charge of Priangan, that the system of land management so recently introduced to the Dutch East Indies was leading to horrific suffering up here in the hills.

The resident's concerns had been well founded. Many of the locals Vitalis passed at the wayside were in a pitiable state. Here and there he spotted a corpse in the long grass beside the road. But there was no epidemic, and there ought to have been no hunger. The calamity that was killing people here was, as far as Vitalis was concerned, entirely man-made. Large tracts of the land on either side of the road had been given over to growing indigo, a spindly shrub producing a blue dye that would, later in the century, give the classic blue tint to the newly invented denim jeans. The emaciated men were labourers on these indigo plantations, and they had, quite simply, been worked to death.

'Truly their situation is lamentable and really miserable', Vitalis wrote. 'What else can one expect? On the roads as well as the plantations one does not meet people but only walking skeletons, which drag themselves with great difficulty from one place to another, often dying in the process'.

When he reached the district headquarters Vitalis grilled the local regent, Raden Anggadipa II. The regent was a scion of a princely dynasty, part of that old stratum of aristocrats that had always run the countryside for indigenous sultans and VOC officials alike. Daendels had despised them, of course, but in the 1830s they were back in favour. Raden Anggadipa reported that 'some of the labourers who work in the plantations are in such a state of exhaustion that they die almost immediately after they have eaten from the food which is delivered to them as an advance payment for the produce to be delivered later'. When Vitalis demanded to know why the bodies of the victims were left to lie at the roadside instead of being given a decent burial, the regent shrugged. There was, he said, no need to make the effort: 'Every night these bodies are dragged away by the tigers...'

It would have been easy enough for Vitalis to dismiss the outrage as entirely the doing of the ossified aristocrat before him, and to place the blame on 'oriental despotism'. But he knew that such excuses would not stand up to much scrutiny, for the regent was merely effecting the orders for a wider system, introduced five years earlier and designed to raise colonial revenues—and, it was claimed, to improve the lot of the peasants in Dutch-held territories. It was painfully obvious, however, that here in Priangan this so-called *Cultuurstelsel*, this 'Cultivation System', had gone horribly wrong.

⊙–⊙–⊙–⊙–⊙

In the years after the British interregnum, and in the run-up to the Java War, the new leaders of the Dutch East Indies had struggled to make sense of how to extract money from what was now a genuine imperial possession. At the time, there was a great tension between the liberals and the conservatives when it came to deciding on a policy for the colony. It is always important to remember that the political designations of the past may not mean quite the same thing as they do today. In the post-Napoleonic milieu, 'liberalism' was first and foremost of the economic variety—that is, an advocacy of private capitalism and free trade. This sentiment might have found inspiration in ideas about the Rights of Man, but as both Daendels and Raffles had demonstrated, real humanitarianism was often nothing more than an airy theory. 'Conservatives' of the day, meanwhile, were unlikely to have much in economic common with their modern-day, right-leaning counterparts: far from it—they were generally the ones advocating an old-fashioned system of government monopoly.

To begin with, the liberals seemed to have the floor. But if ethical liberalism had always been up for compromise whenever there was a road to be built or a war to be fought, then pragmatism had also got the better of free-market ideals from time to time. As liberals, both Raffles and Daendels had fervently believed in free trade. But they had also desperately wanted their cash-strapped administrations to make money, and if there was a particularly lucrative government monopoly, then they were generally loath to let it go. Under British rule, peasants across most of Java were free to grow what they pleased, but in the Priangan highlands the old VOC system of compulsory cultivation of coffee for exclusive sale to the state was kept in place—coffee, after all, was a cash crop of the first rank. By the 1820s, with no sign of a decent financial surplus emerging from the East Indies and with the cost of wars in Java, Minangkabau and Palembang spiralling out of control, the official pendulum had swung firmly in favour of this sort of hard-headed pragmatism. The man who put the pragmatism into play was Johannes van den Bosch.

Van den Bosch had come out to Java as a soldier in 1797. However, his eighteeth-century attitudes led to an almighty falling out with Daendels, and in 1810 the Thundering Marshal had him evicted from the Indies. He shipped home to the Netherlands and set about studying politics and economics. Once the Napoleonic Wars had passed he took to publishing pamphlets condemning the 'perverted Liberalism' of Daendels and Raffles. The establishment in 1824 of the *Nederlandsche Handel-Maatschappij* (Netherlands Trading Society, or NHM), a company owned by the Dutch Crown for the exclusive purpose of trading Archipelago products into Europe, suggested that the pro-state ideals of van den Bosch were beginning to find official favour, and in the aftermath of the Java War he found himself appointed the new governor-general of the Dutch East Indies.

Taking stock of the raw scars of Diponegoro's recent rebellion, the new chief could not deny that there was a great deal of ill-feeling towards his countrymen in the green fields of Java—and, as far as he was aware, elsewhere in the Archipelago. 'Our policies have done nothing to overcome this popular hate towards us', van den Bosch declared. 'On the contrary it has increased whenever we have come into closer contact with the people...'

Back in the days of the VOC, van den Bosch insisted—with rose-tinted spectacles firmly in place—there had been 'not a trace of rebellion or riot' because of the policy of devolving much of the day-to-day administration to the local regents. The trouble, he felt, had all started when Daendels and Raffles set about overturning this system with their new-fangled nonsense. Van den Bosch was never coy about explaining why he felt this way:

> The intellectual development of the average Javanese does not reach beyond that of our children from twelve to fourteen years, while in general knowledge he is left far behind by them ... to give to such people institutions suitable for a fully grown society is just as absurd as to give children the rights of adults and to expect that they will put them to good use ... Only a patriarchal government suits the Javanese. The government must take care of them and must not allow them to do things for themselves, because of their limited capabilities. This, of course, must be done with fatherly consideration...

Here, then, was the ultimate fruition of Enlightenment ideals, the ethos of nineteenth-century imperialism writ large and the final unashamed iteration of the unvoiced idea that had tormented Raffles and Daendels and that had led them to all their untenable hypocrisies as self-proclaimed believers in the universal equality of man. In no time at all, the pukka sahibs would be talking of the 'White Man's Burden'.

In the Dutch East Indies, this new attitude was manifest in the form of the Cultivation System. The idea was simple, and it combined what the likes of van den Bosch considered to be the best of both the VOC and Rafflesian worlds. A colony-wide and carefully constructed land revenue system would be put in place,

but as in the old days its actual enforcement would be left to regents and village chiefs. And what was more, as in the old days,
the emphasis would be on payments in kind. Villagers in Dutch
territories in Java, in Minangkabau in Sumatra, and in Minahasa
in the far north of Sulawesi, would be exempt from paying rent
if instead they gave a fifth of their lands over to the growing of
cash crops prescribed by the government. These crops—coffee,
inevitably, was foremost amongst them, but there was also indigo,
tea, tobacco, cochineal, and sugarcane—would be delivered to
the government at a fixed and rather paltry price, processed in
factories run by Chinese and European entrepreneurs, and then
shipped to Europe to be sold at a vast profit by none other than
the *Nederlandsche Handel-Maatschappij*.

It was said that the system would not only free the peasantry
from the grip of the moneylenders by doing away with a compulsory cash rent; farmers would also have the potential to make
a profit if their haul of government crops sold for more than the
amount they were due to pay in taxes. But in truth, the entire
business was about making money for the government, and within a year of the Cultivation System's launch in 1830 the colonial
budget had been balanced for the first time in decades.

$\odot-\odot-\odot-\odot-\odot$

By the middle of the nineteenth century remittances from the
East Indies, raised through the Cultivation System, were almost
a third of all state revenues in the Netherlands. The Dutch-ruled
Archipelago had been turned into a powerhouse of agricultural
production. There was, however, scant liberalism on the ground,
for in practice the system essentially amounted to one of forced
production. Each season there were fresh demands for coffee, indigo and sugarcane. Any excess was warmly appreciated, and so
there was every reason for Dutchmen in the field, as well as the
local regents and headmen, to push for ever higher yields. In some

places, forced labour was expected in lieu of forced cultivation, and corrupt local governance meant that many villagers found that they still had to pay taxes in cash as well as in crops.

Today, the Cultivation System is popularly remembered as an unmitigated evil of exploitation, a procession of skeletal peasants fed one by one into the grinders of a great colonial sugar mill with pure profit dribbling out the other side. Nothing is ever black and white, however, and had a system which involved around half the entire Javanese population (and an unknown proportion of Minangkabaus and Minahasans) been so unremittingly appalling it surely wouldn't have survived for three decades without prompting either mass mortality or mass rebellion. Around the fringes of the system there were incidental benefits. Carters were called upon to carry cane to the mills; skilled machinists were required in the plants; bridges and roads had to be built for the transport of cut crops; and men whose fathers had been nothing more than part-time artisans found themselves turned into full-time professional craftsmen. And there *was* cash in the countryside for the first time, allowing small purchases and petty indulgences. A proper economic network was beginning to emerge, and at the same time the population was booming.

But reports of the kind raised by Louis Vitalis in Priangan had not simply been invented, and while the Cultivation System did not lead to universal hardship, in very many instances it most certainly did cause suffering. In some places attempts were made to grow cash crops that were ill-suited to the local soils, and villagers were compelled to work for many months planting coffee or indigo that never yielded a harvest. When crops were successful, meanwhile, local administrators tended simply to shunt the land tax assessments arbitrarily upwards and pocket whatever notional profit the peasants had earned from the excess. The coastal regions of the Java Pasisir around Cirebon and Pekalongan were particularly hard pressed; in the 1840s famine broke out there as a result of so much former rice land being used for forced production of cash crops. Louis Vitalis himself was still on the scene, and he reported gangs of starving children haunting the roads in this, one of the most fertile of all Dutch territories:

> It is sad to have to admit that poor, hungry people who came in droves to beseech private people in the Residency of Cheribon [Cirebon] for food did not dare to turn to the government officials. When they were asked why they did not go to the officials for help, the answer was: 'We fear them'!

Inevitably, word of all this began to filter out back home in the Netherlands, and with the liberals still clamouring for private enterprise to be given a free hand, an increasingly critical eye was being cast on the Cultivation System. The critics received an unusual boost in 1860 with the appearance of one of the strangest novels ever published, a positively incendiary tract by the name of *Max Havelaar*.

The book had been written by a bitter former colonial official named Eduard Douwes Dekker—though he gave himself the self-pitying Latin nom de plume, *Multatuli* ('I have endured much'). He had been born in 1820 into a moderately prosperous middle-class family, and had sailed for the East Indies in his teens. He seems to have made a habit of falling in love and falling into debt, but he was also possessed of considerable administrative talents and he was given government posts in Sumatra and Maluku. Then in 1856, after a furlough in the Netherlands during which he lost just about everything at the card tables, he was appointed assistant resident in the West Java district of Lebak. It was here that the trouble began.

His predecessor in Lebak, a rugged district in what had once been the sultanate of Banten, had died suddenly at his post, and Douwes Dekker quickly began to suspect that there had been nothing natural about his passing. The man had been investigating the outrageous abuses of power by the local regent, yet another member of the old co-opted aristocracy that underpinned the workings of the Cultivation System. Douwes Dekker enthusiastically continued the dead man's work, and after just four weeks in Lebak he attempted to charge the regent with various crimes, including the poisoning of the former assistant resident. The colonial authorities were not impressed, and rather than being rewarded for his efforts in the name of truth and justice, Douwes Dekker was roundly rebuffed. He resigned, headed home, and ended up drifting bitterly around the casinos of Europe in the company of a former prostitute.

Embittered former colonial employees pontificating about the wrongdoings of the empire for which they had once toiled were something of a nineteenth-century cliché, and there were plenty of other Dutch and Englishmen doing the same thing. The more energetic of their number might write a letter to a newspaper, or even publish a pamphlet. But Douwes Dekker went one step further—in the autumn of 1859, in a flurry of production in a Brussels garret, he penned an entire novel. He then rather blotted his copybook as a man of high ethics by using the manuscript for a clumsy blackmail attempt: he sent it to the Colonial Minister offering to refrain from publishing if the government would grant him not only a new and prosperous post in Java, but also a knighthood. The response was predictably unfavourable, and so the book appeared in print the following year.

It was a very odd sort of book, and as no less than D.H. Lawrence would later write, 'As far as composition goes, it is the greatest mess possible'. It was certainly chaotic, with multiple changes of narrator and incessant editorial interjections. It is also hard to think of another book that gives such an irresistible impression that the author is *shouting* at you. But for all that, it was very powerful indeed. It was essentially a barely disguised autobiographical account of what Douwes Dekker had seen and experienced in Lebak. Indeed, in the final paragraphs he went so far as to kick his narrator off the page, drop all pretence that the thing was a novel at all, and appear in person as Multatuli to sign off in a welter of ellipses and italics with a demand to know of the King of the Netherlands 'whether it is Your Imperial will ... that yonder Your more than *thirty million* subjects be MALTREATED AND EX-PLOITED IN YOUR NAME?' Unsurprisingly, the book raised a storm of controversy.

Today, casual readers might be forgiven for coming away with the idea that Eduard Douwes Dekker single-handedly brought an end to the Cultivation System. His book certainly helped it on its way. It was not, however, ethical concerns that provided the real impetus. The real drive for change came from the free marketeers, and from 1862 they began to get their way. The government monopoly on pepper was abolished first; cloves and nutmeg came next, and tea and indigo soon followed suit. As the second half of the nineteenth century got under way, commercial agriculture in Java was turned over to private enterprise on an enormous scale, and the cash-rich colonial society became ever more sophisticated. Luxurious hotels and social clubs opened in the towns; new urban technology came into play, and lavish entertainments were laid on for Europeans. Elsewhere in the Archipelago, however, things were rather more wild, as one of the most remarkable of all the foreign travellers to pass between the islands during the imperial heyday was finding out.

⊙—⊙—⊙—⊙—⊙

The house stood amongst the trees where the land angled upwards towards the island of Ternate's central volcanic peak. It was an old building. The space between the low retaining wall and the shaggy thatched roof was filled with palm-leaf matting and the narrow veranda gave onto a gloomy interior. Below the house the rooftops of the little town showed between the palms, stretching away along the shore to the northeast. Across the water, the hills of Halmahera rose dark from a forested shoreline. It was February, and away to the southwest columns of monsoon rain would be marching across Java and Sumatra. But here in Maluku the seasons are reversed, and the breeze that shifted the branches of the trees around the house was fiery and dry. Five and a half thousand feet above, the smoke from the summit of the central volcano made a pale streamer in the bleached sky.

Ternate and its southern twin Tidore—little peaks of land rising from the depths off the coast of Halmahera in northern Maluku—had a troubled past. They were the seats of a pair of feuding sultanates, and in earlier centuries they had found themselves in the very crucible of the spice trade. The Portuguese had settled here and built fortresses in the early sixteenth century. They had tussled with passing Spanish ships and engaged in endlessly appalling conflicts with the locals. One bout of violence in 1529 erupted after a pig escaped from the Portuguese fort and went rampaging through Ternate's Muslim quarter. When the outraged locals killed the offending swine, the Portuguese kidnapped one of their senior religious officials and smeared his face with bacon fat by way of revenge. Unsurprisingly, the mortified cleric then declared a holy war against the pork-loving infidels. There were similarly foul-tempered conflicts throughout the century until 1575, when the Portuguese pulled out altogether. A couple of decades later the Dutch arrived, and more intercultural bickering continued throughout the seventeenth century.

But those days were now long past. It was 1858 and the spice trade was a shadow of its former self. That so much blood had been spilt over this tiny island seemed absurd, and though it was still the headquarters of a Dutch residency claiming nominal authority over a galaxy of islands stretching all the way to the head of New Guinea, it was unmistakably a backwater.

But for the man tossing and turning on his cot in a backroom of the little house, Ternate was what passed for civilisation. He was a thirty-five-year-old Englishman, and he had spent months wandering in the wilder parts of the Archipelago. He was a naturalist and a professional hunter of exotic birds, bugs and beasts. And now he was sick. Long months in the forests had exposed him to the most virulent strains of malaria, and he had been laid up for weeks.

As he lay sweating and shivering and staring up at the rattan ceiling he had wrestled with big questions. Over the course of his meandering journeys he had already noticed the clear distinction between the flora and fauna of the western and eastern parts of the Archipelago, Asian plants and animals giving way dramatically to those of Australia and the Pacific somewhere around the vicinity of Sulawesi. One day the putative line that marked the division would bear his name. Now, though, as the fever wracked his body, he had even bigger issues to contend with.

It was surely the state of his own health that had brought him to the ominous subject of death. He pondered awhile, as the mosquitoes whined around his sweat-drenched form, on the grim theories of Thomas Malthus about the natural—and un-natural—balances that keep human populations in check, and then carried his thoughts into the animal world. The beasts too, he realised, were subject to 'enormous and constant destruction', and he found himself wondering why it was that some survived and others did not. For a sick man on a remote island far from home it was a profoundly unsettling question, and given his current sorry state he can surely have taken little comfort when the answer came to him: 'that on the whole the best fitted live'. But there followed a revelation that was electrifying enough to rouse even an ailing man from his bed:

> [I]t suddenly flashed upon me that this self-acting process would necessarily *improve the race*, because in every generation the inferior would inevitably be killed off and the superior would remain—that is, *the fittest would survive...*

In that one feverish moment Alfred Russel Wallace had grasped the unknown concept of evolution.

◉—◉—◉—◉—◉

Alfred Russel Wallace had arrived in Southeast Asia four years earlier. He was a chronically modest man with a thoroughly un-Victorian talent for self-deprecation, always more inclined to portray himself as a comic bumbler, tripping over roots and tangling his butterfly net in overhanging branches, than as some stiff-lipped imperial hero. But he was a true enthusiast for travel and exploration, and fevers and tropical ulcers did nothing to dampen his zest for stomping through swamps and jungles. He had been born in 1823 into a lower-middle class family on the Welsh Borders. After leaving school at the age of fourteen, he worked as a surveyor and as a teacher, but along the way he had developed a considerable passion for zoology. In 1848, he and a friend headed to Brazil to seek their fortunes by collecting exotic creepy-crawlies to sell in London, where amateur entomology was something of a craze. Unfortunately, after four years in the Amazon, Wallace lost most of his haul in a mid-Atlantic shipwreck, but he had cut his teeth in the world of professional collecting and gained a modest name for himself in scientific circles. As a consequence he was given government funding for his ticket to Singapore.

By this stage there were steamships plying the route from Europe, and a journey that might have taken a year in the days of the spice trade now took just six weeks. Wallace had embarked in Southampton in early March, been hassled and hustled by Egyptian hucksters during the overland hop from the Mediterranean to the Red Sea, and had reached Singapore in the middle of April. He had brought a good supply of pins and nets from England, as well as a fourteen-year-old assistant by the name of Charles Allen. The nets would prove rather more useful than the boy, and by the time they disembarked in the tropics Wallace was already grumbling about the ineptitude of his teenage assistant.

By 1854 the British settlement of Singapore was a bustling port. In 1819, at the end of his tumultuous career in Asia, a sickly

Thomas Stamford Raffles had overseen the founding of an outpost here. The treaty he signed with the local rulers had con-
travened long-standing Dutch agreements with the lords of the
scattered isles of Riau, the archipelago that included Singapore,
and something of a diplomatic crisis between the two European powers had ensued. But in the end British Singapore had
endured, and under the canny administration of its co-founder
William Farquhar and his successor John Crawfurd (Raffles' one-
time point-man in Yogyakarta) the place had prospered, drawing
in trade from those parts of the Archipelago not yet under Dutch
rule and attracting settlers from all over the region. It was, Wallace
noted, already very much a Chinese town, and 'The Chinese do
all the work, they are a most industrious people, & the place could
hardly exist without them'.

After three months in Singapore as the house guest of a French
missionary, who lived in the jungles of the interior (where there
were still a few surviving tigers to provide a frisson for his first
tentative insect-collecting expeditions), Wallace and Charles Allen
clambered aboard a small schooner and sailed two days up the
coast to Melaka, struggling along the way with the unfamiliar
seaboard diet of curry and rice. Melaka, the one-time hub of trade
in the western Archipelago, was a British port by this stage. The
Dutch had captured it from the Portuguese in 1641, but in 1824
Britain and the Netherlands had signed a friendly treaty swapping
ownership of Melaka for possession of that long-standing British
white elephant at Bengkulu on the west coast of Sumatra. The
trade-off certainly made sense: the Dutch were the only serious
colonial presence in Sumatra, and despite their troubles in Palembang and Minangkabau, they looked set to stay. Meanwhile, with
the British settled at both Penang and Singapore, it was certainly
logical for them to hold the third major harbour on the eastern
side of the Straits of Melaka, too. But the 1824 treaty, which drew
a dividing line of imperial influence right down the middle of
the Straits, had arbitrarily cleaved a single region in half. Since

THE HOLY MOUNTAIN The temples on the slopes of the volcano Gunung Lawu—such as Candi Sukuh, pictured here—belong to the final years of Hindu-Buddhist rule in Java, when the refined formality of earlier temple architecture was giving way to an earthier style.

All over the Archipelago, volcanoes have been regarded as homes of ancestral spirits, and in Java and Sumatra these ancient indigenous ideas often blended with Hindu-Buddhist notions about mountains as the homes of the gods. Of all the sacred mountains few have a deeper spiritual character than Gunung Lawu, a dormant hulk 10,680 feet (3,256 metres) tall that straddles the border of Central and East Java. In Javanese traditions this mountain is the realm of the powerful Sunan Lawu, who appears to be a sort of wind god, predating Islam—and probably predating Hindu-Buddhism too.

The slopes of the mountain were the scene for a final flurry of Hindu-Buddhist temple building in the late fifteenth century as Java was increasingly converting to Islam. These temples—most notably Sukuh and Cetho—are packed with images of frightening ogres and with realistic phalluses replacing the abstract lingams of old.

THE WIDOW History and myth are often spectacularly intertwined in Indonesia, and nowhere more so than in the story of Rangda, the nightmarish witch-queen of Balinese folklore.

Rangda—which simply means 'widow'—has her origins in a real-life Javanese queen. In the late tenth century the ruler of Bali was a king called Udayana. He was married to a Javanese woman called Mahendradatta, whom he eventually banished, possibly for her domineering tendencies. After his death she became embroiled in some sort of succession dispute with their son.

Balinese legends have it that Mahendradatta was exiled to the forests for practicing witchcraft. In exile she became the demonic Rangda, leading legions of witches into battle and raining pestilence on the Balinese population before she was defeated by a holy man.

Today Rangda is a key figure in Balinese dance-dramas. Her demonic nature shows a link with the Hindu goddess Kali, the fierce aspect of Durga. The real-life Mahendradatta was reputedly involved in developing worship of Durga in Bali.

THE GODDESS OF THE SOUTHERN OCEAN Of all the mythical forces
that stretch their influence into the realms of real history in the Archipelago,
none is more potent than Java's Kanjeng Ratu Kidul, the 'Goddess of the
Southern Ocean'. She was, it is sometimes said, a princess of the Hindu-
Buddhist Pajajaran kingdom in West Java. She was banished after refusing
her father's choice of suitor, and retreated to the stormy southern coast of
Java to become the Goddess. Kanjeng Ratu Kidul is particularly closely associated with the Mataram, the Muslim kingdom that emerged in Central
Java in the seventeenth century. Mataram's founder, Senopati, pictured here
with the Goddess, is said to have caught her attention while meditating atop
a holy rock close to Parangtritis, south of modern Yogyakarta. She agreed
to lend him her supernatural support in the founding of his new kingdom,
and, legend has it, all the subsequent kings of Mataram consorted with her.
She is still a potent figure today; the Yogyakarta court still makes annual offerings to her, and it is rumoured that even modern Central Java royals still
consort with her.

THE MOUNTAIN OF STONE Borobudur is Indonesia's best known ancient monument. Built by the Sailendra Dynasty in the eighth and ninth centuries, it is still one of the biggest Buddhist monuments on earth. Today it is visited by thousands of domestic and foreign tourists every day, but it wasn't always so well known. Borobudur probably fell out of use when the major centre of royal power shifted to the Brantas delta near modern Surabaya in the tenth century. The earliest known European reference comes from Frederick Coyett, who headed a VOC mission to Mataram in 1733 and

who had some statues from Borobudur taken away to decorate his house in Batavia. In 1814, Thomas Stamford Raffles (who is often wrongly credited with 'discovering' Borobudur) ordered Hermanus Christian Cornelius, a young Dutch surveyor who had already worked on the Prambanan temple, to produce a preliminary survey of the ruin. This illustration is based on his sketch. By the 1980s, over a thousand years after the Sailendras first built the thing, restoration work had returned Borobudur to something like its original glory.

THE LOST TEMPLES OF MUARA JAMBI On the Batang Hari River, downstream from the modern city of Jambi, is the largest expanse of archaeological remains in Sumatra. The Muara Jambi temple complex sprawls across some 1,500 hectares (15 square kilometres) of low-lying, forested land. These are not lavishly decorated stone temples in the style of Java: here in this swampy river basin there was little natural stone, and so the temples were of man-made brick. The structures at the centre of the complex have been restored, but there are dozens of others, unexamined by archaeologists, sometimes just a mound of broken bricks covered with leaf mould.

Muara Jambi was once the seat of the Malayu kingdom. In the seventh century it fell under the sway of the Buddhist state of Srivijaya, but in the eleventh century the centre of political power in the region shifted to the delta of the Batang Hari. By the late thirteenth century, the region had slipped into obscurity. The jungle took over, and the Muara Jambi complex was left to the tigers. It wasn't until the early twentieth century that archaeologists began to clear the forest and take stock of the huge array of structures.

THE TEMPLE MOSQUE In the town of Kudus, on the north coast of Java, stands the Masjid Menara, one of the most unusual Islamic buildings in Indonesia, with split *candi bentar*–style gateways and a remarkable three-tiered drum tower, all built from weathered red brick.

Kudus lies in a region that formed the original foothold of Islam in Java. This was part of the Demak sultanate, which defeated Java's last great Hindu-Buddhist kingdom, Majapahit, in the early sixteenth century.

No one knows the true age of the brick buildings, but they are thoroughly reminiscent of Javanese Hindu-Buddhist temples. Some claim that they actually are an old temple adapted for a new religious purpose. Even if this is not the case, the structures were obviously inspired by the distinctive red-brick shrines of Majapahit.

THE NINE SAINTS In popular belief, Islam was brought to Java by the *Wali Songo*, the 'Nine Saints', a group of men partly historical, partly mytho-logical. They lived between the fifteenth and sixteenth centuries, but their legend was only properly crystallised in the works of eighteenth-century chroniclers. The term 'wali' is Arabic, but individually each of the saints is known by a Javanese honorific, *sunan*. In the standard version of their story, the first of their number was Sunan Maulana Malik Ibrahim, who may have come from Persia or Central Asia, and whose grave at Gresik is dated to 1419. Amongst the other saints is Sunan Giri, who died in 1506, and whose

origin myth has a heavy hint of the tale of Moses, with the saintly child of
a Hindu princess placed in a box and thrown into the sea, only to be raised
by pious Muslims after washing ashore at Gresik. Sunan Kalijaga, meanwhile, was reputedly a son of a Majapahit aristocrat who lived the life of a
highwayman before taking the saintly path. He is credited—although there
is no serious historical evidence—with the invention of *wayang kulit* shadow
puppetry. The Wali Songo still have a powerful hold on popular imagination
in Java, and their tombs—scattered along the north coast of the island—are
major places of pilgrimage.

THE TRADE-OFF Nine tiny pinheads of land, the Banda Islands amount to a total of no more than twenty-three square miles (sixty square kilometres) of solid ground. And yet this clutch of miniscule landfalls, whose main settlement of Bandaniera is depicted here in the nineteenth century, was once the ultimate hub of the spice trade—the only place on earth where nutmeg trees grew. Nutmeg had been finding its way to Europe by way of a relay of trade links since at least the Roman era, but it was only when the Portuguese turned up in 1511 that a direct connection was forged. Portuguese dominance gave way to a protracted tussle for control of the nutmeg trade between the Dutch and the English.

Eventually the Dutch got the upper hand, but the English doggedly maintained their claim to the outlying islet of Run until 1667 when England and Netherlands signed the Treaty of Breda, which declared that both countries would drop all claims to overseas territories they had seized from one another. In practice this amounted to a trade-off, swapping tiny Run in the Bandas for a Dutch outpost called New Amsterdam, nine thousand miles away on the eastern seaboard of North America. An English fleet had captured it three years earlier, and England's King Charles II had noted approvingly that it was 'a place of great importance ... we have got the better of it and 'tis now called New York'.

A CITY OF MANY NAMES The city known today as Jakarta has traded under many different names. The original settlement at the mouth of the Ciliwung River was known as Sunda Kelapa—*kelapa* meaning 'coconut' in a presumed reference to an abundance of coconut palms in the area. In the early sixteenth century it was named Jayakarta, 'victorious deed', to commemorate a conquest by forces from Demak. This name was usually misheard by European visitors, who wrote it down as 'Jaccatra'.

In 1619 the VOC created a new centre of operations there. The governor-general, Jan Pieterszoon Coen, wanted to name the place after his own

hometown, but 'New Hoorn' could hardly compete with an alternative cooked up by some unknown Hollander: Batavia, a name that was used for the best part of 350 years. The city came to resemble a tropical version of Amsterdam, with canals and Dutch-style houses.

When the Dutch were ousted by the Japanese during World War II, the city became 'Djakarta'. In 1946 when the Dutch returned to the stage, Batavia rose from the ashes once more, only to be banished for good in 1949. There was one final change in 1972 when Indonesian spelling was reformed: Djakarta dropped the D and became Jakarta.

THE FALL OF MAKASSAR For many years Makassar rivalled Melaka on the west coast of the Malay Peninsula, and later Batavia, as the major hub of trade in the eastern part of the Archipelago. It got a further boost in 1641 when the Dutch captured Melaka, throwing out its international traders—Indians, Englishmen, Portuguese and others—many of whom drifted to Makassar. For the Dutch the Makassarese were a significant challenge to their own trading power. In 1667 they joined forces with the Bugis of neighbouring Bone, and toppled the Makassarese sultan. As a result of the

conquest, imagined above by a Dutch engraver, all foreign traders were turfed out of Makassar, and control of most of the region was handed to a Bugis pretender named Arung Palakka on an understanding of Dutch-Bugis friendship and exclusive VOC trading rights.

However, both Bugis and Makassarese remained a powerful presence on the sea lanes for centuries to come, trading across the region from Timor to Aceh. Their seafaring skills were formidable, and their high-prowed white boats today still carry a significant proportion of interisland cargo in Indonesia.

THE BUFFALO AND THE TIGER The *alun-alun*, the ceremonial grassy square that was an essential part of a Javanese royal city, was the scene of extravagant entertainments. Troops paraded here; musical performances and sporting contests were held here. And when European officials made formal visits in the eighteenth and early nineteenth centuries, they were almost always treated to the gruesome spectacle of a buffalo and tiger fight. Many of them reported being thoroughly impressed by the bloody struggle. What few of them realised was that for the watching Javanese these inter-species clashes contained a secret symbolism. The tiger—quick-tempered and with a tendency to lash out violently—represented the Europeans; the buffalo— slow, dignified and strong—represented the Javanese. And it was usually the buffalo that won.

THE SHADOW PLAY The *wayang kulit* shadow puppetry is perhaps the best known of all the Archipelago's art forms. The puppets are made from filigreed buffalo hide and then animated against a backlit screen.

Although many Indonesians insist that wayang kulit was invented in Java, shadow puppetry appears in China and India, so there is a possibility that it was originally a cultural import. It certainly existed by the eleventh century, when a court chronicler of the East Java king Airlangga described a performance: 'There are people who weep, are sad and aroused watching the puppets, though they know they are merely carved pieces of leather manipulated and made to speak'.

Today the wayang kulit remains popular, particularly in Java and Bali, and its legendary figures are still used as points of reference in discussions of everything from politics to business.

BRITAIN'S SUMATRAN OUTPOST Bengkulu, pictured here in the early eighteenth century, is today the sleepy capital of Sumatra's smallest and remotest province. But for 140 years this was an unlikely colonial outpost, one of the least profitable of all Britain's Asian possessions.

The first British settlers arrived in 1685, planning to develop Bengkulu as a major pepper port, but it lacked a proper safe anchorage; most passing ships travelled along the other coast of Sumatra, and the pepper crops were never very successful. The colonists died in droves from the endemic tropical diseases of this feverish coastline.

But instead of cutting their losses, the British kept Bengkulu until the nineteenth century. It never made a profit. Eventually a trade-off was organised, and in 1824 the British abandoned their claims on the west coast of Sumatra, while the Dutch gave up Melaka on the Malay Peninsula. Bengkulu rapidly became a backwater of the Dutch East Indies, and then a backwater of Indonesia in turn, though it is still studded with relics from the long British occupation.

A TALE OF TWO PAINTINGS The arrest of the rebel prince Diponegoro
by the Dutch General De Kock in Magelang in 1830 brought to an end
the five-year Java War, and for the Dutch it was the moment at which they
finally achieved uncontested paramountcy in Java. For the Javanese, it was
the moment of final defeat and humiliation.

To celebrate, De Kock commissioned the acclaimed young painter
Nicolaas Pieneman—who had never been to Java—to recreate the moment
of his triumph. The end result, *The Submission of Prince Dipo Negoro to
General De Kock* (above), was calmly paternal. Diponegoro, resigned to his
fate, stands below De Kock, who points decisively to the carriage waiting to
carry Diponegoro into exile, and, with this gesture, also appears to banish all
unseemly resistance from the Dutch East Indies.

Another young painter, an Indonesian aristocrat, Raden Saleh Syarif
Bustaman, who had studied art in the Netherlands under the European

masters of the day, created his own version of events in Magelang. He had obviously seen Pieneman's painting, and was obviously influenced by it. But his painting, *Capture of Prince Diponegoro* (below), is radically different. Diponegoro's distraught followers crowd around the steps of a shabby Dutch building. Instead of Pieneman's bright blue skies and brisk breeze, the air has the heavy look of the late monsoon. The prince looks furious at this moment of betrayal, feet braced and fist clenched. But most striking is that Javanese figures all look natural, dynamic and with expressive faces. By contrast, the triumphant Europeans are stiff and inflexible, with heads a little too big for their bodies and not sitting entirely naturally atop their necks. Raden Saleh had made De Kock and the other soldiers look like the big-headed *raksasa*, the giant demons of Javanese mythology.

Raden Saleh remained a darling of colonial society and a fixture on the European social scene in Batavia. He actually presented his painting of Diponegoro's arrest to King William III of the Netherlands, disseminating an influential, alternative viewpoint of this symbolic moment of history.

THE FINISHING The Dutch conquest of southern Bali in the first decade of the twentieth century featured appalling massacres. Accounts of the killings were contradictory, but all featured the king of a Balinese court and his followers advancing in ceremonial fashion towards a heavily armed column of Dutch soldiers, who opened fire. The illustration above is of the death of the Rajah of Buleleng in an earlier killing in 1849, as imagined by the French newspaper *Le Petit Journal*.

Today these killings are remembered as *puputan* or 'finishings', often described as ceremonial mass suicides. Some decidedly romantic notions have developed around the puputan, with the idea of the killings as a kind of ritual, the ultimate Balinese dance-drama, brought to the fore. But a puputan was sometimes a more conventional fight to the death, a last stand that was anything but ceremonial.

A TALE OF TWO VOLCANOES In 1833, the Krakatau eruption—imagined, below, in an 1838 lithograph—got more worldwide attention than the much bigger Tambora eruption earlier in the century. Gunung Tambora (right) is a huge volcano on the island of Sumbawa in Nusa Tenggara. It erupted in 1815, culminating in a stupendous series of explosions that British soldiers in Java mistook for cannon-fire. The mountain shrank from 13,780 feet (4,200 metres) above sea level to 990 feet (2,800 metres), and a staggering 150 cubic kilometres (36 cubic miles) of material was blasted into the atmosphere. Global weather patterns went haywire, prompting famines in Europe. Over 100,000 people are thought to have died during the eruption.

PHOTO BY: JIALIANG GAO CC BY-SA 3.0

THE POISON TREE OF JAVA Early European accounts of the Archipelago were full of fabulous beasts and fantastical happenings. In the fourteenth century the French Catholic traveller Friar Jordanus wrote of Java (which he had never visited) that there were 'trees producing cloves, which when they are in flower emit an odour so pungent that they kill every man who cometh among them, unless he shut his mouth and nostrils'. Remarkably the tale of 'the Poison Tree of Java', likely to be the *antiaris toxicaria* pictured above, was still doing the rounds some five hundred years later.

In an 1783 edition of The London Magazine, a German doctor, J.N. Foersch who had been employed as a surgeon in the Dutch East Indies, claimed that he had there come across the deadly *Pohon Upas*, or 'Poison Tree'. The tree, he said, was so toxic that it had poisoned a vast swathe of ground, 'and the country round it, to the distance of ten or twelve miles from the tree, is entirely barren'. No man or beast could enter the desert without succumbing at once to the choking gases.

The upas tree, or *antiaris toxicaria*, did in fact exist in the forests of Java, and was used as a source of toxin for assassination, warfare and hunting—though it certainly didn't poison the surrounding air. Foersch's description of a dreary land of lifeless rock where nothing would grow, ringed by a wall of sheer hills and ridges, sounds suspiciously like a garbled report of one of Java's many volcanic craters, such as the Ijen volcano, pictured below, where locals still harvest sulphur in potentially deadly conditions.

THREADS OF HISTORY The best-known traditional textile in modern
Indonesia is batik. The most refined forms are to be found in Java, and it
was here that the technique of making the wax patterns with a *canting*, a
small copper cup with a spout, probably emerged in the twelfth century. In
the court cities of Central Java, batik features abstract geometrical patterns,
but along the north coast there are motifs showing influences from China,
Persia, India and Europe, each speaking of trade across centuries.

Foreign influences are also written into the fabric of another Indonesian
textile tradition—*ikat*, pictured above. The name simply means 'to tie', and
the weft threads for the cloth are tied and dyed before the warp is added,
to create patterns which only become visible on the loom. Ikat is found all
over the Archipelago, but it is commonest in the east, particularly in Nusa
Tenggara, where local designs sometimes show the influence of the Indian
patola clothes shipped into Southeast Asia in the distant past.

KARTINI The role of women in the story of the Archipelago is often obscured by the antics of the men, but one woman who is given plenty of attention is Javanese aristocrat Raden Ajeng Kartini, commemorated below in street art in her hometown, Jepara, in Java, where she was born in 1879. Her father was the local regent, and Kartini received an education in Dutch, even though she still had to go into traditional aristocratic seclusion for the years between puberty and marriage. During this time she struck up correspondences with several Dutch women, writing of her desire to see more education for girls, and for reform of the aristocratic system in which she was trapped. She married the Javanese regent Joyodiningrat of Rembang, who let her set up a school for girls. She died aged twenty-five in 1904, after the birth of her first child.

After her death, the Dutch proclaimed her a figurehead of their so-called Liberal Policy, which sought to improve Indonesian education in the early twentieth century; in 1913 the Kartini Foundation for girls' schools was launched. In 1964 President Sukarno declared her a national hero, implying she had fought against Dutch colonialism. The New Order, meanwhile, turned her into the epitome of ideal womanhood, educated and intelligent but ultimately dutiful.

BUNG TOMO The formidably feisty East Java youth leader Sutomo, known as 'Bung Tomo', became a prominent figure in Surabaya during the resistance to the British Allied troops in late 1945. He was described as 'a slight, handsome man' whose 'eyes shone with an inward fire'.

Foremost amongst Bung Tomo's revolutionary efforts was his pirate radio station, *Radio Pemberontakan*, 'Rebellion Radio'. Ultimately, though, Bung Tomo's role in the revolution was a minor one, once the British had finally taken Surabaya. In later years Bung Tomo remained a fairly obscure figure, though he served briefly as a minister in Jakarta in the 1960s.

THE PROCLAMATOR Of all the iconic moments in the last century of
Indonesian history, few could rival the proclamation of independence on 17
August 1945. And yet, for those present at the modest Jakarta bungalow that
morning, it must have felt like an anticlimax; there were only a handful of
people there, and most Indonesians had no idea that anything had happened.

When Indonesia's Japanese occupiers announced their surrender on
15 August, the leaders of the Indonesian nationalist movement were thrown
into turmoil. In discussion with the Japanese they had been creeping
towards some sort of independence for many months, but now, all that slow
progress was undone, and it looked as though the Dutch might soon return
to pick up where they had left off.

The more radical Indonesian revolutionaries were agitating for a
unilateral declaration, one that was as much a rejection of Japanese rule as
of Dutch control, but Sukarno stepped to the fore and displayed the
remarkably cool-headed pragmatism that was often masked by the
flamboyant antics later in his career. Even after being kidnapped and pushed
to act by radical students he managed to draft a declaration that was
unequivocal but that met with the approval of the Japanese. Read to a small
crowd outside his own home, it was short and simple: 'We the people of
Indonesia hereby declare the independence of Indonesia', it stated.

It was a moment that would fix Sukarno's status as father of the nation
forever. Even twenty-five years later, when his reputation was at its lowest
ebb, he was still quietly celebrated as 'the Proclamator'. No one could take
that away from him.

PRESIDENTIAL TOMB President Sukarno spent his final years under house arrest in Bogor, where he wanted to be buried. But The New Order regime was uncomfortable with the idea of a man that had had such charisma in his glory days lying so close to Jakarta. His tomb would surely have a powerful attraction, maybe becoming a symbol of passive resistance. So when he died in 1970, he was interred in the isolated East Java town of Blitar where his grandparents had lived, in an unmarked grave alongside his mother.

In the 1980s the New Order felt that enough time had passed to allow for a partial rehabilitation of Indonesia's founding father. The Blitar tomb got a lavish overhaul. People had already been making quiet pilgrimages there, but now the place became a tourist attraction. Today hundreds of thousands of people visit the tomb every year. The place has the atmosphere of a popular saint's grave—busy, bustling, and with a party of pilgrims always in attendance.

JOKOWI On 9 July 2014, Indonesians went to the polls to vote for the second directly elected president in the country's seven-decade history. They chose fifty-three-year-old heavy-metal fan and former furniture salesman Joko Widodo, popularly known as Jokowi.

Jokowi had first appeared when he was elected mayor of his hometown, Surakarta, in 2005. He made a remarkable job of shaking up the city administration. There were whispers of presidential promise that turned into a noisy clamour once Jokowi took up the much more challenging role of governor of Jakarta in 2012. He and his gloriously forthright deputy Basuki 'Ahok' Tjahaja Purnama—himself a highly unusual figure as an ethnic Chinese Indonesian in a position of political power—made significant headway with the capital's problems.

No one was surprised when the nationalist party PDI-P made Jokowi their choice for the 2014 presidential race. What made all this remarkable was that Jokowi was a genuine outsider, the first serious presidential candidate in Indonesia's decade-and-a-half of democracy who was not part of the old-established political elite.

But first Jokowi had to head off a challenge from a man very much connected to the old elite: Prabowo Subianto, a former New Order–era military man and onetime son-in-law of Suharto. In the end Jokowi slipped through with a slim majority. His election was deeply symbolic: the outsider triumphing over the insider, the new man trumping the throwback. For many observers it was the moment when the ghost of the New Order was finally exorcised and Indonesia came of age as a democracy.

THE BALI BOMBINGS On the night of 12 October 2002, Kuta was buzzing. The resort town on the west coast of Bali had grown beyond all expectations since the first Australian surfers and hippies turned up three decades earlier, and was packed with thousands of foreign tourists—which was precisely why a small cell of Islamist terrorists had chosen it as their target.

Just after 11 PM that night a suicide bomber with an explosive-filled backpack blew himself up in a crowded bar on the eastern side of Jalan Legian, Kuta's chronically congested main drag. Seconds later, a car bomb exploded across the street outside the Sari nightclub. A total of 202 people were killed, 88 of them Australians. Bali's tourist industry was decimated.

In the coming years there was a rash of other bombings—against a luxury hotel in Jakarta in 2003 and against the same hotel six years later, and against the Australian embassy in 2004. Just as the Balinese tourist industry was beginning to recover, a trio of synchronised suicide bombings struck the south Bali resort area again in 2005. Some predicted that this was the beginning of Indonesia's slide into chronic terrorist violence.

The Indonesian authorities, however, proved adept at tracking down the terrorists, who belonged to one small network. The men who orchestrated the attacks were arrested, tried, and executed. The Malaysian-born ringleaders, Noordin Mohammad Top and Azahari bin Husin were killed in police shootouts, and Abu Bakar Ba'asyir, the supposed spiritual leader of the terrorist movement, was jailed for supporting a jihadist training camp in Aceh.

As for Bali, today a memorial stands close to the site of the 2002 bombings, and the bars and restaurants are busier than ever.

the days of Srivijaya, it had been the Straits themselves which had defined this neck of the woods. Sumatra and the Malay Peninsula had formed a loose, Malay-speaking whole around this storied stretch of sea. Now, however, Melaka, Johor and all those other places that had long played a part in the wider Archipelago story had been hived off altogether. Illogical as it was, from now on Sumatra would have more in common politically with Maluku than with Melaka.

Wallace probably thought little about such matters; he was more interested in the birds and the bees. In Melaka he made his first serious forays into the forests, had his first unpleasant run-ins with leeches and fever, and made an admirable start on gathering a collection of unknown mini-beasts. After two months he returned briefly to Singapore and then set out for Borneo.

$$\odot - \odot - \odot - \odot - \odot$$

Borneo forms a vast, green thumbprint at the core of the western Archipelago. A ragged round of swamp, jungle and mountain, it is the third largest island on earth and until very recently most of it was true terra incognita. For millennia, a thin patina of civilisation has clung to its mangrove-meshed littoral. One of the very earliest Indianised states had emerged at Kutai on the east coast, and in later centuries small sultanates had appeared on the estuaries—Sambas, Banjarmasin, Pontianak, and most powerful of all, Brunei, the place that had given its corrupted name to the entire island. These kingdoms had been the domain of Malays, with settler communities of Chinese and Arabs living amongst them. But they had always faced the sea and kept their backs to the interior. It was not that inner Borneo was empty, of course—this was the realm of wandering bands of Dayaks, Austronesian hunter-gatherers who lived in communal longhouses far up the coffee-coloured rivers, or wandered footloose through the forests armed with blowpipes and spears. Neither Hindu-Buddhism nor Islam had had much impact in their lands, and in the mid-nineteenth century most of the Dayaks were still animists.

Back in VOC days, the Dutch had settled a few unfortunate residents in the various estuary sultanates of southern Borneo, but their outposts had proved singularly unprofitable and notably unhealthy. By the early decades of the nineteenth century, their presence amounted to a handful of ill-fated officials, marooned on the mosquito-infested coastline and looking longingly in the direction of Java. However, the Dutch had been stirred abruptly into action in the 1840s by the moves of the man who was to play host to Wallace during his stay in Borneo: a dandyish Indian-born Englishman who had turned himself into an oriental despot—James Brooke, the first 'White Rajah' of Sarawak.

Brooke was an adventurer in the old and not entirely reputable sense of the word. At the age of thirty he had spent his modest inheritance on an armoured schooner named, appropriately enough for a man who would be king, the *Royalist*. He set sail for Borneo, where he helped the Sultan of Brunei to crush an uprising. The grateful sultan granted him the personal title to the territory of Sarawak at the western end of the island by way of reward. Brooke rapidly expanded his domains inland and along the coast, ruling under the title of 'rajah'. This all prompted considerable embarrassment in official British circles—and outright panic amongst the Dutch, who swiftly set about tightening up their own lackadaisical operations on the southern underbelly of Borneo. By the time Wallace and Charles Allen landed at Brooke's royal capital of Kuching in October 1854, the Dutch had staked a notional claim of suzerainty to most of the southern sections of the island. The British, meanwhile, had tentatively invited Rajah Brooke into the Establishment by giving him a knighthood. The basic outlines of the Dutch and British spheres of influence in southern and northern Borneo had been fixed—though of course, under the canopies of cloud forest, the Dayaks were still going about their business entirely oblivious to colonial machinations.

⊙—⊙—⊙—⊙—⊙

Wallace spent some fifteen months in Borneo. He collected end-less bugs and butterflies, and killed a large number of orangutans in the name of science. He also palmed off his unfortunate assis-tant, Charles Allen, on some local missionaries and replaced him with a Malay boy called Ali. He then set his sights on Sulawesi and the isolated landfalls of Maluku.

En route for Sulawesi—aboard a tramp ship owned by a Chi-nese trader, crewed by a mob of Javanese, and captained by an itinerant Englishman—Wallace stopped off at Buleleng on the north coast of Bali. For several years the Dutch had been bick-ering with the rajas of Bali—mainly over the rajas' irrepressible habit of plundering the ships that frequently ran onto their sharp coral reefs. In the 1840s some semblance of Dutch suzerainty had been established on the north coast, but the bulk of the island still had no experience of colonial control, and a gaggle of competing Hindu rulers still held sway. Wallace was only in Bali for two days, but he was, like the piratical crew of Cornelis de Houtman 260 years earlier, thoroughly impressed: 'I had never beheld so beauti-ful and well-cultivated a district out of Europe'.

His next landfall lay just twenty miles east of Bali, but within hours of arriving in Lombok, Wallace realised that the gulf be-tween these neighbouring islands was bigger than distance sug-gested. There was something unusual about the birdlife: there were cockatoos and parakeets here. That great ecological Rubi-con that would one day been known as the Wallace Line ran slap-bang down the middle of the deep-water channel between Bali and Lombok. Bali was the most easterly part of the Archipelago that had ever been attached to mainland Asia.

Lombok had had even less to do with the Dutch than Bali. Its inhabitants, the Sasaks, had been Muslims since at least the early seventeenth century, and local legend gave credit for the con-version to apostles from the Javanese house of Giri, the dynasty founded by one of the most orthodox of all the Wali Songo. The Sasaks had never proved very successful at organising a robust indigenous sovereignty, however, and the more powerful kings of Bali and Makassar had tussled for control of their island for hundreds of years. By the time Wallace turned up, Lombok was ruled by a line of the house of Karangasem, a powerful Balinese kingdom. In a curious inversion of everything that had happened in the Archipelago in the previous half-millennium, Muslim Lombok was dominated by a Hindu elite who still carried the torch of Majapahit.

Wallace was every bit as impressed by Lombok as by Bali:

> These two islands are wonderfully cultivated, in fact, they are probably among the best cultivated in the world. I was perfectly astonished when on riding 30 miles into the interior [of Lombok] I beheld the country cultivated like a garden, the whole being cut into terraces, & every patch surrounded by channels, so that any part can be flooded at pleasure.

So much for 'the lazy native' and the racist paternalism of Johannes van den Bosch: the locals seemed to be perfectly capable of their own agricultural endeavours, if only they were left to get on with it.

After two-and-a-half months stuck in Lombok waiting for onward passage, Wallace got underway for Sulawesi. He came ashore at the fabled port of Makassar on 2 September 1856. He had been in the Archipelago for two-and-a-half years, but he was only now setting foot in a Dutch settlement for the first time, and he was thoroughly impressed: 'I found it prettier and cleaner than any I had yet seen in the East'. There were rows of white-washed Dutch bungalows set along broad and well-swept streets. The drains were covered over, and each afternoon, by order of a local bylaw, every householder had to water the road before his home to keep down the dust. The commercial quarters thronged with sarong-clad Bugis and Makassarese, and, as everywhere, there were dozens of prosperous Chinese-owned trading houses.

Makassar had, of course, long been a major hub of maritime power, seat of the old Sultanate of Gowa, and for all the impression of calm, dust-free Dutch order that Wallace described, this was still a feisty corner of the Archipelago, a place of usurper pirate princes. The forty-two-gun frigate and the trio of armed cutters that Wallace spotted anchored off the Makassar waterfront were not just for show.

Sulawesi's strange and spidery form was anchored by Dutch settlements at its northern- and southern-most extremities. Makassar was mirrored in the far northeast by the old port of Manado. Wallace would go there too, later in his wanderings, and would call it 'one of the prettiest towns in the East'. Manado was the hub of a region called Minahasa, a peninsula of mountainous land fringed with coral seas. It had been under the sway of both Ternate and Makassar in the past, but the ancestor-worshipping local tribes had proved particularly amenable to European influence. Portuguese and Spanish sailors had stopped here in the sixteenth century and planted white churches between the palms. The Dutch had taken over from the Iberians in 1679. During the VOC years, the authorities had generally frowned on the work of missionaries, and their efforts had been officially discouraged in the regions where Islam dominated. Like the British in India, Dutch officials tended to look on Christian missionaries as meddlesome men whose proselytising could provoke needless hostility amongst the locals. But in places like Minahasa where the people were deemed either uncouth tribal heathens, or were already Christians of an alternate flavour thanks to the efforts of an earlier set of colonialists, the Protestant missionaries were given leeway. By the middle of the nineteenth century, well over half of all Minahasans had been baptised. No other region in the Archipelago would commit itself so closely to the Europeans.

Alfred Russel Wallace was in Sulawesi until the end of 1856, when he and his assistant Ali sailed from Makassar on a local ship bound for points far to the east. Bugis and Makassarese seamen had long sailed for shores beyond the southern horizon in search of slaves, sandalwood and other strange substances. They had even gone as far as the upper reaches of Australia, to the bleached coastline of Kimberley and Arnhem Land in search of sea cucumbers to trade with the Chinese. They called these places *Kayu Putih*, 'White Wood', for the pale eucalyptus trees, and they lent the locals their own word for the Dutch—*Belanda*—long before the Aborigines had ever met a white man.

Wallace would not travel as far as Australia, but over the coming years he incessantly criss-crossed the eastern seas aboard local sailing ships. He reached the Aru Islands off western New Guinea, where he sampled the supposed delicacy of sea cucumbers and was singularly unimpressed ('like sausages which have been rolled in mud and then thrown up the chimney' he thought), and where he captured several specimens of the fabled birds-of-paradise. He also visited Timor, stopping by in the stony settlement of Kupang. This far-flung port had long been a source of slaves and sandalwood. The Dutch had taken over here from the Portuguese in the middle of the seventeenth century, though the place was always a hardship posting. A 1665 report on the state of the VOC's Kupang garrison had condemned the entire force, from the officers downwards, as 'leading a very foul, slovenly, and unruly life, as much with drunken drinking as with whoring'. Moral standards had apparently improved slightly by the time Wallace arrived, but the place was very much a colonial backwater.

The region around Kupang was the one part of the Archipelago where the Portuguese were still, just about, clinging on. Their government was finally settling its affairs with the Dutch, rescinding all claims to Flores on the condition that the Protestant missionaries should leave the local Catholics as they were. But in the eastern half of Timor a relic of the lost Iberian empire still endured, though when Wallace saw their capital, Dili, he declared it 'a most miserable place compared with even the poorest of the Dutch towns'.

All the while Wallace was travelling, he had been corresponding with men of science back in England—with Charles Darwin most significant amongst them. And all the while he had been netting butterflies and shooting birds-of-paradise, he had been pondering the question of diversity and development in the natural world. During that two-day foray in Bali, he had spotted a tiger beetle on the beach that seemed perfectly camouflaged against the dark volcanic sand, and elsewhere, too, he had seen uncanny adaptations to the myriad environments he encountered. The idea of natural selection as the driver of evolution may have come to him in one feverish flash that day in Ternate in 1858, but the inspiration had been all around him for years.

Wallace eventually headed home for England in late 1861. The fevers and the wounds and the endless rounds of bad food in strange places had taken their toll, but he had collected examples of some seven thousand insect species, many hundreds of them new to science. He reached Folkestone on 31 March 1862. While he had been gone, Charles Darwin had published *On the Origin of Species* and everyone already knew all about evolution...

⊙—⊙—⊙—⊙—⊙

The watchwords of the age of high imperialism in the Dutch East Indies were *rust en orde*—'peace and order'. In the book that Alfred Russel Wallace eventually wrote about his journeys there—*The Malay Archipelago*, a masterpiece of sprightly travel writing and popular science—the impression he gave was of a pacific island world where a gentlemanly Dutch order sat lightly alongside domesticated local sultans from Sumatra to Aru. This was not, however, the whole story, as those warships moored off Makassar had suggested. Even at the end of the nineteenth century there were plenty of pockets of territory, whole islands even, where no treaty had been signed, and even when there were long-standing agreements—in southern Sulawesi, in Banjarmasin and elsewhere—many of the local chiefs had a habit of testing the mettle of their notional Dutch overlords from time to time. If a Dutch *rust en orde* was ever truly to be extended to every corner of the Archipelago, then a good deal of mopping up would be needed.

One particular irritant lay at the furthest extremity of Sumatra in Aceh, Mecca's Verandah, that original point of contact with the western Islamic world. The sultanate there had always held itself aloof from the rest of the Archipelago. No tribute had ever been sent to the great Javanese courts from Aceh, and Indian and Arab modes, rather than the courtly culture of royal Java, had set the tone. More importantly still, the place had grown into a major trading power in its own right, and by the early decades of the nineteenth century more than half of the entire global supply of pepper was coming out of the plantations of Aceh. A crucial clause of that 1824 treaty by which the British and Dutch drew an arbitrary line down the Straits of Melaka guaranteed that Aceh would remain independent, assured against British political interference but also, uniquely in all Sumatra, inured against Dutch annexation. At first both European parties respected the arrangement, and merchant ships from Britain, France and America routinely stopped by in the northernmost Sumatran ports to fill their holds with peppercorns. Wealth caused the power of the Acehnese court to swell, and before long it developed modest imperial ambitions of its own, extending its sway south towards the middle reaches of Sumatra just as the Dutch were edging their way north. A clash was inevitable, and though the British initially protested, they quickly acquiesced.

In 1871, some six thousand miles from Aceh and with not a single representative of the Acehnese court in attendance, Britain and the Netherlands signed a new treaty. This was perhaps the apogee of haughty European imperialism in the Archipelago: the fate of huge swathes of distant territory inhabited by neither Hollanders nor Englishmen decided with a scratch of a pen nib in a wood-panelled chamber in The Hague. The British agreed to let the Dutch do as they pleased in Aceh, and in return the Dutch handed over the Gold Coast of Africa to the British. The immediate upshot was some four decades of violence in Aceh as the Dutch struggled to crush first the organised forces of the sultanate, and then a ferocious guerrilla resistance based in the hills—at the cost of some thirty-seven thousand military fatalities and an estimated sixty-thousand local lives.

$$\odot - \odot - \odot - \odot - \odot$$

There was another unconscionable pocket of indigenous sovereignty much closer to the heart of the empire—almost within hailing distance of Java. As the nineteenth century gave way to the twentieth, much of Bali was still doing its own thing—and doing it rather violently at that.

Alfred Russel Wallace had been impressed by Bali, as had Cornelis de Houtman. Thomas Stamford Raffles, too, had been rather taken with the place. But none of these fly-by-night visitors had spent more than a few days in the island, and their opinions stood in contrast to the general European attitude, which was that Bali was a violent place where they burnt widows on their husbands' funeral pyres and sold serfs into bondage.

Bali had long been one of the foremost sources of slaves in the Archipelago. Local rulers shipped out some two thousand of their lowliest subjects every year in the eighteenth century, and around half of Batavia's enormous population of bonded workers were Balinese. The women were particularly favoured by the Chinese as kitchen girls and concubines, for as non-Muslims they had no qualms about cooking pork. The men, however, had a slightly less positive reputation, and though their reported ferocity made them favoured candidates for soldier-slaves in the armies of both the VOC and indigenous courts, their alleged propensity for 'running amok' meant that the Dutch eventually banned their import as domestic staff. By the mid-nineteenth century, the standard Dutch view of Bali had it that 'The Balinese are a fierce, savage, perfidious, and bellicose people, loath to do any work'. This point of view was at least three parts crude imperial racism, but the idea that the island was a rough sort of place was to some extent borne out by events on the ground.

Until the seventeenth century, Bali had come under the sway of a single kingdom, the old house of Gelgel which claimed, like so many other Archipelago courts, a pedigree from Majapahit. Gelgel had gone to pieces in 1651 and a gaggle of nine competing fiefdoms had risen from the ruins, each claiming a small tranche of the Balinese whole. Throughout the nineteenth century there was periodic internecine fighting in Bali, and from the 1840s the Dutch were increasingly involved as powerbrokers and kingmakers—just as they had been in Java in the previous century. By this stage Bali had been suffering from decades of ill-fortune. The slave trade had gone out of fashion with the Europeans and the island had lost its traditional source of income; a relay of plagues, famines and epidemics had scourged the land, and by the second half of the century many of the local courts were tottering. Meanwhile, in the 1890s the much-abused Sasaks of Lombok rose up against their Balinese overlords and made the naïve mistake of calling on the Dutch for help. In 1894 the Dutch invaded Lombok, razed the royal capital to the ground, and established sovereignty. The Sasaks found they had simply replaced one set of alien overlords with another, but the Balinese had lost their own empire on the other side of the Wallace Line.

⊙－⊙－⊙－⊙－⊙

As a new century opened, a new attitude had come into play in the colonial scene. The Cultivation System had been consigned to history, and for several decades the economic liberals had had the floor in the Dutch territories. But so much for 'trickle down economics': standards of living had actually fallen in Java. Wage packets for labourers shrank, and the cost of rice rose. Taking note of all of this, in 1899 a Dutch lawyer named Conrad Theodor van Deventer—a sad-eyed man with a magnificent moustache—had published a powerful article entitled '*Een eereschuld*', 'A debt of honour'. The Netherlands, he argued, had gotten so very much out of the East Indies for so very long, that it was time to return the favour. For even the most intransigent stick-in-the-muds it was a compelling argument, and from 1901 onwards a so-called Ethical Policy was supposed to underpin all Dutch actions in the Archipelago.

On the one hand the policy was manifest in efforts to improve education, healthcare and general standards of living in Java. But in places like Bali it took a rather different form. Not only did the Ethical Policy demand Dutch-built schools, roads and hospitals; it also required the final obliteration of any lingering 'Asiatic barbarism'. Willem Rooseboom, the governor-general when the Ethical Policy came into play, declared that 'wherever there is injustice [we shall] not be able to remain inactive in the protection of the weak and the oppressed'. This all provided the perfect excuse for tidying up messy corners of the Archipelago, and when Rooseboom's successor, Johannes Benedictus van Heutsz, despatched a new resident to Bali in 1905 he allegedly waved his hand across a map of the southern half of the island with its patchwork of independent fiefdoms, and muttered, 'All of this has to change'.

In May 1904 a trading schooner from Banjarmasin had been blown onto the shallow slab of coral that lies off the beach at Sanur on the southeast coast of Bali. Today the beach is backed with a massed rank of hotels, and surfers make the most of the waves that surge onto the reef during the monsoon. A century ago it was a spot notorious for shipwrecks, particularly during the early months of the dry season, as the winds turn fickle and flip from west to east. The ship that drove onto the coral that May day was owned by a Chinese trader called Kwee Tek Tjiang, whose residence in Banjarmasin made him a Dutch subject. When the Sanur locals, subjects of the Balinese kingdom of Badung, looted the wreck, Kwee sent the colonial authorities a claim for compensation—the perfect excuse for a final annexation of Bali.

The Badung king, Cokorda Ngurah Made Pemecutan, refused to pay the compensation, and in September 1906 a Dutch force rowed ashore at Sanur. The Badung palace at Denpasar lay some three miles inland, and for four days the invaders sent shells shrieking towards it. Then, on the morning of 20 September, they advanced towards the capital. As the roofs of the palace hove into view the soldiers caught the acrid scent of burning wood and thatch. And then a strange procession appeared: hundreds of men and women, dressed in ceremonial white and with frangipani flowers tucked in their hair. At their head, borne aloft on a sedan chair, was the king himself. The procession advanced at a steady shuffle towards the Dutch.

What happened next was so utterly horrific and so utterly inexplicable that it is little wonder if the accounts are somewhat confused. In some versions the ghostly procession came to a halt three hundred feet short of the nervous Dutch column. The king stepped down from his chair, gave a signal, and was immediately stabbed to death with a ceremonial kris by his attendant priest. The rest of the courtly entourage then turned their weapons on themselves in a grotesque mass suicide. At this point a stray gunshot startled the Dutch soldiers into action…

In other accounts, the white-clad column simply walked on towards the colonial troops, paying no heed to the increasingly frantic orders to halt. In still other versions, when that three-hundred-foot point was reached they broke into a frenzied headlong charge, the king wielding his sacred *Singapraga* kris at their head. What is not disputed, however, is that, in the words of the senior Dutch commander, 'the artillery opened fire, with horrible consequences for the packed crowd'.

There is a grainy black-and-white photograph of the after-math. In the background a pair of low thatched roofs rise beneath a canopy of trees, and to the left the Dutch troops are standing in the khakis of a modern army. Their arms hang limp at their sides and their hats are in their hands as they try to make sense of what they have just done. In the foreground is a mass of jumbled white forms. They look like boulders on the bed of a dried-out river, until you peer closely and pick out the curve of a hip or the out-line of a head. To the right stands a gilded royal sedan chair, empty.

What happened at Denpasar on 20 September 1906 is remem-bered in Bali as a *puputan*, a ritual 'finishing'. The interpretations are as conflicted as the accounts, however, and whether it re-ally was a meticulously planned suicide ritual, a desperate kami-kaze attack, or simply a fearsome final stand, will never really be known. It was, however, the end of an old order. Two years later the last Balinese kingdom to resist Dutch control, Klungkung, succumbed in exactly the same way. The king had tried to resist Dutch attempts to establish a colonial monopoly on opium sales in its territory. The court was bombarded from the sea, and on 28 April 1908 a Dutch force marched inland to be greeted with a ghastly reprise of the earlier events in Badung. Some four hun-dred white-clad courtiers went down in a welter of gunfire.

The Bali puputans were, to all intents and purposes, the last acts in an Archipelago-wide process that had begun in earnest under Daendels and Raffles a century earlier, but that had in some ways started way back in 1596 when Cornelis de Houtman and his crew had opened fire on the court of Banten. The old order had truly been overturned, and some sort of *Pax Neerlandica* had finally been achieved.

But at the very moment at which the Dutch attained true supremacy in the Archipelago, those with a sharp eye might have noticed that their empire was already set to unravel.

⊙—⊙—⊙—⊙—⊙

Twenty-two days after the last round of gunfire splattered against the palace walls of Klungkung, a meeting took place in far-off Batavia. The men in attendance were students of a medical college developed under the educating ideals of the Ethical Policy. This college was open, in theory, to any 'native'. In practice, of course, virtually the only people with sufficient schooling to get into the college came from the old ranks of the aristocracy, and the vast majority of them were Javanese. Indeed, the name of the organisation which they founded during that meeting on 20 May 1908 was itself Javanese—*Budi Utomo*, 'the Beautiful Endeavour'—and foremost amongst its rather vague initial aims was the idea of reinvigorating a decayed Javanese society by means of Western-style education.

But though most of the members of this rather modest group had been born into old privilege, they belonged to an entirely new sort of elite. They were educated; they were literate in Dutch and Malay; they were ready to engage with modern ideas in science, literature and politics; and before long, they would begin to think of themselves as 'Indonesians'.

CHAPTER 7

BRAVE NEW WORLD: THE RISE OF NATIONALISM

T he hotel stood beside a broad, smooth road running through the heart of the colonial capital. To the south lay the Koningsplein, the King's Square, a huge expanse of scorched grass at the heart of the city laid out by Daendels at the start of the nineteenth century. To the north, the original quarters of Batavia —as built by Jan Pieterszoon Coen—were still a tight-packed jumble of mildewed warehouses. Here, however, the buildings stood well apart from one another, each white mansion nestled in its own manicured jungle of bottle palms and traveller's trees.

There had been a hotel on this spot for the best part of a century, and it had long been the lodging of choice for wealthy passers-by to the city. A disorientated Alfred Russel Wallace, still finding his feet in crowded cityscapes after years in the wilderness, had stopped by on his way home in 1861. Sixty years had passed since Wallace's visit, however, and the old core of the Hotel des Indes, with its pastel-red shutters and neoclassical colonnades, was now hidden under three stark storeys of angular modernism. It looked like the upper levels of a luxury liner, marooned three miles from the sea.

On the hotel's broad balcony a man was sitting, looking out on the scene below and scribbling in a notebook. Now and then a landau or a motorcar would rumble by, carrying a Dutchman in a starched white suit. But the man was more interested in what was happening in the canal on the other side of the road. Directly opposite the hotel a set of steps descended to the water, and the scene at the foot of these steps was in warm contrast to the stiff formality on dry land: local men, women and children had gathered there for their daily bath. The man on the balcony had already decided that 'The Javanese cannot be said to be beautiful', but he was particularly keen to watch when a pair of comely, sarong-clad sixteen-year-olds emerged from the water like 'two dripping Venuses'—and he was a little disappointed when they deftly changed into dry clothes 'in the bright light of this tropical sun without the least exposure of person'.

The man had arrived in Batavia a few days earlier aboard a steamer from Australia. He had jug ears and floppy red hair, and his thin frame seemed a little lost in the folds of his suit. He was sixty-eight years old; he was an American citizen, and his name was Frank Carpenter.

Carpenter was an inveterate globetrotter. He had started out as a journalist in Ohio, and he had funded his first world cruise in the 1880s by selling a series of pithy travel articles to a dozen different publications. He had gone on to author an endless series of potboiler travelogues under the brand of 'Carpenter's World Travels: familiar talks about countries and peoples with the author on the spot and the reader in his home'.

Travellers of all sorts had been wending their way through the Archipelago for thousands of years, but Carpenter belonged to a new breed. Yijing had been a pilgrim; Ibn Battuta was an adventurer; Tomé Pires had been a born reporter and Alfred Wallace was an authentic explorer. But in 1923 Frank Carpenter—for all that he would hastily hack out yet another book about his brief visit to 'Java and the East Indies'—was unmistakably a *tourist*.

After his sojourn at the Hotel de Indes, and still having failed to spot a bathing teenager in total dishabille, he set out on a thoroughly touristic itinerary, ticking off all the must-see sights of Java in fine style. He wandered in the glorious botanical gardens at Buitenzorg, as his counterparts do today (though this country seat of the colonial government has now gone back to its old name of Bogor). He took a comfortable train to Bandung and enjoyed its cool mornings and mountain views, and he was a guest at the huge estate at Sinagar, where they still grow tea for export in the twenty-first century. He visited Borobudur by moonlight—it was now fabulously restored and stripped of all the accumulated debris of a millennium. He took in the sights of Surakarta, enjoyed the luxuries of Surabaya—now surrounded by huge private sugarcane estates—and was left breathless by the infernal fumes of Gunung Bromo. Amongst his enormous luggage he carried a full suit of evening dress, for he had been reliably informed that the Dutch were great sticklers for formality, and that 'It is impossible to travel comfortably and see anything of the country without dress suits'.

Carpenter was by no means the only first-class tourist on the roads. Java had been an essential stopover for well-heeled globe-trotters for several decades, and in Bali, too, just a decade-and-a-half since the puputan bloodbaths at Badung and Klungkung, a nascent tourism industry was already emerging. The first images of the island had appeared in a tourist brochure in 1914 and the steamships of the *Koninklijke Paketvaart-Maatschappij*, the 'Royal Packet Navigation Company' or KPM, were already depositing a trickle of sightseers at Singaraja, the Buleleng harbour where explorers and spice traders had once disembarked. By the end of the 1920s there would be hotels, travel agencies and packaged dance performances for the visitors. Bali would also have become temporary home to a burgeoning international band of itinerant artists, bohemian anthropologists, aristocratic drop-outs and sexual adventurers who would do so much to forge its enduring reputation as an earthly paradise—and a place of irresistible titillation to boot. Frank Carpenter did not make it to Bali, but had he known the name it would shortly attain in travel circles he would perhaps have skipped across the channel in a jiffy: there would be no frustration for an admirer of local bathers there, and Bali would soon be known worldwide as 'the island of bare breasts'.

The early tourists were usually starry-eyed and admiring of the state of affairs in the Dutch East Indies, and Carpenter was no exception. He described the place as a beneficent Eden of well-mannered economic progress and gentle paternalism:

> The railways have already conquered ... Java, and the schools
> of the west are to be found in the towns. New resources are
> being discovered, and new industries are developing ... the
> bulk of our tin is from the islands of Banka and Billiton
> [Bangka and Belitung] ... The petroleum of Borneo and
> Sumatra competes with ours in the markets of Asia...

As for the indigenous population, in Carpenter's eyes they were either ossified relics of oriental splendour at the courts—draped in batik, shaded beneath golden parasols and clinging to the arm of a beefy Hollander in a tropical suit—or smiling peasants ready to drop to their heels in a respectful squat the moment a white man hove into view. The land Carpenter described was a place of timeless tradition, for all the industrial activity, telephone cables and railways.

He did not, of course, invent the scenes he described. He really *had* seen sultans and courtiers performing an ageless routine at the quiet command of the Dutch 'elder brother', and he really had 'travelled for miles through the country where every man, woman, and child I met would squat down on the ground and fold his hands in an attitude of humility until I passed'. But tourists, and indeed travel writers, have always had a tendency to see only what they are shown and hear only what they are told. Had

Frank Carpenter been a better journalist he would perhaps have noticed the tectonic rumblings that were beginning to trouble the *rust* and the *orde* of the colonial regime.

◉—◉—◉—◉—◉

The 1920s were a brave new world. By the time Frank Carpenter came trotting merrily through Java with rose-tinted spectacles wedged on the end of his bulbous nose the plates were shifting all over the globe. The Netherlands had remained officially neutral during World War I and Europe's mud-splattered apocalypse had scarcely ruffled the palm fronds of the Dutch East Indies, but the world beyond had changed. In Russia the Bolsheviks had triumphed in the October Revolution of 1917, while in China the Qing Dynasty had collapsed and an ailing Sun Yat-sen was building a new republic. Elsewhere, Mustafa Kemal 'Atatürk' had overturned the grandest of all old Muslim aristocracies—the Ottoman sultanate—and had forged the aggressively modernist Turkish Republic from the wreck. British India was already home to a sophisticated independence movement: Gandhi's noncooperation campaign against the colonial authorities was earning headlines around the world, and in just about every other tranche of European empire there were strange whisperings on the wind. There was no way that the Dutch East Indies could continue undisturbed.

◉—◉—◉—◉—◉

The first stirrings of what would one day become a revolution had come amongst ink, chalk dust and the declination of irregular Dutch verbs in the early years of the twentieth century.

For the bulk of their time in Asia the Dutch had made little effort to dispense knowledge to their subjects. They did not encourage the locals to use the Dutch language; in some instances it was expressly forbidden, and Malay and Javanese had remained the main mediums of interaction. Even in the second half of the nineteenth century, pidgin Portuguese would often prove more useful than Dutch on Archipelago docksides. This was all in striking contrast to the state of affairs in other areas of European empire in Asia at the turn of the twentieth century. Across the Bay of Bengal in India, for example, the British Raj was at its zenith with stiff-lipped pukka sahibs lording it over 'a fifth of humanity'. Much of the lowly desk work there was being done by a vast native clerical class—an army of Anglophone 'babus' in possession of a cut-price Western education. It was from this new caste that the leading lights of the Indian independence movement would rise, speaking smoothly in the tongue of their oppressors.

But in the East Indies, the Dutch were still governing through those old layers of batik-clad regents and princes, a stratum that was part-administrative apparatus, part-museum piece, and where a bowdlerised version of princely protocol was still the order of the day.

At the end of the 1890s just 150,000 so-called *inlanders*, or 'natives', out of a total population of some 40 million had been enrolled in government primary schools, and even their instruction was mainly in Malay. When it came to a proper European education in the Dutch schools of the cities, a measly cabal of just 1,500 ultra-elite natives—the sons of the most senior of Europhile aristocrats—were studying alongside their European brethren. But under the auspices of the Ethical Policy this had all begun to change.

First, the European lower schools in the cities were opened to any inlander with the ready cash to pay the fees. Then Dutch language, and even Dutch teachers, were brought into the higher class of native primary schools, and the entire school network was greatly expanded. Elsewhere, old institutions set up decades earlier to give young aristocrats a modicum of formal schooling were overhauled and reinvented as serious training colleges designed to turn out well-rounded, Dutch-speaking civil servants.

By the end of the first decade of the twentieth century, the first generation of graduates was emerging from the schoolrooms and lecture halls—earnest young men in possession of ideas that their fathers and grandfathers could never even have imagined. Most of them were still drawn from the ranks of the indigenous elite—and thanks to the simple facts of demographics, the vast majority of them were still Javanese. But many of their number came from a substratum below that of genuine aristocrats. They were the studious sons of schoolmasters, local doctors and junior magistrates: they were, in short, the rootstock of a modern middle class, and they would change the course of history.

One of the earliest manifestations of a nascent native middle-class sensibility came rolling off the backstreet presses of Batavia, Surabaya and Semarang: journalism was coming into its own in the Indies, and for the most part the language was Malay and the type was Latin. Malay had been the major lingua franca of the Archipelago since the days of Srivijaya. But it was usually a spoken rather than a written language. It was what got you by in markets away from home; it was what you used to barter with a Melanesian trader from some lost eastern island, or to beseech the Chinese toll-keeper—and it was what you used when talking to the white men. In the western part of the Archipelago it did take a literary form, but it was usually written in a modified Arabic script called *Jawi*—a script that wedded Malay literacy closely to Islamic scholarship. But over the course of the nineteenth century Romanisation had crept in, *alif-baa-taa* giving way to ABC, and a vernacular press soon appeared. By 1900, there were around thirty Malay-language newspapers printed in the Latin alphabet. Journalism became a legitimate trade for literate locals, and on smudged back pages the first buds of a new literary culture unbound by courtly convention was starting to show in the form of modernist poems and short stories.

But journalism and literature were just the start of it. In no time at all the young men of the new educated class were ploughing headlong into politics.

⊙−⊙−⊙−⊙−⊙

Today, in the received narrative of nationalist history, the founding of Budi Utomo, just two weeks after the mayhem of the Badung puputan in 1908, is proclaimed as Indonesia's moment of 'national awakening'. Hindsight is a fine thing, however, and if the scholarly young men who gathered in a Batavia medical school on 20 May had been told that they were, in fact, anti-colonial revolutionaries, they would doubtless have been utterly flabbergasted.

The founding members of Budi Utomo, this so-called Beautiful Endeavour, were students of STOVIA, the *School tot Opleiding van Inlandsche Artsen* or 'School for the Training of Native Physicians'. This was one of those old institutions, originally a training centre for local smallpox vaccinators, that had received an educational upgrade under the auspices of the Ethical Policy. Its alumni were amongst the first of the new elite. The man who had come up with the idea for the Budi Utomo was a doctor from Yogyakarta called Wahidin Soedirohoesodo (sometimes also spelt Sudirohusodo), and whatever later myth-makers might claim, he was certainly no radical anti-colonialist. He was an aficionado of the traditional arts who believed that Javanese culture could be returned to the heights of Majapahit-style glory through the medium of Western education.

Budi Utomo's main aim was to lobby for more educational opportunities for Soedirohoesodo's own elite class. It was eminently innocuous, and far from viewing the organisation with oppressive suspicion, the colonial authorities actually welcomed its existence. But Budi Utomo *was* one of the first manifestations of a craze for politics that was soon sweeping the Indies. By the time Frank Carpenter noted that the locals were 'as happy as any people of their kind' with the colonial status quo, there was a multitude of political organisations. They came in all shapes and stripes, and some of them were flirting very seriously with revolutionary nationalism.

Some, like Budi Utomo itself, were more like educational organisations than proper political parties, and some were essentially ethnic lobby groups. For example, *Paguyuban Pasundan*, formed in 1914, was Budi Utomo's Sundanese counterpart, seeking to better the lot of the West Java locals. Some groups were basically trade guilds, looking to provide a unified voice for a particular class of merchants, and still others found their drive from religion. In 1912 a batik trader from Yogyakarta named Ahmad Dahlan founded the *Muhammadiyah*. Dahlan was a returned Haj pilgrim, and his organisation belonged to a loose global movement of religious reform that had emerged from Saudi Arabia in the previous century. He and other returned pilgrims of his ilk worried that Islam in Java was not just encumbered with all manner of unconscionable heterodoxies; its community—the local sector of the universal Muslim community or *Ummah*—had also become hopelessly enervated. Muhammadiyah aimed to set that all straight through modern, Western-influenced education. Soon it had its own schools in Java and beyond. The success of the Muhammadiyah would eventually prompt those on the other side of the Muslim coin in Java, the traditionalist orthodoxy of the village seminaries, to found their own group, the *Nahdlatul Ulama*, as a counterpoint to all this internationalist reform.

The biggest organisation of all, however, was neither ethnic nor religious in its inspiration. By the 1920s it was claiming a membership in the hundreds of thousands and it had true politics as its raison d'être (although it had both 'trade' and 'Islam' in its original name).

A year before Ahmad Dahlan founded the Muhammadiyah, another cloth merchant and returned Haji named Samanhudi had started another group, in the old Mataram capital of Surakarta. Samanhudi meant his *Sarekat Dagang Islam*, the 'Islamic Traders' Union', to be a means for local batik merchants to stand together against the inroads of Chinese businessmen in the rag trade. But within twelve months the part about 'traders' had been quietly dropped from the name, and Samanhudi himself had withdrawn as a new man took to the helm, a sharp-tongued former civil servant named Oemar Said Tjokroaminoto (sometimes also spelt Cokroaminoto).

What the Sarekat Islam, or 'SI', actually stood for was never entirely clear, but it was certainly about much more than the batik business. By 1913 it was claiming 150,000 members, with branches in every major Javanese city and outposts in Sumatra, Borneo and Sulawesi, too. Despite the titular 'Islam', the SI was not a religious interest group like Muhammadiyah. What it seems to have represented above all else was a sudden desire, born of a changing epoch, to belong to *something*. And 'Islam' here seemed mainly to stand in for an idea that hadn't yet crystallised: a sense of national identity, setting Archipelago natives apart from Dutchmen and Chinese. This, then, was an embryonic Indies nationalism, even if the feisty Tjokroaminoto himself declared at the 1913 SI conference that 'we are satisfied under Dutch rule'.

It was some measure of the naïve optimism of the Ethical Policy that the Dutch authorities cheerfully gave their seal of approval to all these organisations. The governor-general of the day was the mild-mannered Alexander Idenburg. Here, he felt, was the Policy coming good. If the inlanders were now so far advanced that they could form political organisations, then surely the Dutch were well on their way to paying off that *eereschuld*, that 'debt of honour'. There were, however, some limits to the authorities' tolerance…

⊙−⊙−⊙−⊙−⊙

It would not be until the mid-1920s that the nationalist movement would truly find its feet and its voice. But as early as 1912, a trio of feisty firebrands had founded an organisation that really deserves much more credit for kick-starting a revolution than the innocuous Budi Utomo. While other groups were quietly concerning themselves with batik and education, the *Indische Partij*

('Indies Party'), demanded nothing less than outright independence for the Archipelago in the shortest possible time.

Amongst the Indies Party's leading lights were a Central Java doctor called Tjipto Mangoenkoesoemo (sometimes also spelt Cipto Mangunkusumo) and a minor Yogyakarta aristocrat and STOVIA drop-out by the name of Suwardi Suryaningrat. But its real driving force was a man with a name richly redolent of radicalism: Ernest François Eugène Douwes Dekker. He was the great-nephew of none other than the author of *Max Havelaar*, Multatuli himself, and as his name suggests, he was not, in the colonial scheme of things, an inlander. He was the son of a Dutch father and a German-Javanese mother, born in Pasuruan on the coast east of Surabaya. He was an Indo-European, part of the large mixed-race population colloquially known as 'Indos'.

Colonial society in the Dutch East Indies was classified into three legal layers. At the bottom was the biggest—and lowliest—sector, the inlanders, 'the natives'. Above them, and with rather more by way of rights and status, came the 'foreign orientals', Chinese for the most part, but with Arabs and Indians amongst their number. Finally, at the top of the pile, came the Europeans. This last elite grouping was not strictly defined by race, and it included a number of individual Asians. These 'honorary Europeans' included a few Europhile local aristocrats and some particularly wealthy Chinese businessmen, as well as all Japanese expatriates, who had gained the status through official lobbying by the Nippon authorities. The majority of legal Europeans, however, were actually Indos.

The Indos had existed in the Archipelago even before the Dutch arrived, in the form of the Portuguese creole population of the ports, and there was scarcely an old-established Dutch dynasty in the Indies that didn't have a little Indo blood in its collective veins. But for all their elevated status, they often found themselves caught between worlds—viewed with suspicion by true indigenes, and subjected to patronising sneers from the European paternal side. In spite of this, they had traditionally found a footing as cultural go-betweens. They were railway clerks, post office chiefs and estate managers.

In the latter half of the nineteenth century, however, a larger and larger part of the colonial infrastructure was placed in the hands of fresh-faced professionals straight off the boat from the Netherlands. These were career men with every intention of going home at the end of their tenure, and they felt no need to avail themselves of a mixed-race, Malay-speaking wife—at least, not officially. Meanwhile, with the Suez Canal open and the journey from Europe to Batavia reduced to little more than a holiday cruise, more and more 'pure' Dutchwomen were turning up in the colony. The ladder was being swiftly pulled up and it was no longer easy for Indo girls to get an instant social upgrade through marriage. At the same time, just as the Indo community's social stock was falling, the Ethical Policy was starting to turn out Dutch-speaking, Western-educated inlanders, and Indo men found that they were no longer the indispensable go-betweens they had once been.

It was doubtless these factors that prompted some of the poorer Indos to sign up for the Indies Party cause—an independent East Indies as a homeland for anyone born within its borders, whatever their ethnic origins. It was an idealistic and ill-fated vision, and the Indos would ultimately be written out of the nationalist legend. That they made up more than three-quarters of the Indies Party's seven-thousand-strong membership goes a long way to explain its strangely ambiguous status in the received version of history today.

During its brief lifetime, however, the Indies Party certainly rattled the authorities. Its stated aim was 'to awaken the patriotism of all the people of the Indies … and to prepare its people for independence'. Douwes Dekker had evidently taken a lesson in no-holds-barred rhetoric from his great-uncle, and he declared that 'As we plan to put an end once and for all to the colonial situation, the Indies Party is definitely revolutionary…'

Douwes Dekker's collaborator Suwardi Suryaningrat, meanwhile, was flexing his own rhetorical muscles. As the Dutch community prepared to celebrate the 1913 centenary of Holland's liberation from Napoleonic rule, he published an outrageously sarcastic Dutch-language pamphlet entitled 'If I were a Netherlander'. It was deliberately inflammatory, and it packed a powerful punch:

> I can easily understand the feelings of Netherlands patriots of today who want to celebrate such an important date. After all, I am also a patriot, and in the same way as the genuine Netherlands nationalists love their fatherland, so do I love my own fatherland more than I can express in words ... I wish for a moment that I could be a Netherlander, not a naturalised Netherlander, but a real pure son of the Greater Netherlands, completely free from foreign stains ... How I would rejoice when I would see the Netherlands flag together with the Orange banner flutter in the wind. I would join in the singing until I was hoarse ... but I would not wish the natives of this country to participate in this commemoration ... I would even close off the area where the festivities took place so that no native could see our elation at the commemoration of our day of Independence.

> It would seem to me somewhat impolite, coarse and improper, if we—I am still imagining that I am a Netherlander—let the natives join ... because we would be commemorating our independence here in their country which we keep in subjugation ... [but] I am not a Netherlander. I am only a brown-coloured son of this tropical land...

The pamphlet roused the conservative Dutch-language press to a storm of vitriol, and it was too much even for gentle governor-general Idenburg. He had all three Indies Party chiefs evicted from their putative fatherland on the grounds of 'journalistic excess' and exiled to the Netherlands, where he felt they would do less damage. The party quickly collapsed in their absence.

Douwes Dekker, Tjipto Mangoenkoesoemo and Suwardi Suryaningrat were the first true radicals, and their party had espoused a secular nationalism a decade before a similar ideology became the driving force of the independence movement. They had also become the first political exiles of the coming struggle, but they would by no means be the last, for by this time a strand of radical Marxism was emerging from the broad church of the Sarekat Islam. From amongst the chains and girders of the railway sheds of Surabaya and Semarang modern trade unions were rising, and before long a communist faction had coalesced from the burgeoning membership of the SI under the leadership of a feisty young man named Semaun. In 1921, he was made the first chair of the *Perserikatan Komunis di Hindia*, the 'Communist Association of the Indies', or PKH, and was soon clamouring for revolution. His efforts to start mass strikes were quickly crushed by the authorities, however, and Semaun was shipped off to exile in the Netherlands.

$\odot - \odot - \odot - \odot - \odot$

Frank Carpenter's tranquil, timeless 1920s East Indies was in fact a place humming with intellectual and ideological ferment. The business of discussing Marxism, Islamic reform and political structures was clearly the preserve of a tiny elite, but they were not the only ones starting to stir. By the early twentieth century, the major cash crop in Java was sugarcane. Vast reaches of the stuff stretched across the flatlands of the Brantas delta where Majapahit princes had once paraded in cloth-of-gold, and the workers were pushed exceptionally hard when it came to producing the stuff. In response, a devastatingly simple form of resistance had emerged: cane fields developed a peculiar tendency to go up in flames during the hours of darkness, just as they were being readied for harvest.

Outside of Java, conflict between labourers and landowners was often more violent. In the eastern levels of Sumatra—one-time heartland of Buddhist empires and Muslim sultanates—a frontier-zone agricultural industry had developed. Swathes of virgin jungle were leased to speculating pioneers, who would strip the forest and plant vast acreages of tobacco. In an area largely devoid of local population, the workforce had to be shipped in from elsewhere—be it the crowded spaces of Java or southern China. These Chinese and Javanese coolie labourers were often retained on appalling terms of indenture, and Sumatra was home to what was often little short of a slave economy. For desperate men, resistance itself tended to be more desperate than mere arson: there were sporadic outbursts of bloody violence against European planters by renegade coolies. These were generally dealt with brutally, and usually hushed up by the local authorities, but they brought a permanent atmosphere of mutual hostility to some estates. On one plantation in Asahan, south of Medan, the assistant manager 'never went around to inspect the work of the Chinese coolies because he was afraid of their violence if he criticised their work'. He never went anywhere 'without very visibly bearing a revolver'.

Sometimes, rural resistance would coalesce into an earthy political movement. In the countryside around Blora in East Java, visiting officials found villagers responding to their demands with peculiar passive-aggression and cryptic sexual innuendos. They were the followers of a man called Surantika Samin, who had turned resentment of government interference in the local teak industry into a mystic movement. Meanwhile, in villages all over Java recruiters for the Sarekat Islam were passing off membership cards as magic amulets, and doing nothing to discourage the notion that Tjokroaminoto might just be the latest incarnation of the Ratu Adil...

What was lacking, however, was a unifying drive for all this ferment. Neither Islam nor socialism was a sufficiently inclusive banner for a pan-Archipelago movement against colonial rule. But by the start of the 1920s a whole new generation of educated young men—and they were still all men—was emerging, men born since the turn of the century. Many of the sharpest graduates were now travelling to the Netherlands to continue their studies. Amongst their number were the Minangkabau intellectuals Sutan Sjahrir and Mohammad Hatta, and the future prime ministers Ali Sastroamidjojo (sometimes also spelt Sastroamijoyo) and Sukiman Wirjosandjojo (sometimes also spelt Wiryosanjoyo). In draughty boarding houses these students heard the inspiring words of older exiles, Douwes Dekker and Semaun amongst them.

Back in the Indies, meanwhile, other young thinkers were able to continue their own studies closer to home, particularly at the *Technische Hoogeschool te Bandoeng*, the Bandung Institute of Technology. As Frank Carpenter strolled the civilised streets of Bandung in blissful ignorance in 1923, admiring the Dutch bungalows and declaring the place 'a veritable botanical garden', he might have brushed unwittingly past a slim young man who was studying for an engineering degree by day, but who by night was already delving deep into a new sort of nationalist politics. Sukarno had arrived on the scene.

$$\odot-\odot-\odot-\odot-\odot$$

Sukarno is one of those behemoths that thunder through the narratives of many a new or reinvented nation, standing alongside the likes of Gandhi, Mao and Atatürk. His enormous stature overshadows any number of other significant figures, but there are no two ways about it: he was enormously important in the independence movement and in the new nation that it eventually produced. His ideas may not always have been well-considered or original; he may have been propped up by men of greater intellect; but like a sultan of old, he made for a magnificent figurehead.

Sukarno was born in Surabaya in 1901. His origins are a little murky, and the facts are further obscured by both his own later myth-making and the scurrilous rumours spread by his detractors. Claims that he was a direct descendent of the royal house of Surakarta are probably as ill-founded as the stories that he was the bastard son of a Dutch tea planter. His real father seems to have been a schoolteacher from the lower ranks of the old Javanese elite; his mother was a Balinese Hindu from Buleleng. Like Airlangga, nine centuries earlier, he had an ancestry spanning the narrow strait between Java and its eastern neighbour. And like Diponegoro, he was very clearly in possession of that peculiar thing known in the Archipelago as *karisma*—a potent and almost supernatural personal presence that goes far beyond its direct English translation, 'charisma'. He had an ego fit for a king and a libido to match; when he joined an organisation it flourished, and when he left it withered. He was, in short, a force of nature.

Sukarno had served his political apprenticeship as a lodging schoolboy in the Surabaya house of Tjokroaminoto of the Sarekat Islam, and by 1923, even as a baby-faced undergraduate in Bandung, he was already honing his twin talents for speechifying and philandering. At the start of the year he had caused a stir at a political rally with an oration so militant that the police had to step in. Meanwhile, he had also succeeded in seducing his landlord's wife—a Sundanese woman thirteen years his senior—and ditching his own child-bride in her favour.

The Sarekat Islam was still the biggest political beast of the day, but the failure of either Islam or Marxism to truly ignite the nationalist cause, and the tensions between these divergent streams within the organisation, meant that its day was rapidly passing. Sukarno and his contemporaries, meanwhile, were rapidly forging a new and more mature sort of nationalism, one that was pragmatic for all its radicalism. This was the loosely secular ideology that would dominate throughout the coming decades—one in which Islam was sometimes paid lip-service but was for the most part ignored, and in which full-blown Marxism was exchanged for a milder sort of socialism.

This new generation of nationalists had a new vocabulary with which to articulate their cause, and by the start of the 1920s one word had gradually risen to the top of the boiling cauldron of ideas. A decade earlier, Douwes Dekker and Suryaningrat had demanded liberation for the *Indies*; Sukarno and his fellow travellers would be calling for an independent *Indonesia*.

'Indonesia' was a term that had been kicking around in scientific circles since the middle of the nineteenth century, when an English lawyer in Penang coined it as an alternative to Wallace's 'Malay Archipelago'. Now, however, it found potent new form as an alternative to the Dutch East Indies. What was more, if the Archipelago was now 'Indonesia', then its people—all the glorious gamut of them, from Koran-toting Acehnese to headhunting Dayaks—would be 'Indonesians', and the Malay lingua franca would now be known as *Bahasa Indonesia*, 'the Indonesian Language'.

⊙—⊙—⊙—⊙—⊙

On 28 October 1928, a group of young men gathered for the closing meeting of a two-day congress at a student boarding house in Batavia, to the southeast of the Koningsplein and the Hotel des Indes. The delegates were mostly students and they came in a curious array of dress styles—from sarongs to tropical suits, and with a batik headdress here and a bowtie there. Earlier in the day, they had met in a cinema to discuss the challenges of education, but here things were a little more radical.

First, a young songwriter by the name of Supratman took up a violin and played his latest composition, an anthem entitled *Indonesia Raya*, 'Indonesia the Great'. Once he was done, the delegates read a three-line declaration. They called it the *Sumpah Pemuda*, 'the Youth Pledge'. The word *Pemuda*, 'the Youth', would soon have an enduring potency of its own, a byword for a seething politically literate mass with the power of numbers on their side. The pledge itself, meanwhile, was an unadorned evocation of the new nationalism:

> Firstly: We the sons and daughters of Indonesia, acknowledge one motherland, Indonesia.
>
> Secondly: We the sons and daughters of Indonesia, acknowledge one nation, the nation of Indonesia.
>
> Thirdly: We the sons and daughters of Indonesia, uphold the language of unity, Indonesian.

They could not have put it more simply, or more effectively.

Sukarno, meanwhile, had turned a study club he had founded in Bandung in 1926 into a proper political party, the *Perserikat Nasional Indonesia*, the 'Indonesian Nationalist Association' or PNI. And then he went a step further and formed the PPPKI, the 'Union of Political Organisations of the Indonesian People', an umbrella organisation for parties and pressure groups of all stripes. To join the PPPKI, all that was required was a commitment to Indonesian independence. Everyone who was anyone signed up—including the now rather irrelevant Budi Utomo. Even a few Arab and Chinese lobby groups gave their support. A head of steam for independence appeared to be building up.

And at this point the Dutch authorities decided that the Ethical Policy was dead in the water.

◉ ─ ◉ ─ ◉ ─ ◉ ─ ◉

The first people to feel the heat were the Indonesian students in far-off Holland. While Sukarno had been stirring things up at home, the young Mohammad Hatta had been causing waves of his own in the colonial fatherland. In the years to come, Hatta would be the intellectual anchor of Indonesian nationalism, a stolidly efficient counterpoint to Sukarno's mercurial antics. He was born in 1902 in the Minangkabau town of Bukittinggi, a cool and misty place in the hills of western Sumatra. Like many Minangkabaus, he was a fairly orthodox Muslim, but he always rejected the idea of Islam as a political force in its own right. Similarly, though he inclined in a distinctly socialist direction, he would never commit entirely to Marxism. He shared Sukarno's essentially secular nationalist ideology, for all that their personal styles differed.

Hatta had travelled to Rotterdam to study economics in 1921, and he had soon became embroiled in serious student politics. Back in 1908, a social organisation with a Dutch name, the *Indische Vereniging* ('the Indies Association'), had been set up for the first generation of Ethical Policy scholars to study away from home. In 1922, Hatta and other members of the new and more radical generation had hijacked it and, using their new national language, they had changed its name to *Perhimpunan Indonesia*, the 'Indonesian Association', and turned it into a serious political organisation. Before long they ran into trouble with the authorities. In September 1927, Hatta was arrested and charged with fomenting armed resistance to Dutch rule in Indonesia. He spent five months in jail awaiting trial, and once he reached a courtroom in The Hague, he took the opportunity to make a stirring public condemnation of Dutch colonialism. To his own surprise as much as that of the authorities, the court declared him not guilty.

In the Indies, however, the courts were much less inclined to leniency. By late 1929 Sukarno was an increasingly ubiquitous figure on podiums and in pamphlets. The PPPKI was speaking with an increasingly unified voice, and Sukarno's own PNI had doubled its membership to ten thousand in less than six months. As a consequence the authorities were growing increasingly nervous, and three days short of the end of the decade Sukarno was arrested in Yogyakarta, where he had gone to make a speech. He was charged with all manner of offences under the general catchall of 'disturbing the public order', and locked in a tiny cell in a

Bandung prison. Imprisonment, he later recalled, was a shattering experience:

> I am a man who gratifies his senses. I enjoy fine clothes, exciting foods, love-making, and I could not take the isolation, rigidity, filth, the million little humiliations of the lowest form of prison life.

But if the authorities had hoped that humiliating interment would break his resolve, they were mistaken. It was almost eight months before the trial got underway, but just like Hatta two years earlier, Sukarno took it as an opportunity for showboating. He was a born orator and the courtroom crackled with the energy of his attack on European colonialism.

'Why do the people always believe in the coming of a Ratu Adil?' Sukarno demanded. 'Why are there constant rumours of messianic figures appearing in this or that village?' The answer, he declared, was simply that 'the weeping people endlessly, unceasingly, wait and long for the coming of help as a man in darkness endlessly, every hour, every minute, every second, waits and wonders when will the sun rise'.

They found him guilty and sent him to jail for four years.

⊙—⊙—⊙—⊙—⊙

As the 1930s got under way, a pall of gloom descended over the Archipelago. For both those who thought of it as the Dutch East Indies and those who called it Indonesia—and for the many millions who still mainly considered themselves Javanese, Balinese, Sasak, Bugis or whatever it may be—the tumult of the previous decade had unmistakably passed.

A slow economic tsunami sent out by the Wall Street Crash of 1929 had washed up in the tropics by the start of 1931. Sugar prices collapsed, and an era of hardship set in. Average incomes in Java swiftly fell by more than half, and former free-labouring peasants were soon signing up in their droves for the only option available: indentured coolie work on the grim plantations of Sumatra. All this hardship might have primed the populace for revolution, but most people were simply too busy trying to survive to bother with politics. The nationalist movement, meanwhile, had been effectively decapitated, and within months of Sukarno's imprisonment the PNI had given up the ghost and disbanded, while the PPPKI had lost its way. Meanwhile, there were other clouds gathering on other horizons: in 1931 Japan invaded Manchuria, and on 30 January 1933 Adolf Hitler became chancellor of Germany.

Sukarno served less than two years of his first prison term. In his absence, the veterans of the defunct PNI tried to keep the nationalist cause afloat and had founded a new group, Partindo, the 'Indonesian Party'. Mohammad Hatta and Sutan Sjahrir, meanwhile, had finally graduated from their Dutch universities and returned to Indonesia, where they had set up another new party, *Pendidikan Nasional Indonesia*, 'Indonesian National Education', known as 'New PNI' to distinguish itself from Sukarno's old group. Sukarno sniffed around both organisations for a while, before throwing in his lot with Partindo and swiftly assuming command. Prison had done nothing to strip him of his *karisma*, and within months the membership had reached twenty thousand.

But by this stage, there was a thoroughly conservative governor-general at the helm of the Dutch East Indies. Bonifacius Cornelis de Jonge was a tall, thin man with a bristling moustache and not an ounce of sympathy for the nationalist cause. In August 1933 Sukarno was arrested again, on trumped-up charges connecting Partindo to a recent mutiny on a Dutch naval ship off Sumatra. This time there would be no chance for courtroom theatrics: there would be no trial at all. Instead Sukarno was shipped off into indefinite exile—first to Ende, a former pirate haunt in the shadow of a table-topped volcano on Flores, and then to a tiny bungalow in Bengkulu, the one time British backwater on the wild west coast of Sumatra. With the big man gone, Partindo went to pieces almost immediately. Hatta and Sjahrir were arrested too, on the same spurious charges. They were also evicted from Java, but their place of exile was even more obscure. They were sent to the remotest of all Dutch territories—a jungle-fringed prison camp called Boven-Digoel in the malarial depths of West New Guinea.

$$\odot-\odot-\odot-\odot-\odot$$

By the middle of the 1930s, it looked as if the wind had gone from the nationalist sails. The bright lights of the movement were far away—Sukarno reading books and romancing a local schoolmaster's daughter in Bengkulu, and Hatta and Sjahrir enduring hard labour and high fever in New Guinea. The only political activity was now in a tame parliament in Batavia.

Back in 1918, in the heady days of the Ethical Policy, the authorities had set up a *Volksraad*, a 'People's Council'. Its powers were strictly of an advisory nature, but it was at least allowed to speak. Its membership was drawn in unequal parts from the three tiers of colonial society—European, foreign oriental and inlander. Half of them were appointed, and half were elected. There was, however, a considerable degree of smoke-and-mirrors at play in creating this rudimentary vision of democracy: the electorate that voted for the Volksraad members consisted entirely of the conservative municipal councils from the major towns of the Dutch East Indies. Inevitably, then, those elected to the Volksraad were pliant yes-men. As a consequence, no one had paid it much attention during the 1920s, but now it was the only outlet left for the politically inclined. For the rest of the 1930s, the Indonesian members of the Volksraad would periodically press requests on the governor-general—for the official replacement of the term 'inlander' with 'Indonesian', for example, and for a ten-year plan for Indonesian autonomy. The requests were invariably rejected out of hand, and the councillors could do nothing but meekly comply with the higher decision.

The colonial authorities might, then, have had reason to congratulate themselves: a potential revolution seemed to have been nipped in the bud. But they had many other problems to deal with—not least the economic challenges of the global Great Depression. At home in Europe the political scene was starting to turn ugly, and in Asia there were difficulties with that nation of 'honorary Europeans'.

The ascendant Japanese had long bought huge quantities of raw materials from the Dutch East Indies, and they had shipped plenty of their own cheap consumer goods back in the opposite direction. With the local manufacturing industry now in a parlous state, the Dutch had started to limit Japanese imports. They were also becoming increasingly reluctant to send the Japanese metal ores, oil and the other potential components for a military machine. Recent events in Manchuria had made it clear that Japan was increasingly inclined to use force when it didn't get what it wanted, and the Dutch authorities were becoming increasingly nervous. Then, on 10 May 1940, Hitler invaded the Netherlands.

This had all happened before, of course: way back in 1794 when Napoleon conquered the country. Once again, the East Indies were cut adrift from the fatherland. The authorities in Batavia attempted to follow the example set by Daendels 130 years earlier. They ramped up recruitment to the colonial army and set about improving their defences. In Central Java, some of the raw recruits were sent for training to a fort at Gombong, west of Yogyakarta, which was originally built during the Java War against Diponegoro. Amongst their ranks was a nineteen-year-old village boy by the name of Suharto.

⊙–⊙–⊙–⊙–⊙

On 8 December 1941, Japan launched aerial attacks on British bases in Hong Kong and Malaya, and strafed American facilities in the Philippines. At the same time, on the other side of the international dateline, 353 Japanese planes descended on the US fleet in Pearl Harbor in Hawaii. The Netherlands—in the form of an exiled government in London and a colonial administration in Batavia—joined its allies in a declaration of war. They would not have to wait long for the hostilities to begin.

On 10 January 1942, Japanese troops landed in Dutch-controlled Borneo, Maluku and Sumatra. At the same time they were surging south through the Malay Peninsula. The reputedly impregnable British fortress of Singapore fell in the middle of February, and at the end of the month a final concerted Allied effort to rebuff the Japanese in the Battle of the Java Sea was also a miserable failure. Shortly before midnight on 28 February, a Japanese troop ship dropped anchor in Banten Bay, the very spot where Cornelis de Houtman had hove to in 1596. Within twenty-four hours Japanese troops were closing in on Batavia and Buitenzorg, and by 7 March they were descending from the Priangan highlands towards Bandung, where the Dutch high command was holding out.

On the morning of 8 March 1942 the Dutch forces in Java surrendered, and later that day the governor-general gave himself up. At eleven o'clock that night Dutch rule ended with a final radio broadcast from their official station: 'We are closing now. Farewell until better times. Long live the Queen...' It had taken the Dutch more than three hundred years to achieve supremacy over the entire Archipelago. The Japanese had done it in less than two months.

CHAPTER 8

FREEDOM OR DEATH: WAR AND REVOLUTION

T he trucks came at first light, when it was still cool and there were thin skeins of mist lying over the hills. The plantation headquarters was a complex of bulky, tin-roofed sheds on the banks of a stony river. Scattered around the site were the stolid bungalows of the Dutch overseers, each surrounded by its own patch of clipped grass. In the middle of the complex there was a swimming pool.

The plantation lay deep in the Priangan highlands—that hulk of volcanic uplands at the heart of West Java, the place where the worst excesses of the Cultivation System had played out a century earlier. This was still the heartland of the Indies tea trade, and the hillsides were swaddled in a blanket of tea bushes.

On a normal day the plantation would have been bustling at this hour, workers heading for the hillsides with conical baskets slung across their backs, European managers hurrying between the sheds, and the smells of cooking rising from the bungalows. But this was not a normal day. The eight Dutchmen who had run the place had been taken away by the Japanese weeks ago, and now two trucks had arrived for their wives and children. They had been warned the night before, and were waiting when the trucks arrived: women and children standing stoically be-side the mattresses they had been told to bring. Japanese soldiers herded them into the trucks, and with a crunch of gears they rumbled slowly out of the complex, heading for Bandung.

Amongst the women and children was a seven-year-old boy called Ernest Hillen. He had lived on the plantation with his eleven-year-old brother Jerry, his Dutch father and his Canadian mother. When the convoy stopped at some roadside hamlet for the soldiers to fill the radiators, little Ernest clambered up on to a suitcase and peered over the high side of the truck. Across the road a young Sundanese girl was sitting in the shade beneath a banyan tree, watching the strange scene. For a moment their eyes met, and many years later an adult Hillen would still remember that fleeting connection: 'She had looked so free', he wrote. Everything had changed in the Archipelago.

$$\odot - \odot - \odot - \odot - \odot$$

Many members of the Dutch community struggled to comprehend the disaster that had overwhelmed them. The regime, the structure, the very *idea* of which they were a part had simply ceased to exist the moment the Japanese arrived on the scene.

There were some 220,000 Dutch citizens living in the Archipelago, and for most of them the nationalist ferment of the previous decades had seemed like an obscure irrelevance. Here and there a plantation official might have sucked his teeth as he read of Sukarno's latest shenanigans in the morning papers, but the insistent rhetoric and the talk of 'Indonesia' seemed to have nothing whatsoever to do with the servants and labourers who accounted for most Dutch experience of 'the natives'. Young Ernest Hillen, wandering around his plantation and talking to everyone with a child's cheerful equality, had known the Sundanese locals. They were all poor people, he remembered, who spoke no Dutch and ate with their fingers; he 'never saw one in the swimming pool except to clean it'. Many Dutch adults had a similar vision of the indigenous people of the Archipelago.

As for the threat of Japanese invasion, that had seemed like an impossibly distant prospect. Even as they realised that defeat was inevitable, the upper echelons of the colonial regime had failed to grasp the fact that their power was about to be annihilated. When the governor-general and the high command surrendered on 8 March 1942, they had assumed that the Japanese would require them to stay at their posts to run the colony on their behalf. Instead, they found themselves locked up in prison camps. And when Dutchmen saw the Japanese troops rolling into towns across the Archipelago, they were often in for a sudden and sobering shock. On 18 March, a young Dutchman named Frans Ponder saw the invaders marching into Magelang, that pleasant upland township in Central Java where Diponegoro had been seized at the end of the Java War 112 years earlier. Ponder had been born just a few miles away in Ambarawa and he had spent most of his life in Java, so the sight of the column of heavily armed, highly disciplined foreign soldiers thundering between the ranks of Dutch bungalows was disconcerting enough. But there was something still more discomfiting: 'They were greeted with cheers from the natives'.

At first, it was only the military and senior Dutch officials who were placed in camps. The rest of the Dutch population, including the thousands of mixed-race Indo-Europeans, were issued with identity cards and placed under house arrest. If they wanted to go outside they had to apply for special permission, and had to wear a special armband, emblazoned with the rising sun of Japan. But even this limited freedom did not last long. As the dry season of 1942 began, all across the Archipelago the Dutch were rounded up and transferred to huge prison camps. Soon there were 170,000 internees locked up, either behind palisades of sharpened bamboo in designated quarters of the cities, or within barbed wire compounds in festering jungle clearings. They would be imprisoned for the rest of the war.

⊙—⊙—⊙—⊙—⊙

Ernest Hillen, his mother and his brother were interred in Bloemenkamp, a corner of Bandung walled off with bamboo and filled with five thousand women and children from all over West Java. In the early days an air of unreality hung over the civilian camps. Many inmates clung to the forlorn hope that Allied troops would soon come sweeping over the mountains to restore them to their bungalows and their swimming pools. But as 1942 slipped slowly by and the first rainclouds of the coming monsoon gathered over the hills around Bandung, the gulf between their old life and their current, sorry existence yawned ever wider.

Early in 1943, at the wettest, most malarial part of the year, the Hillens were shifted from Bloemenkamp to another section of Bandung. This was the vast Cihapit camp, a wired-off city within the city, packed with 18,000 women and children—almost a third of all the female and juvenile internees in the entire Archipelago. The Hillens shared a house with eleven other families. They had a single toilet between them. Food rations were cut down; the air of oppression thickened, and summary punishments for minor or imaginary transgressions worsened. And as well as the hunger and the oppression, the internees had to face the crushing monotony of prison life. The worst thing, Ernest Hillen would later remember, 'was not the heat, fear, smells, noise, flies, too many bodies, too little food, scratches that festered and diarrhea—it was the sameness…'

⊙—⊙—⊙—⊙—⊙

There was little chance of boredom outside the camps. In the first weeks after the Japanese arrived, unrest had erupted in several towns across Java. The cheers that sometimes greeted the invading troops showed all too clearly that resentment of Dutch rule was by no means the preserve of the educated elite. Now, with all restraint gone, there was spontaneous violence. Dutch homes and businesses were looted, and here and there Europeans were attacked and even killed. And, as was almost always the case in times of unrest, the nascent mob also turned its ire against the local Chinese community. The Japanese authorities were not in the business of starting a revolution at this stage, however, and they quickly brought the violence to an end. A blanket curfew descended, and it was not just the Dutchmen, with their rising sun armbands, who were banned from walking the streets after dark.

The fundamental reason for the Japanese invasion, and the essential purpose of the 'Greater East Asia Co-Prosperity Sphere' they hoped to create, was to ensure unfettered access to the raw materials, the markets and the great labour pool of Southeast Asia. Their arrival might have been greeted with hope by many, but ultimately the three-and-a-half years during which Japan controlled Indonesia were far more brutal and oppressive than the three-and-a-half centuries that the Dutch had spent in the Archipelago. But the Japanese occupation also ensured that it would never again be possible for a tiny cabal of Europeans to control the region.

The Japanese divided the former Dutch territories into three administrative blocks: Java and Madura were under the control of the 16th Army; Sumatra was run by the 25th Army; everything else fell to the Navy. Conditions in each of these zones varied, but from Sumatra to Timor there was one unifying theme: the obliteration of all traces of European dominance. Speaking Dutch was banned—even in private homes—and Indonesian was given official status as the language of the Archipelago. Batavia, seat of colonial power since the days of Jan Pieterszoon Coen, was abruptly stripped of its colonial nomenclature. Streets had their Dutch names removed; clubs, halls and hotels were rechristened in Indonesian or Japanese, and the city itself had a change of name. The old moniker Jayakarta, dating from distant Demak days, had never fallen entirely out of local usage. Now it made an official return, slightly modified, and the city was called Jakarta. All over the Archipelago clocks were put forward to tally with Tokyo time.

The old economic structures were roundly wrecked. Agricultural, forestry and mining exports were abruptly directed eastwards, away from Europe, and imports now came almost exclusively from within the Japanese sphere. This sudden skewing of the economy—which, however artificial and inequitable it might have previously been, had nonetheless developed over centuries—led to inevitable problems. Inflation was rampant. Japan was never able to supply all the import needs of the former Dutch territories. They also requisitioned both rice and fuel for the war effort, and hardship swiftly set in. There were famines in Java during the years of occupation, and perhaps as many as 2 million people died. For the first time in two centuries the population of the Archipelago stopped growing.

Earlier generations in the countryside might have known to squat respectfully when a Dutch official or an American tourist came by, but now everyone had to make obeisance to the Japanese. In Surabaya, an official order did the rounds telling cyclists that whenever they spotted a Japanese sentry they had to clamber down from the saddle, remove their hats, and execute a stiff, formal bow. Punishments for transgressors were swift and often brutal. The *Kempeitai*, the Japanese secret police, were more dreaded than any of their Dutch predecessors.

But even as a pall of hunger and oppression was descending, something else was happening, too. Radios were pumping out stridently political messages, and the population was being mobilised. Those nationalist politicians prepared to collaborate with the Japanese found they had a better platform than they could ever have dreamed of under the Dutch.

◎──◎──◎──◎──◎

On the eve of the Japanese invasion Sukarno was still in Bengkulu. Compared to the experiences of his nationalist compatriots digging ditches in the jungles of New Guinea it was a rather benign sort of exile. He lived in a pleasant bungalow in its own garden in the south of the town, built high to catch the transient afternoon breezes off the Indian Ocean. He had books to read, and a bicycle if he wanted to explore.

But for a man who liked to be at the centre of things, Bengkulu was positively purgatorial. There was also a certain amount of domestic tension. Inggit, the Bandung landlady Sukarno had married in his student days, had joined him in exile. But with his older wife now in her fifties, Sukarno's roving eye had settled firmly on a local teenager named Fatmawati. As a Muslim—albeit a mainly non-practicing one—Sukarno was allowed to take a second wife. But Inggit, a woman with a decidedly forceful character, refused to give her permission.

At the start of 1942, the marital wrangles and boredom came to an abrupt end. In the final weeks before the Japanese invasion the Dutch made a sudden and belated effort to evacuate some of their senior officials to Australia. They also decided to take the most important political exiles with them, rather than let them become tools of the Japanese. Sukarno, Inggit and a small Dutch escort set out north along the coast towards the bigger port of Padang. A lovelorn Fatmawati was left behind in Bengkulu. The journey was a tough one, by truck and on foot, and by the time they reached Padang the last naval convoy had already left for Australia. Looters were rampaging through the town, and the Japanese were closing in. Sukarno's Dutch escort melted away, and he soon found himself standing before Colonel Fujiyama of the 25th Army, and facing an unenviable choice.

Sukarno's ultimate decision to collaborate with the Japanese certainly earned him the furious opprobrium of many Dutchmen in the coming years. However, their characterisation of Sukarno as a traitor on a par with the quislings of Vichy France was fundamentally flawed. He might have been a Dutch subject when the Japanese invaded his homeland, but he was not a Dutch *citizen.* What was more, he had spent his entire adult life campaigning against the colonial regime. He could hardly have been expected to shun the invaders on grounds of Dutch patriotism. On the other hand, for a man with broadly socialist ideals, a fascist regime of any sort—Asian or European—ought to have been thoroughly unpalatable. Many other members of the Indonesian nationalist movement had wrestled with this same challenge in the run-up to the war, and a fair few had already decided against cooperation. Some had even swallowed their decades-old convictions and prepared to stand by the Dutch. Sutan Sjahrir had declared that 'the Axis was a more dangerous threat to Indonesian freedom than existing Dutch colonialism'.

Sukarno, however, put aside any ideological qualms and decided to collaborate. With hindsight it was the right move, for it would allow him to play an essential role in the forging of an independent state when the Japanese were ultimately defeated.

⊙—⊙—⊙—⊙—⊙

Sukarno arrived in Jakarta on 9 July 1942. Mohammad Hatta and Sutan Sjahrir, freed from their New Guinea exile, were already in town and wrestling with the queasy conundrum of possible collaboration. It was almost a decade since the three men had last met. At that time they had been rivals of a sort, tussling over the direction of the independence movement. Now circumstances forced them more closely together. Ultimately Sjahrir decided to stay aloof from the Japanese regime. Not only would this sit far more easily with his conscience; it would also place him in a strong negotiating position with the Allies should they ever return to dominance in Southeast Asia. Sukarno and Hatta, meanwhile, would cooperate with the Japanese.

Over the coming years the two leaders tried to steer the best course for Indonesian nationalism through the stormy waters of the Greater East Asia Co-Prosperity Sphere. Sometimes their machinations had tangible effects. Sukarno's lobbying led to the establishment of the *Pusat Tenaga Rakyat*, the 'Centre of People's Power', known by the acronym Putera, which also happened to mean 'son', a boon to a lover of deft wordplay like Sukarno. Putera was intended as a united front for the entire Indonesian political spectrum, and though its official aim was to offer 'aid and cooperation to Greater Japan', it allowed Sukarno and Hatta an unprecedented platform from which to mobilise the masses.

Political Islam too, long side-lined in the nationalist movement, was given a Japanese-sanctioned front in Masyumi, the 'Council of Indonesian Muslim Associations'. Meanwhile, the young men of Java and Sumatra were being drafted into a series of paramilitary volunteer groups. The biggest of these, founded under the auspices of Putera in October 1943, was the *Pembela Tanah Air*, the 'Protectors of the Fatherland', generally known, with the insistent Indonesian love of acronyms, as Peta. By the end of the war some thirty-seven thousand young men from Java, around twenty-thousand Sumatrans, and a further one thousand six hundred in Bali had joined Peta, and as many as two million youths in total had undergone some sort of military training.

But at the same time as all this political activity, conditions for most Indonesians were growing ever grimmer. Food shortages worsened, urban infrastructure crumbled, and the economy slid from depression towards outright collapse. At the end of the second year of the occupation the Japanese ordered the drafting of thousands of *romusha*, or 'volunteer labourers'. Some were sent to work in grim conditions alongside Dutch internees and Allied prisoners of war on the Pekanbaru Railway project, an ambitious attempt to drive a train track through some 135 miles (220 kilometres) of Sumatran jungle, which echoed Daendels' efforts to force the Great Post Road across Java a century and a half earlier. As many as seventy thousand people died before the work was complete. Other *romusha* were sent overseas, some to work on the notorious Thailand–Burma 'Death Railway'.

As conditions all over Indonesia worsened, millenarian rumours started doing the rounds. Out in the villages of Java, the old prophecies of Joyoboyo—that twelfth-century Javanese king who had popularised the idea of the Ratu Adil—were common currency. People managed to identify accurate predictions of railways and aeroplanes in Joyoboyo's works, but the prophecy that got the most attention proclaimed that a three-hundred-year span of rule by 'white buffalos' would be ended by the arrival of a race of 'yellow dwarves'. The yellow dwarves, the prophecy had it, would prevail only for the lifespan of a single maize crop; after that, with glorious inevitability, the Ratu Adil would arrive…

Remarkably, this same prophecy had also gained currency amongst the Dutch prisoners in the camps. In the grim military prison at Cimahi near Bandung, a version in which the departure of the 'yellow dwarves' presaged the 'return of the white buffalo to their stables', rather than the arrival of the Ratu Adil, was popular.

⊙ ⎯ ⊙ ⎯ ⊙ ⎯ ⊙ ⎯ ⊙

In the women's camp at Cihapit conditions had become ever more dire. Ernest Hillen's brother had been taken away to join the adult men in another camp, and he and his mother had been shifted to the cramped and filthy upper part of Cihapit. Beriberi, neuritis, chronic ulcers and all manner of other ailments were a part of daily life. Once there was the small miracle of a delivery of Red Cross food packages. 'This was sometime in late 1944', Hillen later remembered, 'when cats and dogs had been eaten long ago and it was no use hunting rats any more—with so little to feed off, they had disappeared…'

But for all the disease and deprivation, news was still seeping into the camp, and in early 1945 most of it was of setbacks for the Japanese. In the early days, the inmates had taken heart at stories of American bombs raining down on Tokyo. Now, however, the idea of a Japanese defeat was terrifying, and rumours were soon circulating that in such an event there would be no gentlemanly transfer or power and prisoners; instead, they would all be massacred as the Japanese troops in Java went down in a suicidal last stand.

There were similar rumours in prison camps all over Indonesia, and when, in May 1945, the inmates began to hear whispers that Germany had surrendered and that the war in Europe was over, the fear of an apocalyptic Japanese last stand only intensified. And then, on the night of 6 August, the prisoners in one of the men's camps in Bandung picked up a crackly news broadcast from Delhi on a hidden radio. The reception was so bad and the message so garbled that they were unable to make full sense of it. However, the gist was clear enough, as one of the prisoners later recalled: 'in the course of the morning of the day which was now ended, something more like an act of God than of man had been inflicted on Japan at a place called Hiroshima...'

⊙−⊙−⊙−⊙−⊙

Nine days after the first atomic bomb fell on Hiroshima, Japan surrendered unconditionally to the Allies. In Jakarta, Sukarno and Hatta found themselves suddenly marooned by the kind of abrupt tidal fall that precedes a tsunami.

During the previous year, the Japanese had started to make sympathetic noises about Indonesian independence, and at the start of 1945, with defeat looking increasingly inevitable, there had been a sudden forward rush. A 'Committee for Preparatory Work for Indonesian Independence' had been formed, and on 1 June Sukarno had given a speech outlining what he called the Pancasila, the 'five principles' that were to be the official philosophy of the new nation: belief in a single but non-religiously specific god; nationalism; humanitarianism; social justice; and democracy. The Committee got to work drafting a constitution.

The Japanese military, meanwhile, met in Singapore and decided that Java should be granted total independence in September, with the rest of Indonesia being freed shortly afterwards.

But then the bomb fell, the Japanese surrendered and everything came crashing to a halt. Sukarno and Hatta had no idea what to do. As part of their official surrender terms, the Japanese were expected to maintain the status quo in their occupied territories until Allied troops arrived to take control. Clearly that meant there would be no independence celebrations in September, and the Indonesian leaders feared that if they attempted some unilateral move the Japanese might well use force to stop them—as the Allied terms would technically require of them. Faced with such an insurmountable conundrum, they vacillated.

But by 1945 there were other forces at play, not least the Pemuda, the militant youth. The thousands of young revolutionaries who had come through the ranks of Peta and the other paramilitary organisations were all fired up for revolution, and the more politically astute of their number quite rightly suspected that a narrow window of opportunity was sliding shut. They decided to take matters into their own hands. At 4 AM on 16 August, a party of young Indonesian revolutionaries roused Sukarno and Hatta from their beds in Jakarta, and telling them that they were acting for their own safety, they proceeded to kidnap them. They drove the two leaders out of the city, and explained to them that they had to stop their prevarications and act. Faced with the insistent Pemuda, Sukarno and Hatta realised that they had no choice but to respond. They returned to the city, and the following morning Sukarno read a proclamation to a small gathering in front of his own house:

> We the people of Indonesia hereby declare the independence of Indonesia. Matters concerning the transfer of power, etc., will be carried out in a conscientious manner and as speedily as possible.

It was short, it was simple—and it would be more than four years before those 'matters concerning the transfer of power, etc.' were finally ironed out.

⊙—⊙—⊙—⊙—⊙

On 15 September 1945 a British warship, HMS *Cumberland*, docked at Tanjung Priok, the commercial harbour at the head of Jakarta, and the troops of the Seaforth Highlanders clomped ashore. In 1811, soldiers of the same regiment had landed at this very same spot as part of the invasion that led to Raffles' British interregnum in Java. Now, in a curious quirk of history, they were back.

When the Japanese surrendered in August there were no Allied troops anywhere near Java or Sumatra. The defeated Japanese were still in place, unmolested and armed to the teeth. The only instruction they had received was to maintain the status quo. The Dutch themselves, despite having been liberated from German occupation at home, were in no position to regain their former colonies immediately. And so the task of taking control of Java and Sumatra fell to Britain, the nation responsible for Southeast Asia Command under Lord Louis Mountbatten. Australia was left with the job of taking over the rest of the Dutch territories in the eastern Archipelago.

Incredibly, given the vast scale of the place, virtually no meaningful intelligence had emerged from Indonesia during the years of occupation. A few whispers of a nascent nationalist revolution had reached the Allied command, but Charles van der Plas, pre-war governor of East Java and one of the first senior Dutch officials to be sent back to Java in 1945, had blithely informed Lord Mountbatten that there was nothing to worry about. 'The Indonesians', he had said, 'are too nice a people to fight really hard...'

The British found a surreal situation in Jakarta. The Japanese were still on the streets and still in possession of their guns. But there was an unfamiliar flag flying everywhere: a simple, two-coloured banner with a strip of crimson at the top and a band of white at the bottom. It was the flag of the Indonesian Republic. The Indonesian flag had originally been concocted by nationalist students two decades earlier, and it was inspired by a banner of Majapahit. Both the Dutch and the Japanese had banned it, but now, fluttering freely in the hot breeze of the late dry season, it was a manifestation not just of an aspiration, but of some sort of reality: the Indonesian Republic actually existed. Sukarno was its president; Hatta was his deputy. They had a constitution and a collection of ministries, and they had even appointed governors for a putative seven provinces spanning the entire breadth of the old Dutch territories—though in practice, outside of Java and Sumatra only the heads of Bali and Sulawesi ever reached their posts.

There were revolutionary slogans daubed on walls all over the city—some of them in incongruous but cannily considered English. And one word was paramount. Alfred Doulton, an English officer who arrived at the end of September, recalled that 'A caller lifting up a telephone receiver would be greeted by a bark of "Merdeka" from the exchange, and if he chanced to raise his eyes to the walls of a public building opposite he would find "Merdeka" glaring defiantly at him'.

Merdeka: it was a word with an old and unusual pedigree. Back in the days of the VOC, the freemen of Batavia—emancipated slaves and 'Black Portuguese'—had been known by that Sanskrit-derived term *Mardijker*. Now, stripped of Dutch and Indian accents, it meant 'freedom' in Indonesian. It had become the rallying call of the revolution.

For all van der Plas' mild predictions, the British forces were faced with an impossible task. At their front they had to deal with an Indonesian Republic that actually existed—even if its writ over the Archipelago beyond Java was mainly a matter of theory. At their back, meanwhile, was a Dutch government absolutely determined to regain control of the Archipelago—for both sensible economic reasons, and as a means to overcome the spectacular humiliation of having lost both homeland and colonies during the course of the war. The British ended up pleasing no one. For the Indonesians, they were imperialist lackeys, come as proxies to do the dirty work of the Dutch; for the Dutch, meanwhile, they were appeasers of 'extremists', who at best failed to bring their full force to bear against a mass of traitorous terrorists, and at worst perhaps even deliberately sabotaged Dutch prospects.

At times the British even had to call on the Japanese to fight alongside them against Indonesian nationalists as they tried to rescue the thousands of inmates, many of who were still marooned in the camps weeks after the end of the war. They succeeded in this, at least: Ernest Hillen was reunited with his father and brother, and the family eventually left for Canada.

⊙−⊙−⊙−⊙−⊙

If the British had an unenviable task, Sukarno, Hatta and the other chiefs of the new Republic were in an equally challenging position. As 1945 rolled on and the monsoon clouds gathered over the Priangan highlands, they gnawed over impossible conundrums in the modest suburban houses that had been turned into makeshift ministries. Outside on the streets the British were struggling to keep control of burgeoning lawlessness. At the same time they were trying to do nothing that might provoke a full-scale Indonesian revolt, even while large numbers of increasingly intransigent Dutchmen were arriving on the scene—either from the camps, or from Europe.

One of the most pressing practical problems was Sukarno himself. For most Dutch officials he was the worst kind of traitor. Many of them regarded his formal interactions with the British as an obscenity: they would have preferred to see him in jail. Even the British were a little queasy about dealing with Sukarno, for he very clearly had been a willing collaborator with the Japanese. Fortunately, however, there was another man with relatively clean hands in the upper echelons of the Republic—the avowed non-collaborator Sutan Sjahrir.

In October there was some brisk ad hoc tinkering with Indonesia's working constitution, and a role which had never previously existed was conjured into being: Sjahrir became Indonesia's first prime minister. Another intellectual with an immaculate record of non-collaboration, the Medan-born Christian convert and socialist Amir Sjarifuddin, became the 'Minister for People's Security'—in essence, the Republic's defence minister. Sukarno and Hatta retained their presidential and vice-presidential roles, but for the moment they became mere figureheads, standing back in the shadows to keep their stains of collaboration out of sight. It was a smart move, and both Dutch and British officials were much more comfortable talking to the new men. But it did nothing to tackle a far bigger and more dangerous problem.

The leaders of the Republican government were veterans of the anti-Dutch struggle, middle-aged men who had cut their teeth in the 1920s. Outside on the streets, meanwhile, there was a whole new generation, trained in the ranks of Peta and the other paramilitary organisations, filled with revolutionary zeal, and with little interest in sober negotiations with their erstwhile colonial oppressors. It had been the Pemuda who had forced Sukarno and Hatta into their unilateral declaration of independence in August; now they were forging ahead with a revolution on their own terms.

Sutan Sjahrir at least understood the phenomenon of massed Pemuda action; he recognised its driving energy and he knew just how dangerous it could be: 'Many of them simply cling to the slogan Freedom or Death', he wrote:

> Wherever they sense that freedom is still far from certain, and yet they themselves are not faced with death, they are seized with doubt and hesitation. The remedy for these doubts is usually sought in uninterrupted action.

Violence was self-propagating; it was becoming an end in itself, and there was nothing Sjahrir as prime minister, Sukarno as president or anyone else could do about it.

⊙−⊙−⊙−⊙−⊙

Revolutionary Pemuda fervour reached its zenith—and British experiences in Indonesia reached their nadir—in Surabaya in November 1945. The East Java capital was the biggest port in the Dutch East Indies. This had once been the site of the main maritime gateway of Majapahit, but twentieth-century Surabaya was a rough and ready industrial city, far removed from courtly sophistication. It was a polyglot brew of Javanese, Madurese, Chinese, Malays, Arabs and more, and the locals spoke the coarsest of all Javanese dialects.

Tensions had started to rise in Surabaya in September as Dutchmen, newly released from the camps, started arriving in town and trying to take control of their former homes and businesses. When a small group of Dutch and British officers arrived in the city on 18 September and set up a provisional headquarters in what had once been the smartest hotel in town, things rapidly turned ugly. The following day, a gang of young Indo-Europeans ran a Dutch tricolour up the hotel's flagpole—to the fury of their watching Indonesian counterparts, who started a riot in response, scaled the hotel roof and tore the blue strip from the bottom of the flag, leaving only the red and white of the Republic. It was a symbolic signal for an outbreak of violence, and by the time the British arrived in force the following month dozens of Dutch citizens had been killed and there were thousands of armed Pemuda at large on the streets.

Early attempts to broker a ceasefire came to nothing, and high-handed British demands for the Indonesians to disarm on pain of death only inflamed the situation. On 30 October the British commander, Brigadier Mallaby, was shot dead in the north of the city, and a month of vicious street fighting ensued before the British were able to proclaim a decidedly shabby victory. Surabaya was left a smouldering wreck. At least six hundred Allied troops had died—most of them Indians, on active foreign service on behalf of the British for the last time before Indian independence. There are no truly reliable figures for local casualties, but the British commander in Java, Lieutenant General Sir Philip Christison, privately estimated that at least ten thousand Indonesians, many of them civilians, had been killed.

The so-called Battle of Surabaya was a crucial moment in the Indonesian Revolution—for a revolution, unmistakably, was what was now underway. It proved to the world that Indonesia's independence movement was much more than a small cabal of over-educated collaborators. And for the revolutionaries themselves it provided a fiery rite of passage, a totemic event to prove that blood would be a crucial component of the struggle.

As for the British, the experience simply proved that they ought to get out as soon as possible before they were unwillingly sucked into a protracted colonial war. In the event, it took more than a year of near-continuous fighting in Java, and in many parts of Sumatra too, before the British were able to establish stable perimeters around the major cities. By late 1946, however, the Dutch were thoroughly established in Jakarta (which they were now calling Batavia once again), and the Republican government had pulled out to a new base in Yogyakarta where the sultan, Hamengkubuwono IX, had come out in favour of the Republic.

In mid-November the two sides met in the small resort of Linggajati, perched on the slopes of the mountains south of Cirebon in West Java, to sign a treaty. It guaranteed a ceasefire, acknowledged the existence of the Republic in Java, Madura and Sumatra, and agreed to the establishment, by January 1949, of an independent Indonesian federation, made up of the Republic and some as yet non-existent states in the rest of the Archipelago, and with the Dutch Queen as the symbolic sovereign. It was clearly not what either side wanted, but it allowed the British the chance to depart, which they did with a good deal of bitterness and no great sympathy for either side of the argument.

As the Seaforth Highlanders clambered wearily aboard their transports at Tanjung Priok in November, finally heading for home almost a year and a half after the official end of World War II, some of the men jeered at their Dutch counterparts on the dockside, raised mocking fists and shouted, 'Merdeka!'

⊙—⊙—⊙—⊙—⊙

The ceasefire brokered at Linggajati did not last long. Its terms appealed to neither side: the Indonesian leaders wanted an Archipelago-wide unitary Republic; the Dutch essentially wanted their old colony back. As the monsoon rains rumbled on and 1946 turned into 1947 violence sparked, flared, and occasionally blazed in isolated spots all over the Archipelago.

In Bali and Sulawesi, where the Dutch were trying to establish the tame states that would join their proposed federation, there was bitter fighting. The worst violence was in southern Sulawesi, where the British-trained Dutch commando Raymond Westerling led a campaign of uncompromising summary justice against anyone suspected of rebellion. Westerling was born in Istanbul and was known to friends and foes as 'Turk'. He had cut his counter-insurgency teeth in Sumatra in 1945, where he had specialised in impaling the severed heads of anti-Dutch agitators on spikes. In Sulawesi in late 1946, he and his men—a hardened core of Dutchmen, Indo-Europeans and staunchly pro-Dutch troops from Ambon in Maluku—launched a reign of terror defined by the impromptu public executions of suspected rebels in what soon became known as 'the Westerling Method'. Local Republican forces were decimated.

Fighting erupted again in Java in mid-1947, as the Dutch launched what they euphemistically called 'police actions'. By this stage there were essentially two states functioning in Java and Sumatra. The Dutch occupied the cities and surrounding pockets of pacified territory. From their base at Yogyakarta, meanwhile, the Republicans had notional control of most of the hinterland. They had ministries complete with a civil service, and were doing their best to establish a functioning economy. The police actions were, in all but name, a war between nations.

Over the first weeks of July 1947, Dutch forces managed to gain uneasy control of all of West Java, Madura, and most of the far east of the island around Malang. In Sumatra, too, Dutch troops forced their way into the jungles around Palembang and Padang. The operation was, militarily, a success. But by this stage the Dutch were finding that international opinion was turning against them.

At the start of 1948, under considerable international pressure, Dutch and Indonesian officials were coaxed aboard an American warship, the USS *Renville*, which had dropped anchor off Jakarta, where they signed a new ceasefire agreement. The most important component of the agreement was a line of control based on the most advanced Dutch military positions. It formalised Dutch authority over large swathes of former Republican territory, established a de facto border, and looked to many Indonesians like the most outrageous sop to the colonial aggressors. So furious was the condemnation of the agreement within the Republic that the government of the day—now headed by Amir Sjarifuddin, who had taken over as prime minister while Sutan Sjahrir went off to press the Republican cause at the United Nations—collapsed and Sukarno had to step in and appoint Hatta to the prime ministership, in addition to his vice-presidential role.

But in the eyes of the world, the Indonesians came out of the Renville Agreement in firm possession of the moral high ground. Dutch propagandists were ever eager to proclaim the entire Indonesian independence movement a tissue of terrorism. But now, with film cameras whirring and reporters scribbling, the Indonesians had politely and pragmatically made enormous concessions.

The Dutch found themselves looking like anachronistic bullies in a post-colonial world.

⊙ ⎯ ⊙ ⎯ ⊙ ⎯ ⊙ ⎯ ⊙

It was not only an outdated imperialist impulse and a need to regain face after the humiliation of wartime defeat that kept the Dutch clinging on. They had spent 350 years in the Archipelago. Generations of Dutchmen had lived out their lives there, and there were plenty of Europeans with a deep emotional commitment to the place. Hubertus van Mook, the lieutenant governor-general in the turbulent post-war years, was an Indies-born Dutchmen. His childhood memories were of Semarang, not Amsterdam, and most of his adult life had been spent in Java. There were thousands like him: men and women who were conditioned to speak of the Netherlands as 'home', but whose natural environment consisted of tea plantations or Batavian bungalows.

For the thousands of Indo-Europeans, the 'Indos', their commitment to the Dutch empire was even more pressing. At the start of the Independence movement, some Indos had signed up for the utopian vision of the Indies Party: an independent Archipelago for all, regardless of their origins. But over the subsequent decades they had seen themselves disenfranchised in the nationalist movement. Neither fully Dutch nor fully Indonesian, the Indos had discovered that their only true homeland lay not in a concrete territory, but in an abstract concept—the Dutch East Indies. For many of them its endurance was an existential matter, and as a consequence, by the end of World War II, they were amongst the most vigorous and at times violent proponents of continuing colonialism.

There were also a good number of Indonesians whose very identity was wrapped up in the Dutch East Indies. From the days of the spice trade, the Christians of Ambon in Maluku had formed the core of the Dutch army in the Archipelago, and colonial military service had become a cornerstone of their culture. Many of the indigenous elite, too—the sultans, the rajas and the regents—owed their status to the colonial state, and saw only uncertainty in a Republican future.

But as the end of the 1940s loomed, all of these people—Dutchmen, Indos, pro-colonial Ambonese and others—found themselves on the wrong side of history.

$\odot-\odot-\odot-\odot-\odot$

In 1948 the Republic might well have had the moral high ground, but it was also riven with internal tension. From the very outset of the independence movement, there had been arguments about how best to defeat the Dutch and how best to forge a new nation. The most essential debate was between those who favoured a slow and steady progress towards independence with negotiation and conciliation along the way, and those who wanted to drive urgently forward to '100 percent merdeka'. In the aftermath of the Renville Agreement in 1948, it was the communists who were carrying the torch of radicalism.

The communist organisation formed from Sarekat Islam membership by the Surabaya railway worker Semaun way back in the 1920s had endured in various incarnations down the decades. Now, as the *Partai Komunis Indonesia*, the 'Indonesian Communist Party' or PKI, it was at the head of the faction that viewed the Renville Agreement as an unconscionable sop. The bloody revolutionary ideals of Surabaya and the angry slogan of '*merdeka atau mati*', 'freedom or death', still had much popular currency, and in September 1948 a revolution within the revolution broke out. PKI supporters seized the East Java town of Madiun and proclaimed a new government. Sukarno, for all his own socialist sympathies, condemned the rebels, and pro-government army units descended on Madiun. Thousands died in the subsequent fighting, and many senior left-leaning politicians were arrested and subsequently shot—one-time prime minister Amir Sjarifuddin amongst them.

The Dutch took obvious delight in all this infighting, and on 19 December they launched another offensive of their own, driving far beyond the Renville Agreement's ceasefire line. They overwhelmed the Republic's capital at Yogyakarta and arrested Sukarno, Hatta, Sjahrir and most of the other senior politicians. On the face of it, the operation was a triumph. But the Republican army, the *Tentara Nasional Indonesia*, the 'Indonesian National Army' or TNI, was now a proficient, if still somewhat ramshackle, fighting force, officered by veterans of the pre-war colonial army and the most senior Japanese-trained soldiers. They were still in the field, and the Dutch were faced with persistent guerrilla tactics in the same Central Java countryside where the battles of Diponegoro's Java War had been fought 120 years earlier. What was more, by this stage the Dutch had earned the opprobrium of virtually every significant international power. Australia, India, Britain—all were firmly on the Indonesian side of the argument. Most importantly of all, with the Cold War getting underway the bloody events at Madiun had established the Republic's anti-communist credentials in the eyes of the United States. The Dutch were fighting a lost cause.

⊙—⊙—⊙—⊙—⊙

On 27 December 1949, the Netherlands finally ceded sovereignty to a Republic of the United States of Indonesia. It was a gimcrack federation that no one really wanted, but it consisted of all former colonial territories—all, that is, except for the western half of the great green island of New Guinea, which the Dutch retained.

As the second half of the twentieth century began, the federation threatened to fall apart before it had even begun to function. Raymond 'Turk' Westerling, now acting as a freelance guerrilla, launched his own terrorist campaign against the Republic from the Priangan highlands near Bandung. He called his eight-hundred-man militia the 'Legion of the Ratu Adil', using the ubiquitous Joyoboyo prophecies to proclaim himself the divine saviour of Java.

In the federal state of East Indonesia, meanwhile, pro-Dutch Ambonese troops were stirring up trouble of their own, culminating in the proclamation of an independent Republic of South Maluku, with Ambon as its capital. Ultimately, however, the Republican army crushed these and other nascent rebellions. Westerling snuck out of Indonesia and ended his days running a bookstore in Amsterdam.

Finally, on 17 August 1950, five years to the day after Sukarno and Hatta had stood outside a modest Jakarta bungalow and read their declaration of independence, the federation ceased to exist and the unitary Republic of Indonesia came into being, with Sukarno as its president and Jakarta as its capital. It was a vast nation, stretching from the northernmost tip of Sumatra, down across the crowded countryside of Java and the deep forests of Borneo, beyond the beaches of Bali and Lombok, and out into the scattered landfalls of Maluku and Nusa Tenggara. It was home to around 80 million people speaking myriad languages and practicing manifold cultures, and there were many who guessed that it would never survive.

CHAPTER 9

YEARS OF LIVING DANGEROUSLY: THE SUKARNO ERA

I t was hot in the crowded hall. The silence was broken here and there by a stifled cough and by the whirring of the cine cameras on the press balcony. Delegates fanned themselves with their conference papers. At the head of the room, backed by a rank of flags, Sukarno rose to the podium. He was dressed in a pristine white suit and a black velvet *peci*, the fez-like cap that had become part of the essential uniform of Indonesian nationalism. He shuffled his papers and began to speak.

The room was filled with delegates of twenty-five countries, including thirteen serving prime ministers. On the dais behind Sukarno, Nehru of India slouched in his seat with the casual confidence of a born statesman. Next to Nehru, U Nu of Burma was grinning enthusiastically. Indonesia's vice-president Mohammad Hatta was sitting at U Nu's left, upright, utterly immobile and unblinking behind thick spectacles, the eternal counterpoint to Sukarno's florid charisma. Also there were Zhou Enlai of China, and the Indonesian prime minister of the day, Ali Sastroamidjojo.

'As I survey this hall and the distinguished guests gathered here, my heart is filled with emotion', Sukarno declared. 'This is the first intercontinental conference of coloured peoples—so-called coloured peoples—in the history of mankind!'

And so, indeed, it was. It was 18 April 1955, and the Bandung Afro–Asian Conference was underway. Over the previous days, dozens of chauffeur-driven cars had made their way to Bandung, travelling up from Jakarta through the mountains where the over-lords of the Cultivation System had worked their labourers to death a century earlier. The passengers were the prime ministers, foreign ministers and sundry hangers-on from new and old na-tions across Asia and Africa. Soon they were all rubbing shoulders in the city where Dutch prisoners of war had been interred ten years before. Foreign reporters had arrived in their droves; the hotels did a roaring trade, and the Indonesian hospitality com-mittee laid on a call-girl service to meet the nocturnal needs of the delegates.

The conference had, in fact, been the brainchild of Prime Minister Sastroamidjojo. But this was unmistakably Sukarno's moment, and as he got into his stride he was making the most of it.

'Our nations and countries are colonies no more', he told the onlookers. 'Now we are free, sovereign and independent. We are again masters in our own house.

'Yes, there has indeed been a *sturm über Asien*—and over Africa too'. This was a standard Sukarno affectation—a random foreign phrase dropped into a speech as a flag of his own masterful in-ternationalism. Out in the hall the reporters scribbled and the assorted Arab princes mopped their brows.

'Yes, there is diversity among us. Who denies it?' Sukarno said, pausing for dramatic effect before filling his voice with passion. 'But, again, what harm is in diversity, when there is unity in desire?'

It was a truly proud moment. Here, just a few years removed from the revolution, was Indonesia on the world stage—even if the Bandung Conference would ultimately achieve little beyond a mild declaration of brotherhood in anti-colonialism and a certain amount of backroom politicking. For Sukarno, too, it ought to have been a great achievement, his confirmation as a world leader. But in 1955 he was a man straining at the limits of a constitutional presidency, the figurehead of a country struggling to come to terms with its newfound independence. He was also watching over a political system sliding into chronic ineptitude. Indonesia's first national election was due just a few months after the Bandung Conference, but Sukarno was already beginning to wonder if democracy was a good idea. Before the decade was out he would have broken his constitutional bounds, appointed himself uncontested and unelected Indonesian supremo, and created a political atmosphere so tense that it would eventually produce the most horrific violence imaginable.

⊙—⊙—⊙—⊙—⊙

The independent unitary Republic of Indonesia that finally came into being in August 1950 was faced with some monumental challenges. For a start, as some of the more radical nationalists pointed out, the independence struggle wasn't entirely over. As part of the final treaty with the Netherlands, Indonesia had been forced to take on the huge debts accrued by the Dutch East Indies administration in its final decades. The new Indonesian nation was faced with the bizarre situation of owing 4.3 billion guilders to the Dutch government, a sum that included the cost of military operations intended to prevent its own existence. Many major industries and institutions—including the bank responsible for issuing and guaranteeing the national currency, the rupiah—were also still in Dutch hands, and many of the biggest plantations of Java and Sumatra were still owned and run by Europeans.

But despite that, Indonesia had the recognisable features of a functioning nation. The vast territories had been organised into provinces—some as big as middle-sized European countries in their own right. Each province broke down into smaller administrative units known as regencies—based on the old colonial system of government through local aristocrats. The 282 royal domains recognising ultimate Dutch suzerainty had been dissolved, and their sultans and rajas had either been turned into government employees or left jobless. Only one royal house had kept its official status in the new republican nation: the firm support that the Yogyakarta court had given to the revolution meant that it endured as a special territory. Sultan Hamengkubuwono IX was made governor for life.

Sukarno and Hatta were president and vice-president, as they had been since the declaration of independence. But the constitution made them mere figureheads, always on the stage but without sanctioned political power. Both men still bore the revolutionary title *Bung*, or 'Brother', but they remained nothing like brothers in character and political attitude, as one young Englishman noticed when he met them in the early 1950s. Harold Forster and his wife Coral were teachers, seconded in 1952 to Indonesia's first university, newly opened and using the borrowed pavilions of the Yogyakarta kraton as makeshift lecture halls. The institution had been named after the legendary Majapahit prime minister, Gajah Mada. In the early days the national leaders would often come calling at the university, and Forster quickly recognised Sukarno for a formidable demagogue: he had 'that dramatic quality which makes a great actor and also a great politician' and when he was on campus 'there was excitement in the air'. Hatta, meanwhile, could not have been more different. He was singularly undramatic: 'short, chubby and bespectacled, in a neat lounge suit'. If you didn't know better, Forster wrote, you would have 'guessed him to be a professor or senior civil servant rather than a fiery revolutionary leader'.

While these two contrasting men stood in the limelight, the actual running of the country was the task of a mishmash of contesting political parties. The original constitution, penned in 1945, had called for an upper house, the People's Consultative Assembly, or MPR, which would meet only once every five years to appoint the president; and a lower house, the People's Representative Council, or DPR, which would have the right to legislate but which would, in practice, often bow to a strong executive president. During the tinkering required to get the Republic through the revolution this had all changed, and by 1950 the DPR was the powerhouse of the government. It had 236 members from 16 different parties divided into three broad groupings: Muslim, socialist (including the communists), and nationalist.

At the outset the largest party was the Muslim Masyumi, which had evolved from the umbrella group established for Muslim organisations under Japanese rule. Despite being the biggest party, Masyumi was a very long way from controlling a majority of the parliament, with less than a quarter of the total seats. Its near equal was the Indonesian National Party, or PNI. Like Masyumi, this party had roots in a wartime organisation, and it claimed the heritage of Sukarno's 1920s party of the same name. Further down the ranks there were myriad small socialist and nationalist parties, a clutch of special interest Protestant and Catholic groups, and the ever-resilient PKI, the Indonesian Communist Party, which had managed a partial rehabilitation since its involvement in the Madiun rebellion in 1948.

At a glance, the wild diversity of ideologies without any single party coming anywhere near holding an absolute majority might have seemed unworkable. And when, in 1952, the Nahdlatul Ulama, the influential organisation of traditionalist Javanese Muslims founded in the 1920s, split from Masyumi and struck out on its own, the prospects of any one party achieving dominance became slimmer still. But in practice, ideological commitments were rarely absolute: nationalism, Islam and socialism often overlapped in Indonesia, and there was usually room for enough compromise to form a coalition, elect a prime minister and attempt some legislation. The situation was hardly conducive to stability, however, and the average life expectancy for an Indonesian cabinet in the 1950s was twelve months. The only hope for real progress, as far as many were concerned, was a national election.

⊙−⊙−⊙−⊙−⊙

On 29 September 1955, Indonesia went to the polls for the first time. In Yogyakarta the English teacher Harold Forster woke that morning feeling decidedly uneasy. Foreign reporters, and more than a few Indonesians, had been prophesying doom for days. There would be carnage, they said; the elections would unleash anarchy on a par with the violence of the early revolution. But when he peered out of his modest bungalow at the bright morning street, Forster was greeted by a scene of the utmost tranquillity: far from seething with unrest, Yogyakarta seemed to be deserted. Baffled, he dressed and went for a walk. It was only when Forster reached the first polling station that he realised why things were so quiet elsewhere: 'The people were not visible on the streets because they were packed in the school yards in enormous sinuous queues, patiently waiting for their turn to vote'.

> There were all sorts, from toothless old hags to young girl students, from smart westernised office workers to peasants from the *kampongs*, dressed in their best and complete with *kris*, as befitted a great occasion. Hundreds of babies, slung on their mothers' hips, suffered for democracy. Despite a staggering proportion of illiteracy Indonesia had universal suffrage over the age of eighteen, and here were the people, quiet, orderly but firmly determined to exercise their right to choose their own government at last.

It was the same all over the country. From hill towns in the Bukit Barisan mountains of Sumatra to tiny islands in Maluku, they had turned out: some 39 million people, more than 91 percent of the registered electorate. Nothing served so well to show that Indonesia, for all its faults, was now a nation.

A staggering eighty-three separate parties and independent candidates contested the elections, and every village square and every bus depot was festooned with multi-coloured party flags. The election was run on the principle of proportional representation, so voters had only to choose a party, rather than an individual. And with such high levels of illiteracy, symbols counted for everything. Everyone entering the polling booths was presented with an enormous ballot card, speckled with dozens of cartoon-like party signs. They had to puncture their preferred picture, fold the sheet into a chunky wad, and cram it into the ballot box. The whole process went off in an air of almost surreal calm. As far as the watching Harold Forster was concerned, 'It was the quietest election I have ever seen, but there was no doubt of its fairness and freedom. If this was not democracy, nothing was'.

And then it was time to wait for the results. The outcome of this unprecedented act of communal decision-making turned out to be rather underwhelming. The biggest losers were the Muslims of Masyumi, who slipped into second place behind the PNI, but neither party had managed to accrue even a quarter of the vote. The Nahdlatul Ulama, meanwhile, had come storming out of leftfield to take 18.4 percent, worth forty-five seats in parliament. And the rehabilitated communists of the PKI had garnered 16.4 percent and thirteen seats. Nobody else managed to get more than 3 percent of the vote.

Ultimately, the election only made it clear that it would be virtually impossible for any of the four biggest parties ever to win a majority. Far from doing away with the permanent coalition-based stalemate that had defined the first five years of the Indonesian parliament, the election had confirmed it. And now the president was getting twitchy…

⊙ — ⊙ — ⊙ — ⊙ — ⊙

At the time of Indonesia's first election Sukarno was a man in his mid-fifties. But he was not, by any means, ready for the quiet role of the elder statesman. He was still full of vigour, and as if to prove it he had just taken a new wife. At the height of the post-war struggle against the Dutch, he had finally convinced his aging second wife Inggit to grant him a divorce, and had flown the fragrant Fatmawati from Bengkulu to Java to become his new bride. The couple had several children—including a little girl called Megawati, born in Yogyakarta at the height of the revolution. But by the 1950s, the president's irrepressible roving instinct was in play once more, and he was pursuing the glamorous Hartini, a sophisticated Central Java woman he had met, legend has it, at the Prambanan temple complex. Sukarno decided to marry her, and this time he would take advantage of his Muslim right to a second wife. The decision earned him the ire of modernist politicians, who felt that multiple marriages were for anachronistic aristocrats rather than the leaders of modern nations. It also caused considerable outrage amongst women's groups, and Fatmawati herself was none too pleased—though she did manage to retain her official status as *Ibu Negara*, 'Mother of the Nation', Indonesia's First Lady.

Sukarno remained Indonesia's undisputed figurehead. He lived in the hulking neoclassical palace in Jakarta that had once been the residence of the governor-general, and which was now known as *Istana Merdeka*, 'Freedom Palace'. It looked out over the grassy expanse of the Koningsplein—now similarly rechristened *Lapangan Merdeka*, 'Freedom Square'—and it was here, each year on 17 August, that Sukarno addressed the crowds celebrating the anniversary of the declaration of Independence.

Sukarno was a formidable orator, and he could have a crowd a quarter of a million strong laughing at his jokes, cheering at his exhortations, and then dropping abruptly to respectful silence when he proclaimed profundity. He called these speeches 'a two-way conversation between myself and the People, between my Ego and my Alter-Ego'. In the mid-1950s, the topic of these great orations was often the areas of the revolution that he felt were unfinished. Foremost amongst them was the question of New Guinea.

⊙ — ⊙ — ⊙ — ⊙ — ⊙

New Guinea sits at the eastern end of the Archipelago. Thickly forested and skewed along the edge of the Pacific Ocean at a forty-five-degree angle, it is the second largest island on earth after Greenland. In 1623 a Dutch explorer named Jan Carstenszoon had reached the south coast and thought that he could see distant snows on the high summits inland. He was roundly mocked when he reported the vision back home, for New Guinea lay just beneath the equator. But Carstenszoon's eyes had not deceived him. There really was snow on the heights of New Guinea's central mountains.

After Carstenszoon's visit, Europeans had for the most part left the place alone. Merchants from within the Archipelago, as well as wandering Arab and Chinese sea captains, traded along the coast, but as far as most outsiders were concerned the island was essentially empty. It wasn't, of course, and though they were scattered very thinly, there were indigenous Papuan people living all over the island—often as nomadic hunter-gathers, but in some places as settled villagers practicing well-developed agriculture.

The Sultanate of Ternate in Maluku had traditionally claimed sovereignty over an ill-defined western chunk of New Guinea, and when the Dutch established suzerainty over Ternate they inherited the claim. But it was only at the very end of the nineteenth century that they made any significant effort to settle in West New Guinea, largely in response to British and German activity in the east of the island. They established the 141st meridian—a clean line running through the middle of the island—as the eastern frontier of the Dutch East Indies, and created a few coastal settlements. Even so, when the invading Japanese troops arrived in 1942, West New Guinea was the single least developed part of the entire colony.

As the independence movement got underway, however, all that changed, and New Guinea became a significant bone of contention. Once it became clear that Indonesian independence was inevitable, the Dutch unilaterally hived New Guinea off from the Dutch East Indies and declared it an entirely separate colony. For the first time they began to invest in the place, proposing, amongst other things, that it might make a suitable homeland for the thousands of Indo-Europeans likely to be disenfranchised in an independent Indonesia. The more strident Indonesian nationalists were understandably furious, but Hatta and the other pragmatists agreed to allow the Netherlands to hold West New Guinea temporarily, on the understanding that a later transfer would be arranged. No one, of course, asked the local inhabitants what they wanted.

$$\odot - \odot - \odot - \odot - \odot$$

Sukarno and Hatta had always represented the two sides of the nationalist movement. The calm, intellectual Minangkabau Hatta belonged to the sector that was prepared to be pragmatic, to negotiate, and to make concessions. Sukarno, meanwhile, tended to side with those who called for '100 percent merdeka' at any cost. In the 1950s he felt that the Indonesian parliament, whether through inclination or ineptitude, belonged to the concessionary group. In speech after speech he expanded on the need to make West New Guinea part of Indonesia, and to sever the Dutch tentacles that still extended deep into the Indonesian economy. In the aftermath of the 1955 election, Prime Minister Ali Sastroamidjojo unilaterally repudiated 85 percent of the debt Indonesia supposedly owed to the Netherlands, but this was not enough for Sukarno.

Sukarno also worried that the government was sliding into very obvious corruption, and as it did so the potential for discontent in the outlying regions of Indonesia increased. There were rumblings of unease with Jakarta rule from Sumatra and Maluku. Even much closer to home, the hills of West Java were host to a low-level rebellion by the staunch Muslims of the Darul Islam movement. This movement had emerged the previous decade, at the height of the revolution, amongst orthodox Muslims who wanted to turn Indonesia into an Islamic state, and who were dismayed by the secularism of the mainstream nationalists. They had support in Aceh and South Sulawesi as well as West Java, and though they were never a serious threat to the government, they were a permanent irritant.

By early 1957, Sukarno had decided that Indonesia was 'afflicted by the disease of parties, which, alas, alas, forever makes us work against one another'. What the country needed, he felt, was 'Guided Democracy'. Parliamentary democracy, he believed, was a Western concept, ill-suited to the culture of Southeast Asia, and as 1955 had proved, a popular vote did nothing to achieve stability. A more appropriate system, he declared, would be based on the Indonesian concepts of discussion and consensus. Since time immemorial, Sukarno argued, wise village elders had gathered in the shade of banyan trees and calmly chewed over the various options until they had decided on the best course of action for their community. He envisaged this model scaled up to take in the whole country. There would be a 'national council' made up not of career politicians, but of representatives of the 'functional groups'— the workers, the artists, the soldiers, the housewives, and so on. This council would, through discussion and consensus, set the direction of policy for a cabinet made up of representatives of every political shade. And the guide in this 'guided democracy' would, of course, be the national village chief, the president himself.

Many later critics would assume that Sukarno's guided democracy was simply the power-grab of a dictator, but this is unfair. His vast ego may well have craved a more decisive role in the running of the country, but his 1957 proposal was a genuine attempt to bring some direction to a floundering nation. What was more, the rejection of parliamentary democracy was nothing new: Sukarno had been arguing since the very start of his career that Western political concepts and systems could rarely be imported wholesale to Indonesia. He had also recognised from the outset that no one of the competing ideologies—socialism, Islam and nationalism—could ever succeed in dominating in Indonesia. The country might have a large Muslim majority, but the orthodoxy of the Islamic parties was anathema not only to the non-Muslims of Bali and the Christian-dominated regions: it was also utterly alien to the millions of rural Javanese whose own adherence to Islam was nominal at best. Socialism and communism, meanwhile, had limits in a society that was in many ways pre-industrial, and there was only so much that nationalism could achieve when it came to social justice. It was necessary, Sukarno had argued publically, even as a young man, to splice these three threads together.

Socialism, Islam and nationalism had, of course, all been well-represented in the parliaments of the 1950s. But the democratic system meant that they pulled against one another, creating an unproductive stalemate. In Sukarno's vision of guided democracy the ideological stalemate would remain—as it needed to, with no single worldview dominating. However, without the crude distraction of ballots and shows of hands, everyone would work together; there would be progress. On paper, at least, it was a very clever idea.

⊙—⊙—⊙—⊙—⊙

Guided democracy crept into being over the final years of the 1950s. Hatta had resigned as vice-president in July 1956, frustrated by his own inability to guide the nation and by Sukarno's increasingly strident behaviour. In March 1957, Ali Sastroamid-jojo's democratically elected cabinet collapsed in the face of re-bellions by regional military commanders in Sumatra and eastern Indonesia, and on 14 March 1957 Sukarno declared martial law.

The president's crucial collaborator in the establishment of guided democracy was the army chief, Abdul Haris Nasution. A Batak from northern Sumatra, Nasution had been working as a teacher in Bengkulu in the 1930s when he first met the exiled Sukarno. During the revolution he had become a commander in the new army of the Republic. He had always had political interests, and he believed in a so-called third way in which the military would play an advisory role in government, reserving the right to nudge the country back on track if the civilians went astray.

By the end of 1957 there was a Sukarno-appointed 'business cabinet', supposedly organised without recourse to party lines, and the 'national council' was in place, complete with its 'functional groups'. At the same time a constituent assembly was attempting to put together a new constitution. Outside of the meeting rooms and presidential palaces, meanwhile, Sukarno had encouraged PKI- and PNI-affiliated unions to start seizing Dutch assets ahead of nationalisation, and the remaining 46,000 Dutch citizens were ordered to leave Indonesia.

The eviction of the Dutch citizens and the seizure of Dutch assets was the first move in what would soon be a programme of wilful confrontation with the outside world. International relations worsened in 1958 when the United States, alarmed by what looked like a leftwards tilt in Indonesia, backed an unsuccessful rebellion by an alliance of Masyumi leaders and conservative nationalists in Sumatra. Nasution's army crushed the rebellion with minimal fuss. Following the precedent of the eviction of the Dutch, the army also began forcing ethnic Chinese traders out of the countryside, in line with a ban on foreign citizens participating in the rural economy. Most moved into the cities where they tried to start afresh, but over a hundred thousand Chinese were actually repatriated to China. Many of them were from families that had been in Indonesia for generations.

In July 1959, Sukarno dissolved parliament and dismissed

the constituent assembly before it had managed to create a new constitution. He brought back the old 1945 constitution, hastily drafted during the Japanese occupation. It made him what he had always wanted to be: a strong president with executive powers. Just for good measure, he decided to make himself prime minister, too. Guided Democracy was now firmly in place, and its leader was spoiling for a fight with the world.

⊙—⊙—⊙—⊙—⊙

By the 1960s Sukarno was showing his age. He was a little overweight; there were dark bags beneath his eyes and a puffiness to his face. Beneath the ever-present *peci* cap his hair had thinned, and he was beginning to have trouble with his kidneys. He was showing no signs of slowing down, however.

Guided democracy had given Sukarno the chance for yet more demagoguery, more opportunities to conjure new phrases and concepts from the air. And he did have a genuine talent for capturing the imagination of the nation. He had survived a number of assassination attempts over the years, and there were rumours that he possessed the mystic Javanese power of invulnerability—a property that had been attached to many a great leader of the past, not least Diponegoro. His sexual appetites had not waned either, and he had availed himself of several more wives, including a nineteen-year-old Japanese girl he had met in a hostess bar in Tokyo in 1959. He also had innumerable mistresses secreted in villas all over Jakarta. Members of the educated elite, the women's movement and some of his former revolutionary fellows might have rolled their eyes at his endless romantic dalliances, but they only increased his potent prestige with the masses. In 1963 he had himself declared 'Leader for Life', and there was no outcry from the streets. His charisma could work its magic on foreigners, too: he had recruited a glamorous New York gossip columnist to help him write his autobiography.

Sukarno's Independence Day speeches, which were delivered on 17 August each year, grew more flamboyant. Each had an overwrought title: in 1962 it was 'The Year of Victory', while 1963 was 'The Ringing Out of the Sound of Revolution'. And when it became time to make the 1964 speech, he declared that the coming twelve months would be 'The year of *Vivere Pericoloso*'. This was one of his more obscure dashes of foreign idiom, and even the international reporters were left scratching their heads. When they looked up the phrase, they discovered that he had borrowed it from Mussolini, of all people, and that he had used it to proclaim 'The Year of Living Dangerously'.

Sukarno had ratcheted up the rhetoric against the Netherlands over New Guinea with fiery threats of military action. The president's theatrics might have been viewed with distaste and growing alarm by many Western politicians, but on this issue he actually had the United Nations on his side. In 1962, the Netherlands bowed to international pressure and handed West New Guinea to the United Nations, which then passed it on to Indonesian control in 1963, on the understanding that there would be an 'act of free choice' by the inhabitants, a plebiscite to decide its future, within five years. The place was renamed 'Irian'.

It was a triumph for Sukarno, but with no more Dutchmen to fight he was in danger of being without an enemy. Nothing, he understood, could unite a decidedly ramshackle nation like an external conflict, so he swung next for the new federation of Malaysia, which Britain had forged from its former territories and protectorates in the Malay Peninsula, Singapore and northern Borneo. The federation, Sukarno believed, would be nothing more than the puppet of the dastardly forces of NEKOLIM, his pet acronym for 'neo-colonialist-imperialists'. Indonesia, he announced in 1963, would 'crush Malaysia'. He began a process known as *Konfrontasi*, 'the Confrontation', whipping up angry street protests in Jakarta, and sending soldiers to the jungle borders of Kalimantan, as the Indonesian portion of Borneo was now known (where they struggled against professional Commonwealth troops).

Sukarno also swung for other Western targets. In 1964 it was the turn of the United States, which had only recently backed Indonesia's claims over New Guinea. During the 'Year of Living Dangerously' speech on 17 August, Sukarno condemned the USA as the biggest of all NEKOLIM forces. Soon semi-sanctioned mobs were attacking American-owned businesses and Hollywood movies were banned from cinemas. At one point the innocuous East Java pop group Koes Plus, Indonesia's answer to the Bee Gees, were arrested for playing American rock and roll. In Jakarta, meanwhile, Sukarno was commissioning ostentatious and expensive symbols of national pride, even with Indonesian debt topping US$2 billion. Most notable was the 'National Monument', popularly abbreviated to Monas, a stark 433-foot (132-metre) tower rising from the middle of Lapangan Merdeka.

Politically, Sukarno was still attempting to strike a balance, keeping the opposing political forces within the country in play as ideological counterpoints. The problem, however, was that his own grip on the situation was slipping, and the most powerful of those opposing forces were heading for a confrontation of their own.

⊙ ⁓ ⊙ ⁓ ⊙ ⁓ ⊙ ⁓ ⊙

Guided democracy had not been good for the traditional parties. Some, including Masyumi, had actually been banned. But one political organisation had flourished, and that was the PKI, the Indonesian Communist Party. By the early 1960s, under the leadership of chairman Dipa Nusantara Aidit—a veteran of the revolution from the island of Belitung off the southeast coast of Sumatra—it had become the largest national communist party in the world outside of China and the Eastern Bloc. It claimed 3.5 million members, and some 20 million affiliates through its connected labour organisations and unions. The sheer scale of the PKI made other political forces nervous. The religious groups were particularly concerned; when the PKI attempted to enforce government land reforms in East Java, redistributing farmland from traditional landlords to peasant farmers, there were violent clashes with the youth wing of the Nahdlatul Ulama, which was always eager to portray the PKI as a religion-hating mob.

The other major force in 1960s Indonesia that was becoming nervous of the rise of the PKI was not a political party or religious organisation: it was the TNI, the Indonesian National Army. The army had, initially, done very well out of guided democracy. One third of the cabinet was made up of army officers and Nasution's concept of the military's 'third way' role seemed to have been formalised. But the top brass was mostly drawn from the old Javanese and Sumatran elites, conservative men who disliked socialism and were increasingly averse to the president's antics. Sukarno was aware that the military was a potentially volatile weight in his increasingly precarious balancing act, and from 1963 he had moved to curb its power, ending martial law and reducing the army role in government.

Both military and religious leaders were worried that Sukarno was not just tolerating the rise of the PKI; he seemed to be actually encouraging it, even if only as a balance against their own influence. Internationally, too, the president was displaying distinctly left-wing sympathies. Sukarno had told the United States to 'go to hell with your aid' after it cut financial assistance in the wake of the anti-American actions of 1964. He initially approached Moscow in search of more cash, but then turned in the direction of communist China, and began to talk of a 'Beijing–Jakarta axis'. The Cold War was getting decidedly hot at this point, with American boots on the ground in Vietnam, and the apparently credible threat of Indonesia turning communist terrified many Western observers.

By the time Sukarno's 'Year of Living Dangerously' drew to a close with a new Independence Day speech on 17 August 1965, the political atmosphere in Indonesia was toxic. There had been clashes between PKI activists and Muslim youth organisations not only in East Java but also in Aceh in Sumatra, prompting an American observer in the US consulate in Surabaya to predict that 'a civil war between the two groups will eventually be fought'. In Jakarta, meanwhile, there were persistent rumours that a cabal of senior right-wing generals were being sponsored by the CIA to launch a coup against Sukarno. It was, in the circumstances, an eminently believable rumour. It does not, however, appear to have been true, and this may be why, when September came and the generals in question heard a report that in fact it was the forces of the left who were plotting a coup against *them*, they dismissed it as nothing more than gossip and propaganda...

⊙—⊙—⊙—⊙—⊙

At 3 AM on 1 October 1965, General Abdul Haris Nasution was in bed at his home on Jalan Teuku Umar, a quiet street south of Lapangan Merdeka in Jakarta. The house was an old-fashioned colonial bungalow, a place of tiled floors, high ceilings and long corridors.

Jakarta nights in the 1960s were dark and silent. There were none of the towering skyscrapers or howling traffic that mark the city in the twenty-first century; by day the potholed streets were plied by a few battered buses and a tiny handful of private cars, but little moved after dark. But despite the heavy, blanketing silence, the general, who was now serving as defence minister, despite Sukarno's efforts to curb military influence in government, was not asleep. The monsoon would begin within weeks and the night was humid and thick with insects. The mosquitoes had kept Nasution and his wife Johanna awake, and they were both quick to rise from their bed when they heard the sound of heavy footsteps in the hall outside. When they opened the bedroom door they spotted a uniformed man with a machine gun. Quickly they slammed the door and slid the bolt, and as they did so a shot rang out. Nasution, dressed only in a sarong, slipped out of a side door and made for the garden. As he crossed the grass a volley of shots exploded behind him and lights came on all over the house. He scrambled over the high brick wall at the back of the property and tumbled into the garden of his neighbour, the Iraqi ambassador, shattering his ankle as he fell. With the sound of shooting and shouting still echoing in the night, he crawled across the lawn and hid under a bush.

Back in the house, soldiers dressed in the uniform of the elite presidential guard were demanding of Johanna to know where her husband was. In the confusion an ill-fated young aide who had been sleeping in the guest quarters had been seized in the mistaken belief that he was the general; a policeman from a neighbouring house had been gunned down; and a trigger-happy trooper had accidentally shot and fatally wounded Nasution's five-year-old daughter. Leaving Johanna and the other women of the house sobbing in the hallway, the men bundled the unfortunate aide into a waiting truck and rumbled away southwards, just as the first stain of daylight was starting to show on the eastern edge of the night.

Elsewhere in Jakarta, six other top generals had also been attacked. Half a mile to the south, the chief of staff, the sprightly forty-three-year-old Ahmad Yani, had been shot as he tried to resist another group of kidnappers in his own home, as had generals Harjono and Panjaitan. Three more generals—Suprapto, Sutarjo and Parman—had been seized from their beds and bundled into waiting trucks. By first light, the seven trucks from the seven suburban homes had converged at the Halim air force base on the southeast edge of the city. There, on a patch of marshy ground beyond the end of the runway, the three surviving generals and Nasution's unfortunate aide were shot. The bodies were thrown into a deep well known as *Lubang Buaya*, the 'Crocodile Hole'. Six of Indonesia's most senior generals were dead; a seventh was incapacitated and hiding in a flowerbed.

⊙−⊙−⊙−⊙−⊙

Even half a century later, there is little consensus about what had really been going on in the early hours of 1 October 1965, but the bones of the affair are this: a group of junior officers, most notably Lieutenant Colonel Untung, the commander of the presidential palace guard, had organised a putsch against the top brass, who they believed were hostile to Sukarno. Having thrown the generals down the Crocodile Hole, they quickly moved to take control of the Istana Merdeka (from which Sukarno himself was absent, having spent the night with wife number five, the Japanese hostess, at her villa in the south of the city), the national radio station, and the telecommunications centre—all three places flanking Lapangan Merdeka. At 7.20 AM, they went on the radio to announce that they were the self-proclaimed *Gerakan Tiga-Puluh September*, the '30 September Movement', and that they had acted to safeguard the president against a cabal of right-wing generals who had been plotting to overthrow him. Later that day they made another broadcast, declaring that they were in the process of forming a revolutionary council to temporarily run the country.

But by this time the nascent rebellion was falling apart. The one man the plotters had injudiciously left off their assassination list—the head of the army's Strategic Reserve, a softly-spoken Javanese general by the name of Suharto—had quickly, calmly and efficiently assumed overall command of the military in Jakarta. Over the course of the day he had established which units were loyal, which were wavering, and which were with the rebels. It soon emerged that there were very few of the latter, and by 8 PM that evening the whole business was over. Most of the rebels had either fled or been arrested, and Suharto was in charge.

The shocking murders of six generals, an aide, a policeman and a little girl notwithstanding, the 30 September Movement could well have been dismissed as a flash in the pan. The whole thing was over in less than twenty-four hours. But it was what would happen in the aftermath that really mattered.

◉—◉—◉—◉—◉

Who, if anyone, was behind the 30 September Movement has never been established with any certainty. The fact that both Sukarno and PKI leader Aidit turned up at the plotters' Halim headquarters during the morning of 1 October has led some to suggest that either the president or the communists—or both—had ordered the putsch. But Halim was a natural place for Sukarno to head if there was unrest in the city: it was where he kept the presidential plane, ready to whisk him to safety if required. And it was also quite natural for Aidit to want to find out what was going on. The leaders of the 30 September Movement clearly banked on the support of the communists, but they were not actually PKI members, and it would not have been entirely logical for the party, which was already doing so well under guided democracy, to launch a revolution at that point.

From elsewhere come seemingly far-fetched claims that the whole business was the doing of Suharto, who had somehow engineered a convoluted chain of events to allow him to seize power. And inevitably there are the suggestions that the CIA had been behind it all, creating a pretext for pro-American right-wingers to take control.

Perhaps the most likely explanation is that things were exactly as they seemed: that the junior officers of the 30 September Movement really had believed that a coup against Sukarno was imminent and had acted on their own initiative, possibly with the tacit support of some elements of the PKI, but without the party's full knowledge or approval.

By the end of the first week of October, however, there was no room for alternative theories: the communists were to blame, and with all newspapers besides those owned by the army now shut down, some particularly grotesque propaganda was taking shape. The bodies had been fished out of the Crocodile Hole and false reports were circulating that they had been horribly mutilated, their eyes gouged out and their genitals hacked off. Soon, there were lurid stories, reported in the international as well as local media, that the killings had taken place in the midst of a deranged orgy, with the unhinged harpies of the PKI women's movement dancing naked as the generals were hacked to death. Rumours spread that all over Indonesia the PKI had dug mass graves and stockpiled special eye-gouging instruments in readiness for a mass slaughter of Muslims, Christians, nationalists and anyone else they didn't like.

A new name for these forces of darkness had also been coined by some unknown propagandist: *Gestapu*, based on the Indonesian name of the 30 September Movement—*Gerakan Tiga Puluh September*. It was a somewhat odd acronym: in Indonesian dates the day always comes before the month, so the abbreviation should really have been *Getapus*. However, the rearranged word order produced a name that would remind many Westerners of the Nazi secret police, even if it meant nothing to most Indonesians. Soon, the acronym had been irreversibly wedded to another abbreviation in military and media pronouncements: the evil entity behind the bloody orgy at the Crocodile Hole and the great existential threat to Indonesia, it was said, was 'Gestapu-PKI'.

In the first weeks of October things were quiet. Reports drifted in that Muslim groups in Aceh had spontaneously slaughtered local PKI cadres, but across most of the country there was an uneasy calm. Suharto might have been in full control of the army and much of the media, but Sukarno was still the president, and he was doing his very best to quell the growing anti-PKI hysteria. Always a man to understand the potency of words, he even tried to stamp out the use of the term 'Gestapu', pointing out correctly that the entire affair had actually taken place on 1 October, *Satu Oktober* in Indonesian, and so should really be called 'Gestok'.

In the wake of the events of 1 October excited cables had bounced back and forth between British and American consulates in Indonesia and their home intelligence headquarters. The CIA and MI6 may not have been behind the bungled putsch, but they were certainly hoping that its aftermath might allow for the eradication of communism in Indonesia. On 7 October, the CIA worriedly reported to the White House that 'Sukarno seems to be making progress in his efforts to play down the 30 September Movement and prevent any effective anti-communist action. The US embassy [in Jakarta] comments that there is danger the Army may settle for action against those directly involved in the murder of the generals and permit Sukarno to get much of his power back'. But they need not have worried.

⊙—⊙—⊙—⊙—⊙

The organised mass killing of communists began in Central Java in late October. The army's elite red beret para-commando unit RPKAD (later rechristened Kopassus) had headed east from Jakarta on 17 October under the command of General Sarwo Edhie Wibowo. Central Java was the one province where some of the local army units had come out in favour of the 30 September Movement, and PKI membership there was huge. In some of the villages they passed through, the troops were jeered by the residents. But Sarwo Edhie had been a close friend of the murdered General Ahmad Yani, and he was out for personal revenge as much as anything. Within weeks he had eliminated whatever power the PKI once had in Central Java, and in the process unleashed all the violent forces of the land.

Sarwo Edhie later explained to the American journalist John Hughes what he had done:

> We decided to encourage the anti-Communist civilians
> to help with the job ... we gathered together the youth,

the nationalist groups, the religious organisations. We gave
them two or three days' training, then sent them out to kill
the Communists…

By November 1965 a mass pogrom was underway all across Indonesia. Some accounts of the killings present them as a vast communal rampage and speak of the entire nation running amok as
the built-up tensions of the previous decades exploded. But what
was often most striking about the slaughter was how organised
it was. Huge numbers of people were rounded up by the army.
They underwent cursory interrogations, and those who were
deemed to be passive supporters of the PKI were thrown into de-
tention; anyone who was considered to be an active party member was handed over to the civilian killing squads. Their bodies
were then dumped in rivers, ravines and mass graves.

Youth groups of every stripe took part in the slaughter. In
East Java the Nahdlatul Ulama's youth wing, Ansor, were a major
part of the process. The Kalimas River in Surabaya was clogged
with bloated bodies that had floated down from the countryside.
Elsewhere it was nationalist militias that did the work. In northern Sumatra the Pemuda Pancasila, the youth wing of the army-
backed IPKI party, carried out much of the slaughter. Catholic,
Protestant, Hindu and other organisations also did their bit, and
entirely new militias were formed, too—groups of young men
raised from villages or street gangs, armed, and sent out to kill. In
many places the killings were coloured by old conflicts: the PKI's
attempted land reforms in East Java were avenged by the Muslim groups; in the plantation areas of Sumatra, locals vented their
hostility against the migrant Javanese communities where PKI
membership had been strong.

Some of the worst violence was in Bali. The PKI had found
strong support in the villages there. But Bali was also home to a
more entrenched pre-colonial aristocracy than many other areas of the country, and there was a certain amount of inter-caste

tension in this, the last part of Indonesia with a Hindu majority. When Sarwo Edhie and his commandos crossed the straits from Java to Bali at the start of December they found that sporadic violence had already begun.

'Whereas in Central Java I was concerned to encourage the people to crush the Gestapu, [in Bali] on the other hand the people were already eager to crush the Gestapu to its roots', Sarwo Edhie later said. By the end of the year, tens of thousands of people—possibly as much as 5 percent of the entire Balinese population—had been killed.

⊙ ⸺ ⊙ ⸺ ⊙ ⸺ ⊙ ⸺ ⊙

By early 1966, the mass killings had petered out in many areas—for the very simple reason that most people who could be connected to the PKI, and a good many more besides, were already dead. Here and there the bloody forces that the army had unleashed showed signs of turning on each other. There were occasional clashes between nationalist and Muslim youth groups, and in some places anti-communist pogroms gave way to riots against the ethnic Chinese communities. The military began to rein in the violence, and by the middle of the year it was almost as if it had never happened. Some killing went on in scattered spots around the Archipelago over the next two years, but it was done quietly now, the victims taken out into the forest after dark. Most of the communists and suspected communist sympathisers who had survived were interred in prison camps in the forests of Sulawesi, or on remote islands in Maluku.

No one really knows how many people died in the violence during the monsoon months of late 1965 and early 1966. The US ambassador to Indonesia at the time plumped for a round figure of three-hundred thousand; staunch critics of the Indonesian military often go for an arbitrary one or two million; and none other than Sarwo Edhie himself, speaking shortly before his death at the age of sixty-four in 1989, claimed that 'three million were killed. Most of them on my orders'. Academics, meanwhile, tend to settle very tentatively on a conservative figure of five-hundred thousand. In the end, all that really matters is that a very great many people died.

Strange voids were left in society all over Indonesia. In Kupang in West Timor in the second half of the 1960s, the locals had to get used to putting up with cracked pipes and leaking cisterns: the city's plumbers had all been killed as suspected PKI members.

Meanwhile, as the slaughter had spread across Indonesia then gradually subsided, there had been a change of regimes in Jakarta.

$$\odot-\odot-\odot-\odot-\odot$$

During the first months after the 30 September Movement, Sukarno still seemed to be in full control of the presidency. He was genuinely horrified by the violence unfolding all across the country, and in one speech in December, when the killings were at their very height, he told his audience that 'If we go on as we are, brothers, we are going to hell, really we are going to hell'. At the start of 1966, he announced the formation of a new cabinet, but it was little more than a ramshackle concoction of appointees, and with the communist constituency quite literally wiped out, guided democracy was now without an essential element in its precarious balance. What was more, Sukarno was now facing growing opposition from a quiet coalition of all manner of anticommunists. Before long this grouping, based around General Suharto, would be calling itself the 'New Order'.

The economy, meanwhile, had inched towards outright meltdown, with inflation running at 600 percent and the country defaulting on its commercial loans. As food costs spiralled and what was left of the national infrastructure crumbled, students came out on the streets of Jakarta, protesting against the economic chaos. Fresh violence looked entirely possible, and though he was still hoping to somehow manoeuvre himself out of the mess and regain the presidential initiative, Sukarno had no wish to see more bloodshed. On 11 March 1966, he signed an order that allowed Suharto 'to take all measures considered necessary to guarantee the security, calm and stability of the government'. The order, in effect, gave the general extraordinary presidential powers.

Over the next twelve months, Suharto and his allies quietly and carefully edged any remaining Sukarno allies out of the military and the political elite. Finally, in a parliamentary session on 12 March 1967, Sukarno was stripped of his title and all his remaining powers. He was shipped off to his residency in Bogor, the old country seat of the Dutch governors-general, where he would spend the last three lonely years of his life under house arrest. General Suharto, meanwhile, had been named acting president.

While Indonesia had been convulsed by a bout of violence that would rank amongst the twentieth century's worst episodes of mass killing, the mild-mannered, smiling Suharto had effected a slow, subtle, and in itself entirely bloodless coup.

CHAPTER 10

A NEW ORDER: SUHARTO, CRISIS, REFORM

T he town of Dili stands at the edge of the Ombai Strait on the north coast of East Timor. Its western suburbs are cut by the Comoro River, a broad smear of braided channels. To the east, a long arm of land reaches out towards the hazy hulk of Atauro Island, riding some fifteen miles offshore. To the south, behind the town, there are hills. They rise sharply, their ribbed flanks marked with patches of scorched grass and a thin speckling of trees. There is none of the rich, tropical vegetation of Java or Sumatra here. The air is different: it is hotter, drier. It smells like the air of northern Australia—which is hardly surprising, for Dili is far closer to Darwin than to Jakarta. It is a town at the limits of the Archipelago's vastness.

In the early 1970s, it was a place that seemed to have been forgotten by history, for in a post-colonial epoch East Timor was still a colonial territory. What was more, it was the possession of a European power that was already past its prime when the Dutch first arrived in the Archipelago almost four centuries earlier. East Timor was a ghostly survivor of the Portuguese empire.

The first Portuguese sailors had arrived in East Timor in the sixteenth century, but they had made little serious effort to take control. Even by the middle of the seventeenth century there were reportedly just eight Portuguese officials in all of East Timor; any real power was split between the 'Black Portuguese', the mixed-race Catholics who made much of their Iberian origins but had no political ties with Portugal itself, the Dominican friars who ministered to them, and the local chieftains of the interior. By the nineteenth century a little more order had been established, but East Timor was hardly the jewel in a glittering colonial crown.

The Portuguese only fixed the border of their Timorese territories in 1914, drawing a line across the island's midriff, with the Dutch in charge to the west. On the eve of World War II there was still virtually no modern infrastructure in Dili, no mains water or electricity, and no paved roads. East Timor had a rough time in the war. Japan invaded, and teams of Australian soldiers harried them from the hills, making it one corner of the Archipelago where Japanese supremacy was not entirely uncontested. Thousands of local people died during the fighting and occupation, but when peace returned and the soldiers departed, East Timor simply slipped back into the same lackadaisical Portuguese rule. It seemed to be a colony in a coma. But in 1975 the territory would come to its senses with an almighty shock.

A year earlier in far-off Lisbon, a group of left-leaning military officers overthrew Portugal's authoritarian regime. It was a singularly bloodless coup—no one was murdered or thrown down a well, and there were no pogroms in its aftermath. But the new government did decide to do away with imperial anachronisms. East Timor was faced with the alarming prospect of independence from Portugal.

As Dili and the surrounding hills came to their senses, two main political arguments, and two main political parties, emerged. One party, the UDT, or 'Timorese Democratic Union', called for a slow and steady move towards autonomy, with old ties to

Portugal maintained. The other, the ASDT—later to be better known as Fretilin, the 'Revolutionary Front for an Independent East Timor'—wanted immediate and absolute independence. In August 1975 the two parties fought a brief but bitter civil war. Fretilin won, and the UDT leadership fled across the border into Indonesian West Timor.

The Indonesian government had been watching events in East Timor with a considerable degree of discomfort. They had backed a third, minority party, Apodeti, which called for Timorese integration with Indonesia, and they had no intention of allowing Fretilin, with their avowedly socialist rhetoric, to establish a turbulent left-wing state within the Archipelago. On 7 December 1975 Indonesia invaded East Timor. It was a messy, ugly war, but in July 1976 East Timor became Indonesia's twenty-seventh province.

The invasion of East Timor received the tacit approval of America and Australia: the Cold War still had a lot of heat at this stage, and the Indonesian government had impeccable anti-communist credentials. But in time this new addition to the Indonesian fold would become a permanent irritant, a financial burden, a military conundrum, and an international embarrassment. It was an albatross slung around the nation's neck, set to ensure that Indonesia would end the twentieth century with an episode of squalid violence, even as it finally achieved true democracy...

⊙—⊙—⊙—⊙—⊙

By the time that East Timor was made the twenty-seventh province of Indonesia, Suharto had been in power for ten years. During that decade the stocky, smiling general had proved himself to be the perfect counterpoint to his flamboyant predecessor. There were no more rabble-rousing rallies and verbal pyrotechnics. When Suharto gave a speech people tended to fall asleep. Sukarno could conjure up literary quotations in French, German and Italian. The best Suharto could manage was a rather hesitant and broken English. Even his Indonesian had the thick, rounded vowels and blurry edges of a man who preferred to speak Javanese at home. The presidential lifestyle had changed, too: there were no more multiple wives and multitudinous mistresses, and Suharto wouldn't have been seen dead with a Japanese bargirl. In short, when compared to the mercurial man he had ousted, Suharto was *boring*. But he had a peculiar charisma all of his own. It came, as much as anything, from the fact that no one really knew what he was thinking.

Suharto was born on 8 June 1921, in a poor hamlet called Kemusuk in the countryside west of Yogyakarta. Suharto's parents divorced before he could walk, and he spent his childhood orbiting through the households of relatives. For a village boy there was nothing out of the ordinary about such an upbringing. Divorce was common in Java, and many children lived in the care of uncles and aunts. But there was something strange about Suharto's childhood: he started school at a young age; at one point he actually moved households just to continue his studies, and he didn't finish his schooling until he was seventeen. This was not only a highly unusual level of education for a child from a farming community; it was also well beyond what Suharto's father, a landless irrigation official, could have been expected to afford. Inevitably, then, there have always been rumours of secret patronage. There are tales of an illegitimate royal descent and money for schooling secretly sent from the Yogyakarta kraton. But there is also the recollection of a former neighbour from Kemusuk, who claimed that Suharto was really the son of an itinerant Chinese trader who passed through the village from time to time.

Whoever his real father was, and whoever had paid for his education, Suharto left school just in time for war. He was caught up in the last-minute frenzy of recruitment by the Dutch colonial army on the eve of World War II. Once the Japanese arrived, he shed his Dutch uniform and joined the ranks of Peta, the paramilitary youth group, and when the war was over he found himself in the vanguard of the makeshift army of the Indonesian Republic. At the height of the revolution, in 1947, he was married, decidedly above his station, to a young woman called Siti Hartinah. She was short, stocky and by no means glamorous, but she came from an aristocratic family, distantly related to the Mangkunegaran, Surakarta's secondary royal house.

By the time he was forty, Suharto was a quiet family man in the middle ranks of the officer class of the Indonesian army. He had proved himself an effective regional commander, despite getting into trouble on one occasion for some over-enthusiastic commercial activities on the side. But he seemed unremarkable, as a soldier and as a personality. Few people would have expected him to make true top brass. But then came 1 October 1965, and all Suharto's superiors ended up dead at the bottom of the Crocodile Hole...

$\odot - \odot - \odot - \odot - \odot$

The New Order that had ousted Sukarno was, at the outset, a genuine coalition of the willing, and its first task was to do something about the economy. When Suharto came to power Indonesia owed a staggering US$2,358 million to foreign creditors; inflation was heading for 700 percent; and the annual income for the average Indonesian was no more than US$50. The country itself, meanwhile, was falling apart. Roads and railways, bequeathed by the Dutch and battered by years of war, were in tatters, and there were famines in this, one of the most fertile places on the planet.

By the end of the 1960s, however, Suharto, his first finance minister, Sultan Hamengkubuwono IX of Yogyakarta, and a coven of American-educated economic advisors—later dubbed 'the Berkeley Mafia'—had managed to turn things around. They had quietly renegotiated the country's debt and politely invited back the American aid that Sukarno had sent to hell. A new law was drafted to make space for foreign investors scared off by Sukarno's anti-

Western posturing, and soon the oil fields of eastern Sumatra were thick with rigs and the logging camps of the Kalimantan jungles were roaring with the sound of chainsaws. Out in the rice fields of Central Java and Bali, meanwhile, peasant farmers suddenly found themselves inundated with new seed types, pesticides, chemical fertilisers and technical advice from the denizens of the 'green revolution'. By 1969 inflation was in single figures. Incomes were rising, and for the next decade Indonesia's gross domestic product would grow at a steady rate of almost 8 percent per annum. The New Order had found its theme: *Pembangunan*, 'Development'.

The New Order had also tackled several other problems. They quickly brought the *Konfrontasi* with Malaysia to an end, and in September 1966, with the sporadic killing of suspected PKI members still going on in the more remote corners of the country, Indonesia re-joined the United Nations, which Sukarno had left in a fit of pique over Malaysia's inclusion in the Security Council the previous year. Suharto's government also deftly dealt with the question of West New Guinea. The UN's transfer of the territory to Indonesia in 1963 had been dependent on an 'act of free choice'. The New Order cannily declared that West New Guinea—now known by its Indonesian name, Irian—was not ready for democracy. The territory amounted to 200,000 square miles of forest and mountain with hardly a single road. Many of the inhabitants had had no contact with the outside world.

In 1969, instead of holding a referendum in West New Guinea, Suharto's government carefully selected a thousand local leaders and asked them, with UN observers looking on, for a show of hands if they wanted to join Indonesia. The architect of this rather compromised act of free choice was a loyal Suharto lieutenant, General Ali Murtopo; the practicalities were managed by none other than Sarwo Edhie Wibowo, the man who had sent the people of Java and Bali out to kill communists four years earlier. Unsurprisingly, the New Guinea leaders did what was expected of them. Every hand went up.

At the start of the 1970s it looked as though the New Order had dealt with most of the mess that Sukarno had left behind, and tied up any number of other loose ends, too. Thousands of alleged communists were still locked up in prisons and labour camps, but they were out of sight and out of mind, and the killings of the previous decade had taken on the air of a bad dream. Indonesia was calm, and development was underway. What Suharto needed now was some kind of democratic mandate, and he got it with the election of 1971.

It was more than fifteen years since Indonesia's last—and only—national election, and Suharto's government did a certain amount of tinkering before the polling stations opened. Firstly, the make-up of the parliament, the DPR, was fixed so that a quarter of the 360-strong membership would be appointed by the government, rather than elected by the people. This parliament would form a part, as it always had done, of the larger MPR, the Consultative Assembly, which also appointed the president. But now a full third of the MPR membership was appointed by the very president it was tasked with electing.

Next, the New Order created an electoral vehicle for itself in the form of an enormous pseudo-party called Golkar. The name was short for *Sekretariat Bersama Golongan Karya*, the 'Joint Secretariat of Functional Groups'. It was, in fact, a relic of Guided Democracy, an umbrella organisation for the apolitical 'functional groups' that Sukarno had made so much of—the farmers, the trade union members, the housewives, and the government workers. Now it was lavished with funds. Golkar had no individual membership and no declared ideology, but it automatically accounted for a huge swathe of society. A new regulation banned civil servants from being members of proper political parties, but their automatic attachment to the civil service union made them all de facto members of Golkar.

Finally, Ali Murtopo, fresh from his successful stage-management of the New Guinea vote, was tasked with getting the real political parties into line. Independent candidates were banned from contesting elections, and the remaining nine parties had their leadership firmly nudged in a pro-government direction.

Golkar won 62.8 percent of the vote in the 1971 election. The nearest runner up was the traditionalist Muslim group, Nahdlatul Ulama, with its loyal constituency in rural Java, but it trailed in a very distant second with only 18.7 percent. Even the government was taken aback by the scale of this victory, which was at least in part a genuine expression of popular approval for its developmental achievements. But they wanted more tinkering before the next election. In 1973, the surviving political organisations were corralled into just two umbrella parties: the *Partai Persatuan Pembangunan*, the 'United Development Party' or PPP, for all the Muslim groups, and the *Partai Demokrasi Indonesia*, the 'Indonesian Democratic Party' or PDI, for everyone else.

The New Order had presented itself as an absolute break with the chaos of the Sukarno era, but the new system was, in some ways, simply the perfection of Guided Democracy. Sukarno had wanted rival ideologies held in a balance that permitted consensus and progress, and that was also a feature of the New Order's system. But instead of feuding openly in parliament, the rival political factions now bickered within the two umbrella parties, which were hobbled and acquiescent as a consequence. The New Order had effectively taken the politics out of frontline politics, and elections were nothing more than a formality.

Suharto's critics have often told tales of electoral corruption, of voter intimidation and ballot-stuffing. But while such practices doubtless did occur from time to time, there was ultimately no need for them. The vote of 1955 had proved that Indonesia was unlikely ever to elect a majority government from amongst the parties, even in truly democratic conditions; they were even less likely to do so now. Every five years throughout the three decades of New Order rule, there was a general election that was ostensibly free and fair. Every five years the PPP and the PDI got to campaign openly, actively and occasionally violently. And every five years Golkar won. There was no way they could lose.

But even if the New Order had no need to practice electoral violence, it was by no means entirely benign. The state security services had a long and ominous reach, watching over the general population for signs of rebellion. The unspoken memory of the 1965 nightmare lingered, and virtually any dissent could, with a little imagination, be interpreted as 'communism'—and to be accused of communism in New Order Indonesia was no joke. At best it could mean a ruined career; at worst it meant imprisonment and even execution. The press was watched closely too, and any newspaper publishing unfavourable reports was liable to be shut down. Protests, which did occur from time to time over all manner of complaints, were dealt with aggressively by the omnipresent army. For most Indonesians the New Order was not some crude and brutal dictatorship, and outside a few restive territories at the fringes of the country most people went about their daily lives unmolested. But there was a sense, a presence, a dull ache born of the 1965 killings, which engendered quiet compliance.

The unspoken demand for compliance was bolstered by the national philosophy. In lieu of a proper political or religious creed, the Pancasila, Sukarno's set of bland 'national principles', was firmly established as Indonesia's national ideology. Pancasila's five vague requirements—belief in a non-specific god, nationalism, humanitarianism, social justice and democracy—were hardly demanding for the average Indonesian. But their very blandness meant that virtually any opinion could be deemed anti-Pancasila if needs be. Every single organisation in the country, from sports clubs to political parties and religious groups, was obliged to make Pancasila its sole 'guiding principle'.

The national motto was the Pancasila slogan, *Bhinneka Tunggal Ika*. It was an Old Javanese phrase, taken from a Majapahit-era poem on the topic of Hindu-Buddhism, and it is usually translated as 'Unity in Diversity'. But a more accurate translation would be something along the lines of 'From Many One'. What Suharto's 'Pancasila Democracy' really demanded was not a boisterous, multifarious diversity, but a uniformity.

⊙−⊙−⊙−⊙−⊙

By the 1980s Jakarta looked nothing like the gimcrack capital of the Sukarno era. The potholes had been filled in and the street lights were working. Multi-storey office blocks and apartment buildings were beginning to appear. The first toll road, a six-lane strip of tarmac stretching thirty-seven miles (sixty kilometres) from Jakarta to the old country seat of the Dutch governors-general at Bogor, had opened in 1978, and there were plenty of new cars to make use of it.

Indonesia weathered a sharp drop in oil prices in the middle of the 1980s. Over the course of 1986 and 1987 the banking sector was deregulated. New private banks blossomed, and with licensing regulations and tariffs reduced, business was booming. Smiling beneficently over all this was the fleshy visage of President Suharto, who now liked to be portrayed as *Bapak Pembangunan*, 'the Father of Development'. He had considerable justification for being proud, for his rule had brought tangible benefits to many Indonesians. At the start of the 1980s annual per capita income, which had been a measly US$50 just fifty years earlier, stood at US$600. Around 100,000 new schools had been built and virtually every primary-age child, even in the remotest of eastern islands, was getting some sort of education. There had also been a remarkably successful family-planning campaign—carried out mostly without the coercion that had marked similar programmes in India and China—which had brought the fertility rate down to levels similar to those of Western Europe. But in private, out of print and out of earshot of the authorities, there was another word beside 'development' associated with Suharto's regime, and that word was 'corruption'.

The graft started close to home, within Suharto's own household. Even in the earliest days of the regime there had been low-level grumbling about the irregular business benefits enjoyed by the aristocratic Mrs Suharto, Siti Hartinah, now better known Ibu Tien. Jakarta wags started calling her 'Ibu Tien Percent' for the cuts she was believed to take on all manner of projects and contracts. The couple had six children, and they, too, had sprawling business interests. Just beyond the family circle, meanwhile, was a cabal of tycoons, many of them of Chinese origin.

The lot of the Chinese Indonesians had been a strange one for centuries. Their role in the Dutch colonial economy, running tollgates and tax concessions as well as private businesses, had bolstered both their disproportionate wealth, and a near-permanent current of hostility towards them. In independent Indonesia, they remained a tiny proportion of the population—probably no more than three or four percent of the total. But there was no denying the fact that a disproportionate number of private businesses were Chinese-owned. Even in the remotest of island outposts in Maluku and Nusa Tenggara, chances were that the local hardware store was run by an ethnic Chinese family. Mindful of the ancient hostility towards the Chinese, the New Order had created oppressive anti-Chinese rules in the name of forced assimilation. From the late 1960s, Chinese script was banned in public places; Chinese-language newspapers and schools were closed down; public celebration of Chinese festivals was forbidden; and ethnic Chinese were pressured to take new 'Indonesian' names.

Yet despite this official oppression, and despite New Order efforts to further the lot of *pribumi* or 'indigenous' businessmen, some of Suharto's closest cronies were ethnic Chinese magnates of astronomical wealth. Amongst them were Sudono Salim (real name Liem Sioe Liong), head of the vast Salim Group conglomerate, and Bob Hasan (originally known as The Kian Seng), chief of the sprawling Nusamba Group, with its timber concessions and banks. Both of these huge groups had Suharto children as partners in many of their constituent businesses.

Suharto himself did not really regard any of this as corrupt, or even problematic. Patronage had always played an important role in Javanese culture, and Suharto was now occupying the position of some great king of Mataram or Majapahit, dispensing favours to those around him as part of his royal prerogative. And crucially, there was a sense that as long as the development continued year by year, as long as the growth figures stayed high and as long as the little people felt some tangible benefits of all the economic progress, then everyone would be happy.

Canny observers pointed out that a burgeoning middle class, an educated generation born under New Order rule and increasingly connected to the wider world, might eventually grow tired of being treated like children by their government. But for the moment things were quiet. In February 1991 the first branch of McDonalds opened in Jakarta, three blocks south of Lapangan Merdeka. People queued for hours to buy their first Big Mac.

⊙ — ⊙ — ⊙ — ⊙ — ⊙

There was no McDonalds in East Timor.

The former Portuguese territory had not come quietly into the Indonesian fold. In the aftermath of the 1975 invasion, the Indonesian army had found itself mired in exactly the kind of guerrilla campaign it had fought against the Dutch in Java in the heady days of the revolution. Now, however, the boot was on the other foot and the insurgents were the ragtag troops of Falintil, the military wing of Fretilin, the Timorese independence movement. In an effort to isolate the rebels from the populace, between 1977 and 1979 villagers from across East Timor were rounded up and herded into new, supervised settlements around the towns. It was hardly a move designed to win hearts and minds, and though Fretilin's campaign was never more than a badly armed effort by a handful of hungry men, hostility to Indonesian rule had never gone away.

The result was a vicious circle. The Indonesian security forces responded brutally to Timorese intransigence. Summary arrests, torture and extrajudicial killings became a part of life in the territory. And taking a lesson from both the Japanese with their youth militias and Sarwo Edhie Wibowo with his communist-killing civilians, the army sought to make use of the bored young men who hung around the towns. Those who weren't already committed to the resistance were recruited, indoctrinated, and turned into spies or petty, pro-Indonesia street gangs. All of this only made the wider population more hostile to Indonesian rule. And that hostility only made the Indonesian response more brutal. At the same time, the New Order lavished development money on East Timor, bringing Dili's crumbling Portuguese infrastructure up to modern standards, and providing education and healthcare to the locals. It was a crude sort of bribe in the circumstances, however, and it earned Indonesia little gratitude.

By the time McDonalds opened its doors in Jakarta, East Timor was a bitter and brutalised place, and international observers were beginning to take notice of that fact. Portugal, the old colonial power, planned to send a delegation to Dili at the end of 1991 to assess the situation, and many Timorese hoped that this would be the moment for the world to recognise their plight. They began planning protests to greet the delegates. But at the last minute the visit was cancelled, and the Indonesian military began cracking down violently on those who had hoped to demonstrate. In one clash at the Motael Church, a sturdy white building amongst the trees on the Dili seafront, an independence campaigner named Sebastião Gomes and another young man who had worked for the military were killed. Dili's activists, frustrated by the cancellation of the Portuguese visit, latched onto Gomes' death. Two weeks after the killing they held a huge demonstration in the heart of Dili.

The day began early with a requiem mass for the dead man at Motael. Then, at around 7 AM, a large crowd began to march from the church towards the Santa Cruz Cemetery, a sprawling graveyard in the middle of the city. As they marched they unfurled banners, championing the Fretilin leader, Xanana Gusmão, and calling for independence. Roars of 'Viva Timor-Leste' swept back and forth along the street, using the old Portuguese name for the territory rather than the Indonesian 'Timor Timur'. They waved the flags of Fretilin and the UDT, and the banned flag of East Timor itself. Without the talismanic presence of the Portuguese delegation in the city, the demonstration was a spectacularly brave statement, and that bravery gave the crowd an exhilarated, but also a faintly hysterical, edge. They moved through Dili far faster than any normal protest march, and as they thundered past the docks Indonesian sailors eyed them from the decks of their navy cruisers with perhaps a hint of fear.

When the crowd—it was thousands strong by this point—reached the Santa Cruz cemetery, some people went inside to pray at Sebastião Gomes' grave. But most stayed outside the narrow gate and milled around in the hot morning sunlight. They climbed up into trees and onto the wall and unfurled banners, many of them in English, championing Xanana, demanding freedom for political prisoners, and calling for independence. And at this point the military turned up.

What happened next is unclear. Some reports speak of scuffles and attacks on soldiers; some blame the presence of agents provocateurs in the crowd; others say there was no provocation at all. But one thing is certain: the army opened fire at point blank range on the unarmed protestors. There is grainy video footage, filmed from inside the cemetery. The stillness of the morning has all gone to pieces in a chaos of dust. Terrified protestors are tumbling in a floodtide through the narrow gate of the cemetery and bolting amongst the gravestones, and there is a barrage of noise, screams and sirens punctured repeatedly by gunshots.

The Indonesian authorities claimed that 19 people had died and 91 had been injured in the shooting—until it was pointed out that they seemed to have simply conjured up this figure from the year in which the killing took place. They later upped the official death toll to 54. The East Timorese, meanwhile, say that at least 271 people were killed at Santa Cruz, and another 200 simply vanished in the aftermath.

The video footage of the massacre was smuggled out of Indonesia and shown around the world. And with the Cold War over, the New Order found that its anti-communist credentials were now worthless when it came to buying acquiescence from the international community. From now on, Indonesia would be perpetually pestered with criticism over its human rights record in East Timor—even if many Western nations continued to sell it arms.

⊙–⊙–⊙–⊙–⊙

East Timor was not the only peripheral territory marred by unrest. In West New Guinea some of those who had been disenfranchised in the 1969 Act of Free Choice were also resisting Indonesian rule. They had rejected the new Indonesian name for their homeland, 'Irian'. They called it 'Papua' instead, and they formed the *Organisasi Papua Merdeka*, the 'Free Papua Organisation' or OPM. By the middle of the 1980s, there were sporadic attacks on Indonesian outposts there and on the huge international mining concession at Grasberg on the flanks of the central mountain range.

Worse still was the violence at the opposite end of the Archipelago, in Aceh. Always more staunchly orthodox in its local version of Islam than Java, Aceh had bridled furiously against Dutch incursions in the nineteenth century, then been a hothouse of the Darul Islam movement in the 1950s. The *Gerakan Aceh Merdeka*, the 'Free Aceh Movement' or GAM, had first appeared in the

1970s. By the end of the 1980s it was fighting a concerted campaign from the mountains of the province—and the Indonesian military was responding just as brutally as in East Timor.

These other insurgencies only strengthened Indonesia's resolve on East Timor. The New Order had made a stony bed for itself when it invaded in 1975, but it was determined to lie in it, for there was an unspoken fear that if this one small tranche of territory ever managed to peel away, then it might presage the unravelling of the whole nation. Indonesia's unlikely national identity had been first forged in resistance to Dutch rule. Sukarno had understood that the end of the revolution would leave a void, and he had tried to fill it with his own forceful personality—and, more importantly, through confrontation with the outside world. But the New Order had turned the confrontation inwards, against communism, and had replaced a demagogic figurehead with the bland exhortations of Pancasila. No one really knew if that would be enough to hold the country together if its peripheries began to fall away or, worse yet, if economic development faltered.

$$\odot-\odot-\odot-\odot-\odot$$

In 1991 Suharto turned seventy, but he had no intention of standing down. The genuinely imaginative collaborators from the early days of the New Order—men like Adam Malik, the Sultan of Yogyakarta, and Ali Murtopo—had gradually fallen away, and the president was increasingly surrounded by pliant yes-men and cronies. And all the while his children—Tutut, Sigit, Bambang, Titiek, Tommy and Mamiek—seemed to grow ever richer on their myriad business interests.

In 1992 Indonesia went to the polls. Golkar, which by this stage had been turned into a formal political party allowing individual membership, but which still had no conventional political ideology, won, and the following year Suharto was elected unopposed to his sixth presidential term. There was no discussion of a future succession, and for the moment the top man was unchallenged. But something wasn't quite right. For the first time ever, Golkar's share of the vote had dropped—by 5 percent. Most of the voters who had abandoned the party seemed to have plumped instead for the PDI, the amalgam of old nationalist parties, which was occasionally beginning to raise a voice of tentative opposition. There were even hints of disquiet from within Suharto's own military faction. Meanwhile, the president had been flirting with political Islam.

Indonesia had an enormous Muslim majority, and both its presidents had been Muslims themselves. But history had left the members of the Islamic parties with a minority mentality—and at times a justified sense of persecution. They had been largely sidelined in the struggle against the Dutch, and Sukarno had made it very clear that Islam could never be the dominant political force in his guided Indonesia. When Suharto came to power, many Muslim leaders believed that their moment had finally come. After all, their youth groups had done much of the dirty work during the anti-communist pogroms. But Suharto himself came from the depths of Central Java, and he belonged to the syncretic tradition of the rural majority there, a tradition that rejected many of the formalities of orthodox Islam. He was happy for the world to know that he dabbled in mysticism and meditation, and for the more credulous of his subjects to believe that he had the supernatural powers of an old-style Javanese king. And like Sukarno, he knew that letting the orthodox constituency have too much power would do nothing for national unity.

But in 1991, entirely out of character, Suharto had gone on the Haj pilgrimage to Mecca, with Ibu Tien and his playboy sons in tow. There had also been a number of nods to Islam in public life: headscarves were no longer frowned upon in schools and offices, for example. Suharto probably understood that growing Muslim orthodoxy was by no means a uniquely Indonesian phenomenon, and that Islam was gaining a greater role in public and political life across the Muslim-majority world. If some global shift was underway, then Suharto probably felt that he should try to harness it.

But many observers believed that the president's sudden displays of public affection for Islam were also a cynical ploy to create a counterbalance against both the military and the PDI's nationalist constituency, should either begin to stir against him. Sukarno had tried a similar trick with communism in the 1960s, of course, and the consequences had been catastrophic. The idea that Suharto might be trying to follow his example suggested that he was starting to lose his grip.

Out on the streets, too, there were hints of disquiet. There had been attacks on churches by Muslim gangs in 1992, and in 1994 rioters had destroyed Chinese-owned shops in Medan. The regime responded oppressively, stifling any press reports of communal violence that might disturb the vision of Pancasila calm. But the trouble continued. In 1995, rioters in East Timor destroyed the mosques of immigrants from other parts of Indonesia, and in Java more churches went up in flames. Meanwhile, those with a sharp eye could see that something was very wrong with the economy.

$$\odot - \odot - \odot - \odot - \odot$$

The great surge of economic development that had come with the first decades of New Order rule had been born not only of raw materials—timber from Kalimantan, oil from Sumatra, and copper and gold from the mountains of West New Guinea—but also from manufacturing for export. Hundreds of factories had risen around the fringes of Indonesia's biggest cities, vast sheds and tall, smoking chimneys sprouting on the flatlands south of Surabaya, around Medan, and on the coast east and west of Jakarta. A huge workforce of women who had once laboured in the rice fields had been freed up by the tractors and chemicals of the 'green revolution', and now they turned up each morning for shifts, stitching t-shirts and sports shoes for export.

But by the middle of the 1990s, Indonesia's manufacturing sector was weakening. Its working practices had never been the most efficient, and now its wages were no longer the lowest, for China was unleashing its cheap and formidably disciplined manufacturing prowess on the world. On paper Indonesia's economy was still booming, and foreign investment was still gushing in. But it was now more speculative and more unstable.

Local interest rates were high and the rupiah was strong, so it was cheaper for Indonesian entrepreneurs to borrow dollars to finance their projects, while the plethora of private banks could use dollars to fund loans in rupiah and make a profit. Dollar-funded five-star hotels and upscale office blocks mushroomed across Jakarta. In Bali, huge plots of coastal land were marked out for luxury resorts. In Medan and Bandung they opened vast, echoing shopping malls, full of luxury boutiques. And in Surabaya they threw up endless luxury housing complexes and apartment blocks, all marketed at vastly inflated prices. It was, unmistakably, a bubble, floating free of any solid foundation. What was more, the universal benefits in development, infrastructure and education that the New Order had brought in the 1970s and 1980s now seemed to have reached their natural limits. All that the factory workers, farmers and migrant labourers could see now was a clutch of cronies and Suharto's children getting very rich.

Meanwhile, Suharto's regime was using cruder, rougher tactics to deal with its political opponents. In the wake of their striking electoral gains in 1992 the PDI had elected as its leader none other than Megawati, the daughter of Sukarno and his third wife Fatmawati, born in Yogyakarta in the heady, revolutionary days of 1947. Megawati, virtually everyone agreed, was no chip off the old block. She was singularly lacking in charisma, could produce no rousing oratory, and having dropped out of university twice, she appeared to have little of her father's fiery intellect. She looked, talked, and as far as anyone knew *thought* like an utterly conventional middle-class Javanese housewife, and for most of her adult life that's exactly what she had been. But by the time two decades of New Order rule had passed, the Sukarno era had begun to take on a rosy tint in the memories of many Indonesians. It had been, they seemed to recall, a time of high ideals, a period when the president was a passionate man of the people rather than a blandly smiling kleptocrat. Megawati had joined the PDI in 1987, and she quickly became one of its most valuable assets—as a sort of human *pusaka*, an heirloom loaded with sacred energy, if not as a serious political thinker.

But with a new round of general elections scheduled for 1997, the Suharto regime wanted her gone. In 1996 they managed to manipulate the party to have her unseated as leader, and when Megawati and her supporters refused to acknowledge the imposed change, a mob of military-sponsored street thugs and off-duty soldiers attacked the Jakarta PDI offices where she was holding out.

The 1997 elections went ahead—but with much violence in the run-up to polling day. Without Megawati the PDI vote collapsed, and Golkar took its biggest share yet, 74.5 percent of the total. Suharto—portly, seventy-six years of age, and widowed following the sudden death of Ibu Tien the previous year—looked set for another five-year term.

But then, two months after the election, the economy of Thailand collapsed.

$\odot-\odot-\odot-\odot-\odot$

For years Thailand had been enjoying a similar speculative boom to that which had driven Indonesia. The deluge of trade and foreign investment there had been helped by a currency pegged to the US dollar, but as problems with the Thai economy became apparent in the 1990s the baht had come under huge pressure. By mid-1997, the Thai government had spent around two-thirds of its international reserves propping up the currency. They simply couldn't keep it up any longer, and when, on 2 July 1997, the authorities were forced to let the baht float on the international currency markets, it sank like a stone, dragging the great balloon of the Thai economy down behind it. And then, like some viral infection, the contagion spread to booming cities across the region—to Kuala Lumpur, Manila, and of course, Jakarta.

As investors realised that should the Indonesian currency also collapse, then the huge dollar debts that had fuelled the booming economy would take on nightmarish proportions, they panicked. And the panic led, inevitably, to the very thing they feared as people scrambled to sell rupiah and buy dollars. In July the rupiah had been worth 2,400 to the dollar; by October the cost of buying a single US dollar was heading towards 4,000 rupiah and Suharto had to call in the International Monetary Fund (IMF) for a bailout of US$43 billion. The bailout came with demands for economic reform, but they focused on cutting government spending rather than the enormous private debts that provided the foundation for Jakarta's forest of skyscrapers.

The value of the rupiah continued to fall, and with the economic turbulence came real trauma. In cities all over Indonesia building projects fuelled by speculative investment suddenly ground to a halt, and when the labourers turned up for their morning shifts on half-built high-rises, they found the site offices shuttered. The skylines of Jakarta and Surabaya took on an eerie aspect: unfinished skyscrapers were left silhouetted against the pale sky, concrete and steel skeletons that would never get their cladding of plate glass, still less their tenants.

In December there were rumours that Suharto had died, and the rupiah plunged on downwards towards a value of 6,000 to the dollar. The president was by no means dead, but when the government released its annual budget statement on 6 January 1998 some did begin to wonder if he was slipping into senility. The budget was based entirely on a rupiah trading at pre-crisis values, but the currency was by now burrowing furiously down the international markets towards the 10,000 mark. Panicky middle-class families descended on the supermarkets to stock up on groceries as their savings vanished before their very eyes. By the end of the month the rupiah was worth 17,000 to the US dollar.

And in the midst of all this, in early March, the tame MPR elected Suharto to another five-year term as president, with B.J. Habibie, his loyal former technology minister, as deputy.

By now there was open protest. Opposition figures were beginning to speak loudly against Suharto, and students were starting to demonstrate. People had given the situation a name by this stage—Krismon, short for *krisis moneter*, 'monetary crisis'—and it was finding unsettling form all over the country. When, on 4 May, the government cut subsidies on fuel—in line with the demands of the IMF—rioters hit the streets and the Chinese-owned shops of Medan came in for another barrage of mob violence.

Suharto, however, seemed unable to understand what was happening around him. On 9 May he left the country bound for a conference in Cairo. By the time he returned a week later, Jakarta would have been ransacked by its own inhabitants, hundreds of people would have been killed, and his own position would have become completely untenable.

⊙–⊙–⊙–⊙–⊙

The final conflagration of the Suharto era began in the aftermath of a rainstorm at a modest private university in the western suburbs of Jakarta on 12 May 1998. That morning, the Trisakti campus had been thronged with young men and women with placards, banners and loudhailers. These were the children of the middle classes, a demographic largely born of the New Order's economic development in the previous two decades, but now watching its future prospects disintegrating. They and thousands like them all over Indonesia had been demonstrating for weeks, condemning corruption and nepotism and demanding reform. But until now the students had stayed within the campus gates. On 12 May, however, the Trisakti demonstrators came out onto the street. They wanted to march to the parliament to deliver a petition, and when they spilled out onto the toll road that ran past the university, a daylong stand-off with the police developed.

Throughout the hot, late morning as rainclouds gathered over Jakarta, throughout the downpour that followed in the early afternoon, and on towards evening the two sides faced off against one another. But then, just as some of the demonstrators were starting to pack up their banners, the security forces opened fire. As always, there were cloudy and conflicting accounts of what had actually happened—and as always there was talk of agents provocateurs. But by the time the shooting had stopped four students were dead.

A decade, a year, and even a month earlier many Indonesian newspaper editors would have baulked at running graphic details of the killings at Trisakti; they would, perhaps, have baulked at running the story at all. But by May 1998, dissent was running high. The next morning the Jakarta papers printed front-page images of the faces of the dead students, and flags flew at half-mast all over the city.

And by lunchtime there were mobs on the street. These were not students: these were poorer, thinner people, young men from the *kampungs*, the sprawling working class quarters. They had first appeared on the fringes of the memorial ceremony held for the dead students at Trisakti on the morning of 13 May, and once the gathering was over they went on the rampage. For the next forty-eight hours, Jakarta succumbed to an orgy of looting, arson and vandalism. Smoke rose in columns across the city as the violence flowed back and forth, east and west, from district to district. In some places there was straightforward looting as men, women and children cleared the shelves of places where they could never afford to shop, taking clothing, food and electrical goods. But elsewhere, the rioters seemed to be gripped by an uncontrollable rage against anything remotely connected with wealth or authority. They overturned cars; they burned petrol stations; they even attacked traffic lights and street signs.

Nowhere suffered as badly in the riots as Glodok, the Chinese quarter halfway between Lapangan Merdeka and the old colonial districts in the north of Jakarta. Chinese homes, Chinese businesses and, all too often, Chinese people were attacked. Some families died in the upper floors of their burning shop-houses. Many Chinese women were raped.

And all the while the security forces did nothing to stop the violence. They put sentries outside the big hotels (and outside McDonalds, too), and then let the mob get on with things. It was only when Suharto returned from Cairo, winging his way into the Halim airbase—the same spot where the 30 September Movement plotters had killed his superiors three decades earlier—on the morning of 15 May that the army brought an end to the rioting. Forty shopping malls, twelve hotels, sixty-five banks and thousands of shops and homes had been destroyed. More than a thousand people had been killed. There had been riots elsewhere, too: in Medan there was unrest, and in Palembang, the old seat of Srivijaya. In Surakarta mobs burnt cars and trashed shops.

By now, few people believed that Suharto could cling to power for much longer. The student movement had picked itself up after the shock of the Trisakti shootings. On 18 May a huge cavalcade of student demonstrators descended on the Indonesian parliament in Jakarta, a peculiar building with a roof like a massive green mushroom standing southwest of the city centre. And the security forces let them in. There could have been no more potent symbol of the great change that was underway: a mass of students—eighty thousand of them by some accounts—thronging the chambers and even the roof of the building, with the army standing by and doing nothing to stop them.

Suharto's lieutenants were abandoning him now. Even Harmoko, the speaker of the MPR and a long-time Suharto loyalist, turned up amidst the protesters at parliament to read a public declaration calling on the top man to go. The army, meanwhile, was prevaricating, riven by its own internal power struggles, not quite backing the chief, but not quite condemning him either. They went so far as to threaten dire consequences if a proposed million-man march against the president went ahead on 20 May, but they did nothing to clear the parliament building.

Finally, at 9 AM on 21 May 1998, the man who had ruled Indonesia for more than three decades appeared before the cameras at Istana Merdeka, the presidential palace that had once been the seat of the Dutch governors-general. Dressed in a black *peci* hat and a short-sleeved blue safari suit, coughing occasionally, it took Suharto several minutes of rambling platitudes before he got to the point. When he did, he delivered it with little discernible humility: 'I have decided to declare that I have ceased to be the president of the Republic of Indonesia as of the time I read this on this day, Thursday, May 21, 1998'. He wanted Indonesia and the world to know that it had been entirely his own decision.

After that, in line with the constitutional provisions for what ought to happen should a president depart his post before the end of a five-year term, Suharto's deputy B.J. Habibie—who looked utterly terrified at this point—was sworn in as Indonesia's third premier. Suharto walked casually out of the palace, flanked by his oldest daughter Tutut. He smiled and saluted the press photographers, and then stepped into a sleek black car, which carried him away to his home on Jalan Cendana.

⊚–⊚–⊚–⊚–⊚

Once the students had gone home, and once the shopkeepers of Jakarta, Surakarta and all the other towns wracked by rioting emerged to clean up the mess, a sense of anti-climax set in.

Suharto might have gone, but B.J. Habibie was very much the ex-president's man, and many wondered if a deft trick had in fact been played: perhaps nothing had changed. But they underestimated the frightened little man who had sworn the presidential oath on the morning of 21 May.

Bacharuddin Jusuf Habibie might have had form as an arch New Order crony, but he was an unusually complex character. Small, dapper and faintly elfin in appearance, he was just short of his sixty-second birthday when he became Indonesia's third president. He had been born in southern Sulawesi in the 1930s, the son of a Bugis man and an aristocratic Yogyakarta woman who had met while studying in Bogor.

Habibie was fourteen when he first met Suharto. The future president's regiment had been based for a while across the road from his family home in Makassar, and over the subsequent years the New Order chief kept his eye on the bright young man. Habibie had gone to Germany to study engineering, and had stayed in Europe to work in the aircraft industry. But in 1974, Suharto had called him home to join the great developmental drive of the New Order. A confirmed technocrat, his interest was always in hi-tech industries—aircraft manufacture and the like, fields that many other economists felt were ill-suited to Indonesia's conditions. He was by no means free of the kleptocratic taint of Suharto's regime, but in 1998 he embarked on a brisk bout of reform.

Within days of coming to power, Habibie had freed hundreds of political prisoners locked up under Suharto's rule—including many who had been detained for their alleged communist inclinations. He did away with virtually all restraints on the media, and a raucous press blossomed almost overnight as a result. He allowed new political parties to form at will, and he set about curbing the almighty power of the armed forces, separating the army, the police and the other branches of the military so that they no longer formed a single monolithic entity. But despite all that, Habibie was not universally lauded by Indonesians. The economy was still in dire straits. Inflation was running at close to 80 percent, and a staggering proportion of Indonesia's companies were technically bankrupt. Most damningly, Habibie showed little inclination to curry public favour by pressing charges of corruption against his former mentor. When he set a date for fresh elections on 7 July 1999, he must have known that he would not emerge the winner.

The vote of 1999 was Indonesia's first truly open election since 1955, and once again public enthusiasm was enormous. Across the country cavalcades of campaigners traipsed through the towns, and politicians spoke in front of huge crowds. No less than forty-eight different parties contested the election, and the ballot papers were huge charts speckled with a multitude of symbols. Most people predicted that the PDI-P, the party that Megawati had formed from her faction of the original PDI, would top the polls. Megawati herself even managed to channel a little of her father's speech-writing skills, if not his charisma in delivery. 'Please children', she exhorted one crowd of supporters in Magelang, that upland town in Central Java where Diponegoro had finally given in to the Dutch in 1830, 'do not just cause a stir without really understanding the history of our nation':

> I don't want to be called a Balinese, Javanese, Sumatran, Irianese, Sundanese, whatever—I want to be called an Indonesian...

More than 90 percent of registered voters—almost 106 million people—turned out on polling day, and once the votes had been counted, it emerged that the PDI-P had indeed taken the biggest share of their support. But that share amounted to only 34 percent of the total, and that old reality, first demonstrated back in 1955, was confirmed once more: in a truly democratic election Indonesia was unlikely ever to elect a majority government. Many people still assumed that Megawati would end up as president. But ultimately, once all the horse-trading and coalition building was done, it was not Sukarno's daughter but the blind, bumbling Muslim leader Abdurrahman Wahid who the MPR elected to the presidency when they met in October, with Megawati as his deputy.

Wahid—known to all as Gus Dur—was the leader of the traditionalist Muslim group Nahdlatul Ulama, and the grandson of its founder Hasyim Asy'ari. But though he had studied in the Islamic seminaries of Egypt and Iraq, he was no religious conservative; far from it: he was a genuine champion of liberal values across races and religions. Amongst the first things he did as president was remove the remaining legal discrimination against the ethnic Chinese. His informal style, his tolerance and humour, and the way he wore his intellect so lightly gave him a hint of the beneficent aura shared by the likes of Nelson Mandela and the Dalai Lama. But as a president tasked with running the fourth most populous nation on earth his wildly erratic style was disastrous, and he would be unseated by parliament and replaced by his deputy long before he completed his term.

But as Indonesia lurched towards the close of the millennium, perhaps what it needed above all was someone to speak up for peace and tolerance—because right across the country, from Aceh to Irian, those values were in very short supply.

⊙—⊙—⊙—⊙—⊙

The patchy violence that had marked the final years of Suharto's rule all over Indonesia did not end with his departure. It got worse. Sometimes the violence was based on old ethnic tensions or jealousies; sometimes it was born of religious conflict. Sometimes it simply had no rational explanation whatsoever.

In early 1997 the first reports had leached out of Kalimantan that the Dayaks, the indigenous people of inner Borneo, were killing their Madurese neighbours. All across southern and western Kalimantan there were communities of settlers from Madura, people who had shipped out to these under-populated regions as part of a nationwide transmigration scheme begun by the Dutch in the early 1900s and continued in independent Indonesia. There had long been tension, and as the oppressive calm of the New Order began to dissipate it gave rise to nothing short of ethnic cleansing. Certainly hundreds, and probably thousands, of Madurese were beheaded by gangs of young Dayaks armed with spears and machetes, and Madurese settlements were left ruined and empty.

In places where Muslims and Christians lived side by side, neighbours turned against one another. In Poso at the fulcrum of Sulawesi, and in the old Spice Islands of Maluku, communities embarked on an appalling cycle of reciprocal violence, Christians and Muslims bombing each other's markets and murdering each other's children. In Aceh, meanwhile, the insurgency against Indonesian rule was heating up once more, and even in the remotest places, where there was no obvious religious divide, unrestrained violence could erupt, seemingly without warning.

In rural East Java, meanwhile, the violence took on the form of a disembodied nightmare. Here, in the beautiful, volcano-studded countryside around Jember, Bondowoso and Banyuwangi, traditional Muslim leaders were murdered in the night. The victims were rumoured to be practitioners of black magic; the killers, meanwhile, were said to be black-clad squads of 'ninjas' armed with samurai swords, who emerged from the forest after dark and swept silently through the villages on their gruesome task. Soon the violence had flipped in the opposite direction, and village mobs murdered those they suspected of being ninjas.

No one knew who—if anyone—was behind this violence, but in Indonesian political gossip people always speak of the hand of the unseen *dalang*, the puppet-master of the *wayang kulit* shadow play, and the dalang here was rumoured to be none other than Suharto himself. In fact, there were those who said that all the violence, from Kalimantan to Maluku, was the doing of the old dictator, and that from his modest home on Jalan Cendana he was using all his dark powers—be they political or supernatural—to wreak a terrible vengeance on the nation.

Rumours aside, there was one corner of the Archipelago where vengeance of the most terrible kind really was driving the violence, and that place was East Timor.

⊙ – ⊙ – ⊙ – ⊙ – ⊙

Of all the unexpected reforms that B.J. Habibie announced during his brief stop-gap presidency, none was more surprising than what he offered to East Timor in early 1999. In the years since the Santa Cruz massacre there had been ever more international criticism of Indonesia's behaviour in East Timor. Even Australia, the only country ever to have formally acknowledged Indonesia's annexation of East Timor, was pressing for change. In early 1999, Habibie announced that the people of East Timor would be offered a referendum. This would not be some stage-managed New Guinea-style 'act of free choice', but a genuinely universal vote in line with the democratic ideals of post-Suharto Indonesia. The Timorese would be asked a simple question: did they want a deal for special autonomy within a unitary Indonesia? And if they didn't want it, then they could have their independence.

Quite why Habibie made this startling decision is a mystery. It was rumoured that he had come up with the idea in the middle of the night, quite literally on the back of an envelope. Most members of the military elite were appalled. They had spent decades fighting in East Timor, and had lost thousands of men and millions of dollars in their efforts to drag the province, kicking and screaming, into the Indonesian fold. Many civilian politicians—including Megawati and Gus Dur—were similarly outraged. National unity was the ultimate watchword of Indonesian nationalism. It was what the revolution, with its rejection of federalism, had been all about; it was the one thing both Sukarno and Suharto had had in common, and it was at the very soul of Pancasila.

Habibie may have believed that the East Timorese would actually vote to remain with Indonesia: that, after all, is what New

Order propaganda had always insisted they wanted. He may have been enthusiastically continuing his efforts to place clear blue water between himself and Suharto. Or he may have simply been tired of the endless expense and continuous international whining. But whatever his reasoning, the upshot was the same: a referendum to be held under United Nations supervision in August.

On 30 August 1999 the people of East Timor came out to vote. A total of 446,953 people queued to cast their ballots, 98.6 percent of all registered voters in a place with around 800,000 inhabitants. Polling was peaceful, with international observers looking on. They announced the results of the vote five days later: 78.5 percent of adult East Timorese had chosen to reject Indonesian rule. And by that evening the firestorm had begun.

There had already been much violence in the run-up to the referendum. The Indonesian military presence in East Timor had always been huge, and by 1999 there were more boots on the ground than ever. But there were also the chaotic pro-Indonesia militias that the military had created over the years. Mobs of young men dressed like rock stars and with a distinct propensity for drink and drugs, they adopted the vaguely fascistic insignia of motorbike gangs and took names like *Besi Merah Putih*, Indonesian for 'Red and White Steel', and *Aitarak*, the local word for 'thorn'. And by 1999, in a country where the police and the military kept a very tight grip on ownership of firearms, they also had guns.

No one really knows the details of everything that was going on in smoky military offices in East Timor in 1999. But many believe that the Indonesian army was expecting a referendum result that would at worst be equivocal, a rough balance providing a legitimate excuse for the military to remain in the name of preventing civil war. But when the resounding verdict was announced on 4 September, they unleashed all the darkest forces they had at their command. If East Timor was really going to leave Indonesia, then the departing army would make certain there was nothing left of East Timor.

In the first weeks of September, East Timor succumbed to carnage. Indonesian soldiers burnt mounds of documents from the twenty-four years of occupation, and then put the torch to their own barracks as they pulled out. Their sponsored militias were left to run wild. Thousands died. International observers and journalists found themselves holed up in the UN compound, and then evacuated to Australia. Most of the development of the previous decades was undone and Dili was left a smouldering wreck.

The Indonesian government had previously declared that, whatever the result of the referendum, its rule in East Timor would end no earlier than 1 January 2000. But by the end of September it was clear that the place was imploding. It was obvious that no one, least of all the president, could do anything to stop it. And so, on 12 September, Habibie agreed to allow a force of UN peacekeepers into East Timor under an Australian command. They arrived eight days later, and on 20 October the Indonesian parliament formally gave up all responsibility for the ruined East Timor.

$$\odot - \odot - \odot - \odot - \odot$$

As a new millennium dawned the Indonesian nation had shrunk. A small fragment of the Archipelago had broken away after twenty-four unhappy years. Many observers suspected that the destruction of East Timor had been not just an act of spite on the part of a military fearful of losing its potency in a post-New Order nation, but also a stark warning to any other corner of the country that might harbour its own secessionist dreams. But whether such a warning would be heeded was anyone's guess.

Indonesia had been independent of the Netherlands for half a century. It had been free from Suharto's grip for a little over a year and a half. It had had a democratically elected government for six months, and a new president for ten weeks. But its future as a nation had never looked so uncertain.

Epilogue
Indonesia, Rising

A t a minute before eight o'clock in the morning on 26 December 2004, the Indo-Australian Plate suddenly slipped at the point where it drives under the Eurasian Plate off the west coast of Sumatra.

All the while that the history of the Archipelago had been unfolding the ancient collision between these two huge slabs of the earth's surface had continued, one plate bending ceaselessly beneath the other. The subduction zone was a submarine trench, shadowing the entire southern arc of the Archipelago, 23,000 feet (7,000 metres) deep and 186 miles (300 kilometres) offshore. Throughout history it had caused earthquakes, toppling the uppermost blocks from the Hindu-Buddhist temples and cracking the roofs of the mosques. And throughout history the material forced down into the bowels of the earth had fuelled the volcanoes that defined the landscape of the Archipelago. Ancient chroniclers had written of them; they had taken them as portents.

But this earthquake of 26 December 2004 was entirely out of the ordinary. For a start it was quite simply enormous, measuring somewhere in the region of 9.0 on the Richter scale, one of the most powerful quakes ever recorded. It also went on for an inordinately long time—almost ten minutes. The epicentre was somewhere off the northern tip of Simeulue, a small island off the coast of Aceh in the north of Sumatra. But all across the region people felt the earth move. In the regional capital of Banda Aceh, the morning bustle came to a halt as people crouched or lay in the shifting streets, waiting for the moment to pass. An earthquake is not usually a sudden jolt, or a high-frequency tremor like the passing of a freight train; instead it is a deep rocking to and fro, as if a giant has taken hold of the edge of the land and is trying to work it free of its foundations. In Banda Aceh the palm trees swayed back and forth to the beat of the earth.

When the shaking finally stopped people got carefully to their feet. The damage was actually not as bad as it could have been after such a long and powerful quake. But the real impact had yet to come. Offshore, some 18 miles (30 kilometres) below the surface, a vast gash had been torn into the crust of the earth. The wound had opened at the epicentre of the quake, then ripped its way northwards at 6,200 miles (10,000 kilometres) an hour, all the way to the Andaman Islands. Above this rupture huge submarine ridges had collapsed under the strain, and great blocks of the ocean floor had been shoved suddenly upwards, forcing a huge bulge of water towards the surface. As this liquid mountain reared up it sucked the water from the coastal shallows out to join it, leaving mudflats and beaches dry in a sudden and ill-omened spring tide. And then, with devastating speed, the water surged back, powered by an energy equal to 1,500 atomic bombs.

This tsunami fanned out across the Indian Ocean. It tore through beach resorts in Thailand and levelled fishing villages in Sri Lanka. It smashed the seafronts of southern India and overwhelmed low-lying atolls in the Maldives. Its energy refracted around continents and between islands and out into other oceans, and by the time it had finally spent itself, some sixteen hours after the quake, it was lapping ashore as ripples on the west coast of North America.

But nowhere was hit as badly as Aceh. There, the tsunami surged across the coast, a wall of water and debris rising a hundred feet (thirty metres) in places. Banda Aceh itself was devastated, and all down the west coast the narrow strip of land between the shore and the steep green hills of the interior was left flayed and blackened. Well over a hundred thousand people were killed.

⊙ — ⊙ — ⊙ — ⊙ — ⊙

By the time of the 2004 Tsunami, Indonesia was on to its sixth president. At the start of the twenty-first century the country had been in a truly parlous state. It was riven by any number of violent conflicts; it had just lost its twenty-seventh province, and there were prophesies of doom aplenty, from both outsiders and from many Indonesians. But somehow, none of the grimmest predictions had come to pass. East Timor had gone—finally declaring its own sovereignty in 2002 after two years under United Nations administration—but its departure had not presaged the disintegration of Indonesia. The ethnic and religious violence that had erupted with the end of the New Order seemed to be burning itself out, too. Peace accords in 2002 had brought the worst of the Muslim-Christian fighting in Maluku and central Sulawesi to an end, and the patchy violence that had occurred all over the country had gradually dissipated. There was still an anchor of unrest at each end of the Archipelago—in Aceh and West New Guinea, where entrenched resistance to Indonesian rule continued. But the foreign journalists who had predicted civil war after the fall of Suharto had been proved wrong.

Not that there weren't problems. The presidency of the bumbling, near-blind Gus Dur was a political shambles. He might have been lauded by liberals at home and abroad for his avowed nonsectarianism, but his erratic style alienated even his closest allies in government. His visits to Israel and sympathy for other faiths outraged Islamist hardliners on the one hand, and his successful effort to change the official name of West New Guinea from 'Irian' to 'Papua', in line with local preferences, angered the nationalists on the other. As for his suggestion that Indonesia's ban on Marxism-Leninism should be lifted and some sort of reconciliation process over the pogroms of 1965 attempted, it horrified just about everyone. Once he had been forced from power in 2001, under a vague cloud of suggested impropriety that seemed to have more to do with incompetence than actual corruption, he returned to the more effective role of gentle elder statesman. By the time he died at the end of 2009 he was one of very few Indonesians who could claim the status of 'national treasure'.

His replacement, Megawati, was unlikely to ever achieve such a position, but the students and the poor farmers cheered her on, and she proved more effective as president than some cynics had predicted. She did not do enough to win re-election, however, when the country went back to the polls in 2004. This was the first time that Indonesians were allowed to elect individual candidates, instead of simply casting a vote for a party. The result was the predictable mish-mash of minorities, with Golkar and the PDI-P taking the biggest chunks of the parliament. But voters were now also allowed to choose their own president. The constitution had been amended to allow for US-style presidential elections. Candidates had to get at least a 50 percent share of the national vote, and they were limited to two terms in office. In 2004, after a run-off, the winner was a fifty-five-year-old former general named Susilo Bambang Yudhoyono, who would be known forever more in the interests of brevity as 'SBY'.

He might have been a one-time soldier in the New Order army, but SBY came to power with convincing reformist credentials, promising to tackle corruption, improve education and healthcare, and deal with any number of Indonesia's other woes. One of his biggest headaches on entering office in October 2004 was Aceh, where the army was still locked in a vicious fight with GAM, the Acehnese rebel group. But then, before SBY even had a chance to take stock of the situation, came the tsunami. As the waters receded, the Aceh conflict came to an abrupt halt. International aid agencies descended to help rebuild the province and a peace agreement followed. GAM, which had been fighting the Indonesian government for three decades, signed up for democracy. It had taken plate tectonics to bring one of Indonesia's most intractable conflicts to a close.

Even before the tsunami, Aceh had been given a special degree of autonomy in an effort to appease the separatists. After the peace agreement that autonomy was extended, and in this staunchly orthodox corner of the country, sharia, the Muslim legal code, underpinned many local bylaws.

⊙—⊙—⊙—⊙—⊙

By the time SBY came to power, a good number of international pundits and journalists were claiming that Indonesia was edging towards some sort of Islamist rule, either through the ballot box or through violence. On an October night in 2002 a suicide bomber had blown himself up in a crowded bar in Kuta, the biggest tourist resort on Bali. Moments later, a huge car bomb exploded outside a night club on the other side of the road; 202 people were killed, most of them from Australia. Other bombings followed, in a luxury hotel in Jakarta the following year, and again in Bali in 2005. Meanwhile, during the 2004 election the Muslim parties dramatically increased their showing, collectively taking 38 percent of the vote, while in society at large the shift towards a more orthodox sort of Islam continued. On university campuses and on city streets there were thousands of candy-coloured Muslim headscarves where there had been almost none a generation earlier, and new concrete mosques were rising in neighbourhoods across the country.

With the global 'war on terror' in full swing following the 9/11 attacks in New York in 2001, some foreign observers tried to conflate these three phenomena—terrorism, electoral success for Muslim parties, and an increasing Islamic influence on society. But they were, as it turned out, quite separate. The violence was the preserve of a tiny minority, and one of Indonesia's most notable New Order inheritances was a powerful security apparatus with absolutely no fear of a fight. The men behind the bombs in Bali were tracked down, arrested, tried, and executed, without prompting a hint of the popular backlash that some pundits had predicted. As for the Muslim political parties, their Islamism was of a moderate sort, and after the successes of 2004 their share of the vote fell away to well below 30 percent in the subsequent election. Many young Indonesian Muslims might well be becoming inclined to sign up for a more formal personal interpretation of their faith, but they seemed to have little appetite for electing an Islamic government.

⊙—⊙—⊙—⊙—⊙

Ultimately, the major challenges of SBY's presidency were not terrorism or the breakup of the nation, but the old issues of corruption, inefficiency and infrastructure. Efforts to get to grips with corruption rarely seemed to be effective, and a regional autonomy package that had been brought in at the start of the decade had, if anything, made matters worse. In an effort to tackle grumblings in the outer islands about the neglect and arrogance of the central government, more power had been devolved to the regencies, the administrative units below the level of the provinces. It had appeased many of the original complainants, but before long others were claiming that it had simply created new opportunities for corruption amongst local politicians, and hampered effective provincial government.

Regional autonomy also made it harder for the central government to deal with Indonesia's appalling environmental problems, to tackle the large-scale illegal logging operations in Kalimantan, or to take any sensible steps to slow the pace of deforestation there or in Sumatra, where vast swathes of what was once jungle were being turned over to the sterile monoculture of palm oil plantations.

One of the fundamental problems was that, for all the high drama that had surrounded the fall of Suharto, there had never really been a clean break with the New Order. Suharto himself had died in a Jakarta hospital on 27 January 2008 at the age of eighty-seven. He had passed his forced retirement quietly at home on Jalan Cendana, and he had never been brought to book for the corruption or the excesses of his long rule. Whenever there were moves towards a trial, his failing health was cited as an excuse not to proceed. But there had never been a serious appetite for pursuing him amongst the new political elite anyway, for the fact of the matter was that many of Indonesia's post-reform politicians were simply veterans of the regime that had gone before. And even where there was no direct New Order link there were sometimes queasy continuities. SBY was married to the daughter of the great communist killer of 1965, Sarwo Edhie Wibowo.

By the start of SBY's second term in 2009, a fair degree of voter cynicism had crept in, and little more than a decade after the wave of popular protest that had toppled Suharto, some Indonesians, both poor and middle class, were starting to make nostalgic comments about the days of the New Order, when, they seemed to recall, things had been somehow less chaotic.

But one thing was certain: Indonesia had thoroughly recovered from the economic meltdown of the late 1990s. The country had crept back into very modest growth under Gus Dur's presidency, and then picked up speed under Megawati. During his first term, SBY had put competent officials in charge of the economy, tightening up the banking system, reducing public debt and cleaning up the notoriously corrupt tax office, in the face of considerable hostility from the old-style oligarchs and surviving New Order cronies. As a result, Indonesia rode relatively smoothly through the turbulence that crippled Western economies in 2008.

In 2014 Indonesia went to the polls once again to choose SBY's successor. This was the first time that power had passed from one directly democratically elected president to another, and the choice was a dramatic one. The frontrunner during most of the campaign was a whippet-thin former furniture salesman from Surakarta named Joko Widodo, popularly known as Jokowi. He had served as governor of Jakarta, but unlike every serious presidential candidate who had gone before, he was not a member of the established political elite. What was more, he had seriously impressive reformist and anti-corruption credentials from his time in charge of the capital and a previous stint as mayor of his hometown, Surakarta.

On the other side of the contest, meanwhile, was a man whose ties with the *ancien régime* could hardly have been more obvious. Prabowo Subianto was not just a retired officer of the New Order era army, one-time head of the Strategic Reserve Command and implicated in some of the military's most heavy-handed efforts to crush the student democracy movement during the late 1990s; he was also the former son-in-law of Suharto.

During the 2014 campaign, Prabowo did everything he could to tap into any latent nostalgia in the Indonesian electorate, dressing and speechifying like Sukarno, while at the same time channelling Suharto's ideas about strong leaders with iron fists. Backed by funds from his billionaire businessman brother, Prabowo's nostalgia-fuelled campaign soon built up a considerable momentum, and by the day of the vote only a hair's breadth separated the two candidates in the polls.

In the end Jokowi won, with a modest but incontestable majority. Few serious observers really supposed that he would be able to instantly change the traditional style of Indonesian politics, with its cynical horse-trading and its entrenched culture of patronage. But Jokowi's election as Indonesia's seventh president was nonetheless a powerful symbolic moment. It had been a close-run thing, but in the end the country had chosen the new man, rather than the figure who harked back, quite literally, to the past.

☉—☉—☉—☉—☉

By the middle of the second decade of the twenty-first century, many admiring observers were proclaiming Indonesia a rising economic superpower, all set to take to the podium alongside India and China. Across Jakarta and Surabaya and Medan and Bandung, the malls and multiplexes and apartment blocks and luxury housing complexes were rising once more, and foreign cash was pouring in. Whether the hyperbolic proclamations of coming glory would ultimately prove as ill-founded as the prophecies of doom and gloom a decade earlier was not entirely clear, for Indonesia certainly still had its problems.

Corruption still stretched down through the deep layers of government, and healthcare and education, though universal, were frequently of woeful standards. The old violence could still flare up at unexpected moments in odd corners of the Archipelago—an attack on a church here, a riot against a transmigrant community there; unseemly blemishes on the glittering developmental façade. In the east of the country in West New Guinea, or Papua as it was now called, there was still much resentment of Indonesian rule. There was active resistance, too, and this was the one part of the country where the army could still show its teeth, just as it had done in East Timor and Aceh in the decades past.

But one thing was clear: Indonesia existed. If only through sheer dogged perseverance and shared traumatic experience, it was more than a disparate collection of islands inside an old colonial border. It was a nation.

$$\odot - \odot - \odot - \odot - \odot$$

History is everywhere in Indonesia. *Bhinneka Tunggal Ika*, the national motto of this, the world's largest Muslim-majority nation, is a fragment of a fourteenth-century poem celebrating the unity of Shiva and Buddha. There is not a city in the country that does not have a street named for Diponegoro, the rebel prince who fought the Dutch in nineteenth-century Java, and a street named for Gajah Mada, the Majapahit prime minister who wanted to conquer all of Nusantara. These same cities also all have streets named for

Ahmad Yani, the senior general thrown down the Crocodile Hole at Halim Airbase in the early hours of 1 October 1965. The bank notes, too, are adorned with a motley array of soldiers from the revolution, and recalcitrant royals and rebel chiefs from the more distant past co-opted as 'national heroes', although they lived and died long before the idea of Indonesia was ever invented. Every year on 17 August the whole country is swamped in a mass of waving red-and-white flags in commemoration of Sukarno's ad hoc proclamation of independence in 1945. On 10 November, meanwhile, children across the nation line up to pay homage to the memory of the heroes who fought the British in the Battle of Surabaya. And 20 May is 'National Awakening Day' in honour of the founding of Budi Utomo in 1908.

This is all official history, of course, fragments appropriated—or misappropriated perhaps—in the name of nationalism and drained of all life and colour in the process. It does little to create a real connection with the past. Few Indonesians and few foreign visitors walking down a Jalan Diponegoro in some town in Maluku or Sumatra will get any sense of the righteous prince's character or motivations, still less the contexts of his rebellion. Indeed, all these sanctioned, sanitised dates and names can sometimes cut people off from the historical realities. The generals killed in the 30 September Movement might have hundreds of streets named in their honour, but there is no memorial to the many thousands of suspected communists who were killed in the aftermath.

But there is another kind of tangible history, one that cannot easily be corralled to meet the needs of authority. It is there when Indonesians speak of churches or flags or windows, and unknowingly use a Portuguese word to do so. It is there when they talk of the exhaust pipe of their car or the washbasin in their bathroom, and use a Dutch term for the purpose; or when they speak of thoughts and breaths and books and schedules and use Arabic words, but then use Sanskrit terms when they describe stories and colour and language, and even simple things like bread and hats. It is there in the words for 'you' and 'me' in Jakarta patois, *lu* and *gue*, which come from the Chinese Hokkien dialect. It is there in the food carts selling Chinese-style noodles and meatballs at every street corner in every town on every island in the country.

This other history is there in every single bite of Indonesian food flavoured with chilli, first brought to Southeast Asia from South America by Portuguese traders. It is there in the little offerings of petals still left by Muslim villagers at old Hindu-Buddhist temples in Java. It is there in the patterning of the hand-woven *ikat* cloth from Nusa Tenggara, echoing the marks of Indian fabrics shipped in centuries ago. It is there on the island of Alor, where the traditional bride price is still paid with *moko* drums made to the same patterns of those imported from Dong Son in Vietnam three thousand years ago.

It is there in the Islam and the Christianity and the Hinduism. It is there in the veneration of ancestral graves, and in the claims of ancestry in Majapahit or Makassar, told everywhere from tiny islands in Maluku to mountain villages in Sumatra—a web of diverse links and common threads, stretching from shore to shore, from volcano to volcano, and from island to island, binding the Archipelago together.

Further Reading

There is a vast scholarly literature on Indonesian history, as well as an intriguing array of nonacademic books. Detailed notes, explaining the key sources for each of the chapters in this book, can be found online at **www.timhannigan.com**, along with a complete bibliography and extensive suggestions for further reading—from florid nineteenth-century travelogues to ground-breaking works of modern anthropology. Below are recommendations for eleven essential reads for anyone looking to find out more about the history of the Archipelago, and a select bibliography listing the other important sources for this book.

The Cambridge History of Southeast Asia, edited by **Nicholas Tarling**. This hulking two-volume behemoth looks intimidating but is surprisingly accessible, setting Indonesia clearly in its regional context.

The Digital Atlas of Indonesian History, **Robert Cribb**. Available both online for free, and as a CD-ROM, this utterly brilliant resource takes maps—hundreds of them—as its starting point, and uses them to highlight all sorts of unusual aspects of Indonesian history.

A History of Modern Indonesia since c.1200, **M.C. Ricklefs**. Now in its fourth edition, this big book is essential reading, covering the history of the Archipelago since the arrival of Islam in formidable detail.

Indonesia: Peoples and Histories, Jean Gelman Taylor. A scholarly book with an unusually literary style, Gelman Taylor shines a light on individual lives, as well as tackling the big picture.

Nathaniel's Nutmeg by Giles Milton, and *Krakatoa: The Day the World Exploded* by Simon Winchester. A rare pair of pop history page-turners, these two books cook up ripping yarns from events during the colonial era, the first tackling the early years of the spice trade, and the second dealing with a very big volcano.

The Power of Prophecy: Prince Dipanagara and the end of an old order in Java, 1785–1855, Peter Carey. Nothing short of a masterpiece, this scholarly biography of the rebel prince Diponegoro doubles as a gloriously detailed social and political history of Java at the turn of the nineteenth century.

The Malay Archipelago, Alfred Russel Wallace. Victorian travel writing at its very best, full of adventure, scientific insight, and colourful snapshots of the remoter corners of the Archipelago.

A History of Modern Indonesia, Adrian Vickers. Written by a scholar with a wry eye and a sharp pen, this unusual account—not to be confused with M.C. Ricklefs' similarly titled book—covers the turbulent twentieth century in Indonesia in fine style.

Indonesian Destinies, Theodore Friend. From the mayhem of the mid-1960s to the high drama of the fall of Suharto, this very readable book combines a scholar's insight with a lively personal narrative.

Indonesia, Etc., Elizabeth Pisani. A wonderful introduction to modern Indonesia delivered in travelogue form by an author with an intimate knowledge of the country.

Bibliography

Anderson, Benedict, *Java in a Time of Revolution*, Ithaca 1974

Anderson, Benedict, and McVey, Ruth, *A Preliminary Analysis of the October 1, 1965 Coup in Indonesia*, Ithaca 1971

Bayley, Christopher, and Harper, Tim, *Forgotten Wars: The End of Britain's Asian Empire*, London 2007

Bellwood, Peter et al, *The Austronesians: Historical and Comparative Perspectives*, Canberra 2006

Bellwood, Peter, *Prehistory of the Indo-Malaysian Archipelago*, Honolulu 1997

Boers, Bernice de Jong, 'Mount Tambora in 1815: a volcanic eruption in Indonesia and its aftermath', in: *Indonesia 60*, New York 1995

Bosma, Ulbe, Giusti-Cordero, Juan A., Knight, G. Roger (eds), *Sugarlandia Revisited: Sugar and Colonialism in Asia and the Americas, 1800-1940*, Oxford 2007

Breman, Jan, *Taming the Coolie Beast: Plantation Society and the Colonial Order in Southeast Asia*, Oxford 1989

Brown, Colin, *A Short History of Indonesia*, Crows Nest 2003

Carey, Peter (ed), *The British in Java 1811-1816: A Javanese Account*, Oxford 1992

Carpenter, Frank G., *Java and the East Indies*, New York 1923

Cortesão, Armando (trans), *The 'Suma Oriental' of Tomé Pires: An Account of the East, from the Red Sea to China*, New Delhi 1990

Cribb, Robert, *Gangsters and Revolutionaries*, Honolulu 1991

Cribb, Robert, *Historical Atlas of Indonesia*, Richmond 2000

Cribb, Robert, and Brown, Colin, *Modern Indonesia: A History Since 1945*, Harlow 1995

Cristalis, Irena, *Bitter Dawn: East Timor, a People's Story*, London 2002

Crouch, Harold, *The Army and Politics in Indonesia* (2nd edition), Ithaca 1988

Dick, Howard W., *Surabaya, City of Work*, Singapore 2003

Doulton, A.J.F., *The Fighting Cock: Being the History of the 23rd Indian Division 1942-1947*, Aldershot 1950

Elson, R.E., *Suharto: A Political Biography*, Cambridge 2001

Farram, Steven, 'Revolution, religion and magic: The PKI in West Timor, 1924-1966' in *Bijdragen tot de Taal-, Land- en Volkenkunde 158*, Leiden 2002

Farram, Steven, 'The PKI in West Timor and Nusa Tenggara Timur 1965 and Beyond' in *Bijdragen tot de Taal-, Land- en Volkenkunde 166*, Leiden 2010

Forster, Harold, *Flowering Lotus: A View of Java*, London 1958

Fox, James, *Harvest of the Palm: Ecological Change in Eastern Indonesia*, London 1977

Furnivall, J.S., *Netherlands India: A Study of a Plural Economy*, Cambridge 1944

Gelman Taylor, Jean, *The Social World of Batavia* (2nd Edition), London 2009

Gomperts, Amrit, Haag, Arnaud, and Carey, Peter, 'The sage who divided Java in 1052' in *Bijdragen tot de Taal-, Land- en Volkenkunde 168*, Leiden 2012

Hägerdal, Hans, *Hindu Rulers, Muslim Subjects: Lombok and Bali in the Seventeenth and Eighteenth Centuries*, Bangkok 2001

Han Bing Siong, 'The Japanese occupation of Indonesia and the administration of justice today; Myths and realities' in *Bijdragen tot de Taal-, Land- en Volkenkunde 154*, Leiden 1998

Han Bing Siong, 'Sukarno-Hatta versus the Pemuda in the first months after the surrender of Japan' in *Bijdragen tot de Taal-, Land- en Volkenkunde 156*, Leiden 2000

Hanna, Willard, *Bali Profile: People, Events, Circumstances 1001– 1976*, New York 1976

Hillen, Ernest, *The Way of a Boy*, London 1994

Hughes, John, *The End of Sukarno*, London 1968

Ibn Battuta, *Travels in Asia and Africa*, Routledge and Kegan Paul, London 1929

Jordaan, Roy, 'Why the Sailendras were not a Javanese dynasty' in *Indonesia and the Malay World 34, Issue 98*, London 2006

Jordaan, Roy, 'Belahan and the division of Airlangga's realm' in *Bijdragen tot de Taal-, Land- en Volkenkunde 163*, Leiden 2007

Kahin, George McTurnan, *Nationalism and Revolution in Indonesia*, Ithaca 1952

Kammen, Douglas, and McGregor Katherine (eds), *The Contours of Mass Violence in Indonesia, 1965-68*, Singapore 2012

Klingaman, William K., and Klingaman, Nicholas P., *The Year Without Summer: 1816 and the Volcano that Darkened the World and Changed History*, New York 2013

Koentjaraningrat, *Javanese Culture*, Oxford 1985

Krancher, Jan A., *The Defining Years of the Dutch East Indies, 1942-1949*, London 1996

Kratoska, Paul H. (ed), *Asian Labor in the Wartime Japanese Empire*, Singapore 2006

Kumar, Ann, and McGlynn, John, *Illuminations: The Writing Traditions of Indonesia*, New York 1996

Knight, G. Roger, 'A Case of Mistaken Identity? Suikerlords and Ladies, Tempo Doeloe and the Dutch Colonial Communities in Nineteenth Century Java' in *Social Identities* Vol. 7, London 2001

Knight, G. Roger, 'Descrying the bourgeoisie: Sugar, capital and state in the Netherlands Indies, circa 1840-1884' in *Bijdragen tot de Taal-, Land- en Volkenkunde 163*, Leiden 2007

Laffan, Michael, *The Makings of Indonesian Islam: Orientalism and the Narration of a Sufi Past*, Princeton 2011

Legge, J.D., *Sukarno: A Political Biography*, London 1972

Lindsey, Timothy, *The Romance of K'tut Tantri and Indonesia*, Oxford 1997

Locher-Scholten, Elisabeth, *Sumatran Sultanate and Colonial State: Jambi and the Rise of Dutch Imperialism, 1830-1907*, Ithaca 2004

Lloyd Parry, Richard, *In the Time of Madness*, London 2005

Madureira, Luis, 'Tropical Sex Fantasies and the Ambassador's Other Death: The Difference in Portuguese Colonialism' in *Cultural Critique No. 28*, Minnesota 1994

McMillan, Richard, *The British Occupation of Indonesia 1945-1946*, Abingdon 2005

Miksic, John, *Borobudur: Golden Tales of the Buddhas*, Singapore 1991

Miksic, John (ed.), *Indonesian Heritage. Volume 1: Ancient History*, Singapore 1996

Morwood, Mike et al, 'World of the Little People' in *National Geographic* April 2005

Munoz, Paul Michael, *Early Kingdoms of the Indonesian Archipelago and the Malay Peninsula*, Singapore 2006

Nas, Peter, and Pratiwo, 'Java and de Groote Postweg, la Grande Route, the Great Mail Road, Jalan Raya Pos' in *Bijdragen tot de Taal-, Land- en Volkenkunde 158*, Leiden 2002

Nicol, Bill, *Timor: A Nation Reborn*, Jakarta 2002

Nordholt, Henk Schulte, *The Spell of Power: A History of Balinese Politics 1650-1940*, Leiden 1996

Pringle, Robert, *A Short History of Bali*, Crows Nest 2004

Penders, C.L.M. (ed), *Indonesia: Selected Documents on Colonialism and Nationalism, 1830-1942*, St Lucia 1977

Penders, C.L.M., *The Life and Times of Sukarno*, London 1974

Retsikas, Konstantinos, 'The semiotics of violence: Ninja, sorcerers, and state terror in post-Soeharto Indonesia' in *Bijdragen tot de Taal-, Land- en Volkenkunde 162*, Leiden 2006

Ricci, Ronit, 'Conversion to Islam on Java and the Book of One Thousand Questions' in *Bijdragen tot de Taal-, Land- en Volkenkunde 165*, Leiden 2009

Ricklefs, M.C., *Jogjakarta under Sultan Mangkubumi 1749-1792*, London 1974

Ricklefs, M.C., *Mystic Synthesis in Java*, Norwalk 2006

Ricklefs, M.C., *Polarising Javanese Society*, Singapore 2007

Ricklefs, M.C., *Islamisation and its Opponents in Java*, Singapore 2012

Robinson, Geoffrey, *The Dark Side of Paradise: Political Violence in Bali*, Ithaca 1998

Roosa, John., *Pretext for Mass Murder: The September 30th Movement and Suharto's Coup D'état in Indonesia*, Madison 2006

Schwarz, Adam, *A Nation in Waiting: Indonesia's Search for Stability* (3rd edition), Singapore 2004

Steenbrink, Karel A., *Catholics in Indonesia, 1808-1900: A Documented History*, Leiden 2003

Stockdale, John Joseph (ed), *Sketches Civil and Military of the Island of Java*, London 1811

Stoler, Ann Laura, *Capitalism and Confrontation in Sumatra's Plantation Belt, 1870-1979*, Ann Arbor 1995

Takakusu, Junjiro. (trans), Yijing's *A Record of the Buddhist Religion as Practiced in India and the Malay Archipelago*, Oxford 1896

Thorn, William, *Memoir of the Conquest of Java*, London 1815

Van der Meulen, W.J., 'In Search of "Ho-Ling"' in *Indonesia 23*, Ithaca 1977

Van der Post, Laurens, *The Night of the New Moon*, London 1970

Van Wyhe, John, and Rookmaaker, Kees (eds), *Alfred Russel Wallace: Letters from the Malay Archipelago*, Oxford 2013

Vickers, Adrian, *Bali: A Paradise Created*, Singapore 1990

Viviano, Frank, 'China's Great Armada' in *National Geographic* July 2005

Wade, Geoff, *The Zheng He Voyages: A Reassessment* (Asia Research Institute Working Paper Series No. 31), Singapore 2004

Wiener, Margaret J., *Visible and Invisible Realms: Power, Magic, and Colonial Conquest in Bali*, Chicago 1995

Index